The Paris Commune

European History in Perspective

General Editor: Jeremy Black

Benjamin Arnold *Medieval Germany*
Ronald Asch *The Thirty Years' War*
Nigel Aston *The French Revolution, 1789–1804*
Nicholas Atkin *The Fifth French Republic*
Christopher Bartlett *Peace, War and the European Powers, 1814–1914*
Robert Bireley *The Refashioning of Catholicism, 1450–1700*
Donna Bohanan *Crown and Nobility in Early Modern France*
Arden Buchotz *Moltke and the German Wars, 1864–1871*
Patricia Clavin *The Great Depression, 1929–1939*
Paula Sutter Fichtner *The Habsburg Monarchy, 1490–1848*
Mark Galeotti *Gorbachev and his Revolution*
David Gates *Warfare in the Nineteenth Century*
Alexander Grab *Napoleon and the Transformation of Europe*
Martin P. Johnson *The Dreyfus Affair*
Paul Douglas Lockhart *Sweden in the Seventeenth Century*
Graeme Murdock *Beyond Calvin*
Peter Musgrave *The Early Modern European Economy*
J. L. Price *The Dutch Republic in the Seventeenth Century*
A. W. Purdue *The Second World War*
Christopher Read *The Making and Breaking of the Soviet System*
Francisco J. Romero-Salvado *Twentieth-Century Spain*
Matthew S. Seligmann and Roderick R. McLean
Germany from Reich to Republic, 1871–1918
David A. Shafer *The Paris Commune*
Brendan Simms *The Struggle for Mastery in Germany, 1779–1850*
David Sturdy *Louis XIV*
Davi J. Sturdy *Richelieu and Mazarin*
Hunt Tooley *The Western Front*
Peter Waldron *The End of Imperial Russia, 1855–1917*
Peter G. Wallace *The Long European Reformation*
James D. White *Lenin*
Patrick Williams *Philip II*
Peter H. Wilson *From Reich to Revolution*

European History In Perspective
Series Standing Order
ISBN 0–333–71694–9 hardcover
ISBN 0–333–69336–1 paperback
(outside North America only)

You can receive future titles in this series as they are published by placing a standing order. Please contact your bookseller or, in the case of difficulty, write to us at the address below with your name and address, the title of the series and the ISBN quoted above.

Customer Services Department, Palgrave Ltd
Houndmills, Basingstoke, Hampshire RG21 6XS, England

The Paris Commune

French Politics, Culture, and Society at the
Crossroads of the Revolutionary Tradition and
Revolutionary Socialism

DAVID A. SHAFER

First published 2005 by
PALGRAVE MACMILLAN
Houndmills, Basingstoke, Hampshire RG21 6XS and
175 Fifth Avenue, New York, N.Y. 10010
Companies and representatives throughout the world

PALGRAVE MACMILLAN is the global academic imprint of the Palgrave Macmillan division of St. Martin's Press, LLC and of Palgrave Macmillan Ltd. Macmillan® is a registered trademark in the United States, United Kingdom and other countries. Palgrave is a registered trademark in the European Union and other countries.

ISBN-13: 978 0333–72302–9   hardback
ISBN-10: 0–333–72302–3   hardback
ISBN-13: 978 0333–72303–6   paperback
ISBN-10: 0–333–72303–1   paperback

This book is printed on paper suitable for recycling and made from fully managed and sustained forest sources.

A catalogue record for this book is available from the British Library.

A catalog record for this book is available from the Library of Congress.

10 9 8 7 6 5 4 3 2 1
14 13 12 11 10 09 08 07 06 05

Printed in China

To my parents, Harry and Ruth Shafer
And my children, Andrew, Alison, and Annèlise

Contents

List of Illustrations

Acknowledgements

After having struggled for so long with the completion of this book, I thought back to all the individuals whose friendship and support assisted me in finally finishing this project. Many of my colleagues, students, and teaching assistants at California State University, Long Beach, and fellow scholars in the French history community extended a high degree of encouragement, confidence, and interest in seeing me complete this project.

Particular thanks go, in no special order, to my department chair, Sharon Sievers, who, in reducing my teaching load, provided me with much needed time. The two anonymous readers commissioned by Palgrave Macmillan gave me frank and insightful critiques and suggestions. Pamela Pilbeam originally recommended me to Palgrave Macmillan; over the years, she has been an outstanding mentor and her comments at various stages of this project have been invaluable. P. M. Jones, S. Hollis Clayson, Greg Brown, and Jane Dabel also read chunks of the manuscript and supplied me with useful feedback. I would also like to thank my various editors at Palgrave Macmillan, and especially Terka Acton and her assistant, Sonya Barker, both of whom have been patient and supportive. My gratitude extends, as well, to Penny Simmons who has been a thorough and reliable copy editor and correspondent.

At the Musée Carnavalet's graphics department, Philippe de Carbonnières, and Scott Kraft and R. Russell Maylone at Northwestern University's McCormick Library of Special Collections were extremely helpful in assisting me in locating, selecting, and providing me with the majority of illustrations that appear herein. I am grateful to the McCormick Library for permission to reproduce images from their collection and to Photothèque des musées de la ville de Paris for permission to reproduce copyright material.

Very special thanks go to Pascal Dupuy and Anne Gardiner, very long-term and special friends; I cannot begin to express my appreciation for all the encouragement, hospitality, and assistance they have extended me over the years. Pascal and I had a friendly competition as to whose book would appear first. I lost.

Jan, Andrew, Alison, and Annèlise – demonstrated great equanimity and consideration in putting up with my anxieties, unconventional working hours, and the clutter that spilled out of my office into our shared living spaces. I think Alison and Annèlise might actually have become a little interested in French history, and I want to thank Andrew for reading bits and pieces of the manuscript and giving me a UCLA Theatre major's perspective on its clarity.

My greatest appreciation goes to my parents, the Honorable Harry and Ruth Shafer, who have demonstrated a level of support and confidence in me (at times unwarranted) that I hope I can return to my children. It is to them that this book is dedicated.

Author's Note

The cover illustration depicts Paris, nineteenth-century Europe's most spectacular and revolutionary city, at its most anguished moment. Alternatingly chastised as opulent, decadent, precious, and as the quintessence of urban pathology, Paris incarnated the contradictions of the nineteenth century. Its physical destruction during the third week of May, 1871, though sometimes exaggerated, served as the coda for the French revolutionary tradition with which the city was indissolubly associated, at once a jarring and expiatory spectacle.

The image portrays an identifiable Paris, putting the final days of the Commune in stark relief. Privileged by its position in the image's foreground, the Tuileries Palace, flanked by the Seine, and the adjacent Ponts Royal, Solférino, and de la Concorde, writhes in the final throes of its immolation. Less prominently situated in the background, the Portes Saint Denis and Saint Martin provide recognizable landmarks to a line of fire that engulfed an otherwise anonymous working-class swathe of the capital from Place de la République in the tenth *arrondissement* to the Père Lachaise Cemetery in the twentieth *arrondissement*. The torched city became the enduring image of the Commune, a conflagrant diaspora capable of marking the denouement of the last French revolution of the century, but incapable of conveying what the Commune signified.

Yet it is precisely the risk of this image contributing to the Commune's indelible association with fire and destruction, in general, and the Communards' unproven responsibility for this destruction, that I hoped to avoid in suggesting this otherwise striking image as the cover of the book. In other words, while this cover puts a topographical face on the final act of the Commune, the face is a mere set design, capable of obscuring more than revealing the essence of the story. As a moment of historical theatre, the final tragic act of the Commune defies comprehension when removed from the context that preceded it.

Introduction: Revolutionary Antecedents

Both in its ideals and its modes of action, the French Revolution established a staggering array of precedents that would resonate throughout the succeeding century. Although it is too simplistic to characterize the Commune as imprisoned by the Revolution, Communards drew from that seminal experience both meaningfully, as a guide and aspiration, and trivially, through slavish mimicry. In addition, the lessons and disappointments of 1848, when republicanism fragmented along class divisions, also factored into the Communards' collective historical memory, providing evidence that, for revolutionary republicans, the Revolution does not conclude with the establishment of the republic.

The French Revolution forged the modern understanding of revolution. By 1789, revolution had only recently transcended its astronomically based reference to the complete movement of one planetary body around another. In the seventeenth century, the English used revolution to describe their withdrawal of authority from Charles I; however, consistent with the astronomical definition, they claimed that their action represented a return to a prior state of liberty, thus completing a 360° turn. During the French Revolution, though, revolution did not so much refer to the completion of a process, but more as an irrevocable break with the past. In other words, a revolution implied a sudden and dramatic action that entailed monumental change.

The contribution of the French Revolution to the modern dynamic of revolution was not simply limited to semantics, but, more significantly, extended to the very ways in which popular protest would, hereafter, be conceptualized. The most common type of popular protest in pre-Revolutionary France occurred over ephemeral issues – for example, food riots during years of bad harvests. The protest did not carry large implications and its resolution either ended in repression or in the satis-

1

faction of the rioters' demand. Though sharing many of the same features and attributes as the other forms of popular protest that occurred with some frequency during the *ancien régime*, revolutions connoted, henceforward, something far more expansive in their aims.

In contrast to riots, a revolution is directed at some fundamental societal dysfunction which cannot be satisfied by palliative measures; in fact, nothing short of a restructuring or regenerating of society will put an end to the conflict raised by the revolution. Although riots and revolutions are both initiated by a problem, revolutions transcend the limitations of the immediate crisis, situating it, instead, as integral to the overall structure of society and as a contest for authority in the public space. One of the most significant contributions of the French Revolution to the succeeding century was the bequest of a revolutionary *mentalité*.[1]

In propelling the Revolution forward and serving as the site of its most crucial events, the Revolution established Paris as the foyer of revolution not only for France, but also for all of Europe. Yet to its detractors, the Revolution represented, at best, the imposition of Paris's will over the rest of the nation, and at worst, the dictates of the capital's worst elements. To its supporters, the Revolution would not have succeeded had it not been for the initiative of Parisians and their spirited defense of it when it seemed most threatened.

The model of revolution forged during the French Revolution was not restricted to the pursuit of power within the political arena. Republicanism was far more expansive than that and, in the revolutionary understanding of it, required that its citizenry have an emotional investment in the republic. To this end, revolutionary republicans promoted virtue as the republic's guiding ideal and inextricably connected it with the idea of regenerating individuals into worthy citizens of a republic. Between 1793 and 1794 the revolutionary agenda included plans for remaking humankind, an objective that required the forging of distinctly republican ideals based on reason and individual conscience and the creation of cultural institutions that promoted virtuous citizenship.

Essentially, the years of revolutionary republicanism, while fostering the period of greatest idealism, was bound to have a fleeting existence. For the bourgeoisie who provided direction and purpose to the Revolution, revolutionary government became necessary only after the liberal consensus of 1791 could not be sustained; at no time did they anticipate that extreme measures adopted during exigent circumstances would become the defining principles of the Revolution. However, once the forces undermining that consensus – the monarchy, foreign powers, aristocratic plots, the Catholic Church – had been neutralized by the revolutionary government, the Revolution would, inevitably, return to the less abstract, more pragmatic, ideals largely associated with the bourgeoisie.

Though confirmed by the Napoléonic Empire, maintenance of these ideals proved to be more fragile during the Bourbon Restoration. In the face of Charles X's assault on the revolutionary settlement, liberals and artisans resurrected their revolutionary coalition in defense of 'liberty.' Liberty proved to be an elusive concept, though. Capable, on the one hand, of superficially forging a revolutionary coalition of liberals and artisans against the Bourbons, it was, on the other hand, bound to divide them over matters of essence and substance. For liberals, 'liberty' meant political freedom and a *laissez-faire* economy; for artisans, 'liberty' connoted the protection of their occupational hegemony by the government.

Seeking to limit the impact of the revolution to political reform and to take advantage of the absence of a republican movement, France's economic and social élite hastily installed Louis-Philippe on the throne, the candidate of the 'liberal' Orléans branch of the monarchy. Within a month of the revolution, Louis-Philippe shed the revolutionary credentials in which he once cloaked himself as officials of the July Monarchy and workers became engaged in what Edgar Leon Newman referred to as 'a strange dialogue of the deaf.' While workers continued to petition the new government with demands for economic regulation, the monarchy and its supporters were determined to limit the revolution to moderate political change. With memories of the 1790s fresh in their heads, they were equally committed to restoring order and halting social upheaval, even if this meant abridging many of the civil freedoms at the core of liberalism. Although it might be too facile for historians to characterize *les trois glorieuses* as 'a bourgeois revolution,' the fact that a burgeoning republican movement interpreted it as such was of large significance to the contemporary political culture.

In the urban political cultures of Paris and Lyon, disappointment with the July Monarchy gave rise to a revived republican, and a nascent socialist, movement. Rekindling their prior association with the *sans-culottes*, republicans in the early 1830s built a base of support amongst artisans by capitalizing on a growing realization that 1830 had been *une révolution escamotée* (a stolen revolution).

Republican political clubs, whose names served as reminders of the

French Revolution, incorporated artisans into their structure, providing them with political answers to their largely economic grievances. Accordingly, many workers in Lyon and Paris connected the advent of a republic with the amelioration of their plight. This was especially true when some republicans tinged their message with socialist ideas. A poorly performing economy and increasing social polarization during the first third of the nineteenth century fostered interest in socialist theoretical frameworks aimed at the remaking of society. Seeking to enrobe their seemingly radical ideas in the legitimizing cloak of the past, socialists claimed, for their precedents, sources ranging from the evangel to the French Revolution.

Under the influence of Philippe Buonarroti, a member of Gracchus Babeuf's Conspiracy of the Equals which, in 1796, attempted to overthrow the republican government and replace it with a communist dictatorship, a young generation of revolutionary socialists, including Auguste Blanqui, reconfigured Jacobin republicanism as having initiated, but failing to complete, socialism's triumph. In reality, in a Revolution dominated by liberal ideals of individual freedom and merit, socialism, with its emphasis on social and economic equality had a very short shelf life. Buonarroti's memoirs rehabilitated the ideals of 1793–4, reconfigured them as the progenitor of socialism, and established both a filial duty and a primer for conspiratorial politics. A new cadre of revolutionary republicans found guidance in a romanticized and teleological view of the Revolution and set itself to the completion of the Jacobin mission.

Though it benefited from revolution in the last decade of the eighteenth century and, again, in 1830, the bourgeoisie now feared a revolutionary dynamic that turned its rhetoric into a clarion for those who were disaffected by the prevailing norms. Bourgeois fear of, and antipathy towards, the working class found its expression in characterizations of revolution as an unrestrained emotional outburst by individuals incapable of rising to the heights of rational, reflective thought.

If the working class was the agent of irrationality, Paris was its locus. Beginning with *les trois glorieuses*, Parisians reaffirmed the public space as the revolutionary theatre for contests of power and authority. The distinctly Parisian complexion of republicanism and the latter's inextricable connection with political violence and revolution further reinforced, in bourgeois eyes, the capital's disorderly image.

Bourgeois commentators, social theorists, and politicians chastised the poor for being predisposed to their own condition while characterizing

Paris as the epitomy of urban pathology. Much of the condemnatory discourse depicted the capital, degenerating in the aftermath of the *ancien régime*, as fostering an environment populated by an anonymous collection of violence-prone reprobates; in essence, for bourgeois Parisians and provincials, the French Revolution's disruption of established hierarchies rendered it the handmaiden of disease, destruction, and decline, and Paris the Petri dish that bred these forces.[2]

Thanks to an intemperate Blanqui-led uprising in 1839, easily repressed by the authorities, republicanism suffered through a near moribund existence in the 1840s; many of the secret societies that sustained it disbanded. Yet at Paris and Lyon, workers found their own, more militant republican, voice in attaching greater relevancy to Babeuf and Buonarroti's conception of a republic premised on political, economic, and social equality and the collective ownership of property than to the more nationalistic message of neo-Jacobinism. As was the case with neo-Jacobins, the neo-Babouvists situated their message within the legitimizing authority of the French Revolution, drawing conclusions about what to do in the present through references to the past.[3]

Studies of revolution often limit its application to successful contests for power. Accordingly, February 1848 was a revolution, whereas the uprisings against the July Monarchy in the 1830s were merely insurrections. However, such a definition ignores certain features of the French revolutionary tradition. First, in the wake of the French Revolution, all insurrections at Paris were contests for power; the fact that February 1848 succeeded whereas June 1832 or April 1834 did not has more to do with variables such as propitious circumstances, the extant regime's structural solidity, or happenstance. With the promise of control over the public space as their ultimate stake, insurrections in nineteenth-century Paris were revolutionary in intent, if not in result. Second, revolutionary successes in July 1830 and February 1848 appear to have been predicated on the participation of the bourgeoisie (in contrast to failed uprisings in the 1830s and in June 1848). Such bourgeois support in 1830 and 1848, though, largely came *ex post facto* the insurrection and, thus, was extraneous to the contest for power by artisans, workers, and students. Third, whereas insurrections put in motion the revolutionary process, it is only completed through a transformation of society's political, cultural, and social bases.

In February 1848 various sectors of French society celebrated the fall of the July Monarchy. The declaration of the Second Republic occurred less out of widespread acclamation for the republic than from the absence of a viable alternative. In other words, in the immediate aftermath of the Revolution, as France was awash in fraternal feelings, those most likely to oppose the Revolution instead chose the path of least resistance, enrobing themselves in the republic in the hope that their fidelity would hasten the revolution's concluding act.

For the workers and artisans whose hopes for some semblance of social and economic equality had been raised by Louis-Philippe's overthrow, the Second Republic turned out to be a cruel deception. Outside of the insitution of manhood suffrage, republicans had demonstrated a decided lack of dedication to meaningful social reform. While workers built barricades in defense of the National Workshops, their motivation was less a commitment to the Workshops than a final effort at exercising control over the revolution they had created. By 1851 workers demonstrated their discouragement by neglecting to defend the republic; having been seduced into believing it to be the panacea for their problems, workers now saw the seduction as more of a violation.

The experiences of 1848 left an indelible imprint on political and social outlooks; arguably, it was the formative experience for the future Communards. On one level, it was a more immediate phenomenon than the French Revolution. Just as in 1830, a political regime borne on the barricades proved itself more inclined to restore order rather than take advantage of an opportunity to effectuate revolutionary change. Socialists became more circumspect about republicanism, no longer viewing its institution as a magic bullet for society's ills. The Second Republic also revealed the folly of wrapping oneself too tightly in the cloak of the French Revolution. For many *quarante-huitards*, the Revolution, in general, and Jacobinism, in particular, was their political profession of faith; leaving aside the almost slavish veneration of Robespierre or Danton by some *démoc-socs*, 1848's version of Jacobinism had not effectively responded to the challenges of the nineteenth century. However, whereas by any measure the Revolution accomplished a major transformation and charted a path for future revolutionaries, the *quarante-huitards* would be measured only by the disappointments they engendered, discredited as a revolutionary exemplar.

Chapter 1: The Second Empire

On 26 March 1871, nearly 230,000 Parisians defied their national government and voted in elections for a municipal government, the Paris
Commune. The vast majority of those elected to the Commune were veterans of revolutionary movements and beginning with its first pronounc-
ments two days after the election, the Commune set itself up as a rival,
revolutionary source of authority to the national government whose legitimacy the Commune openly questioned. On one level, the election of the
Commune was the result of short-term factors, a response to a succession
of events that commenced on 4 September 1870 with the declaration of
the Third Republic, amidst the Franco-Prussian War. On another level, the
Commune flourished out of the roots of France's revolutionary history,
entrenched in the French political soil for more than 80 years, and fertil-
ized by events, personalities, and ideas of the nineteenth century. The
Commune and its supporters drew inspiration from France's revolutionary
past, but also interpreted the French Revolution, as well as the revolutions
of 1830 and 1848, as having challenged the Commune to complete the
revolutionary mission its revolutionary progenitors had fallen short of fulfilling. The Commune, though, was not simply an attempt by revolutionary
republicans at recapturing lost opportunities; it also resulted from French
workers' burgeoning class consciousness, and their resultant politicization,
during the Second Empire. Revolutionary republicanism, socialism, anarchism, utopian socialism all found their expression in the Commune that,
in turn, represented the culmination of these distinct movements.

Introduction

True to his word, Louis-Napoléon reinstated manhood suffrage and,
over the ensuing 19 years, several times provided voters with the oppor-

tunity to register their opinion of him in plebiscites. However, the plebiscites were skewed in favor of his approval. Between 1848 and 1852, large numbers of potential dissidents were in exile or prison. No precise figure exists for those punished for their opposition to the coup d'état, but estimates range from around 10,000 all the way up to 100,000! Furthermore, those tempted to vote against Louis-Napoléon had to go to extra lengths under the gaze of local Bonaparte-appointed officials.[1]

Louis-Napoléon's electoral success was not strictly the result of a repressive machinery which foreclosed the development and expression of opposition. On the contrary, the Emperor was a master of public relations and at least one historian has referred to Bonapartism as 'the great synthesis of post-revolutionary French political culture,' capable of blending such seemingly opposing concepts as revolution and order in the same package. The inability to tag Louis-Napoléon with a label gave him the enigmatic qualities so confounding to the French populace.[2] Fearing a *démoc-soc* resurgence, moderate republicans and conservatives, alike, viewed Bonapartism as a bulwark against social revolution. Louis-Napoléon stood for economic progress – in fact, he had been a follower of Saint-Simon; if parliamentarianism was a victim of the march of progress and the deliverance of social order and stability, so be it. Even some former *démoc-soc* adherents supported Louis-Napoléon out of the belief that he was a populist. In fact, with the ability to bypass the two-house legislature and appeal directly to the voters through plebiscites, Louis-Napoléon appeared to be the epitomy of direct democracy.[3]

Ideological mysteries aside, Louis-Napoléon understood the advantages to be gained from inextricably identifying his regime to his person and becoming a national political figure. In this respect he took a page out of the book of royal absolutism, but in rendering himself more personally accessible, Louis-Napoléon generated strong personal affection. Advance teams would precede his numerous stops at French towns and cities generating 'a buzz' about the Emperor's impending visit.

Public relations junkets, democratic rhetoric, and fear of socialism would not, alone, stabilize or legitimize an extraconstitutional regime. Louis-Napoléon also benefited from a fortuitous economic climate. The discovery of gold in California and Australia worked as a stimulus for the export sector of the French economy. Through an increase in the global circulation of precious metals, manufacturers and exporters of French luxury goods were the first to realize the benefits as the European economy broke out of the slump in which it had been mired since 1846.

Though circumstances played a large part in France's economic rebound, the Empire also deserves some credit for capitalizing on a favorable economic climate. The Empire strove to increase investor confidence in the private sector and the Paris stock-market, the Bourse, provided early venture capitalists with all sorts of speculative opportunities. In addition, it encouraged French banks to modernize through emulation of the British model of lending money to entrepreneurs. No bank better epitomized this new approach to banking than did the Crédit Mobilier. Formed by the Pereire brothers, adherents to the Saint-Simonian creed that economic modernization through cooperation between the financial and industrial sectors holds the key to social harmony, the Crédit Mobilier provided the capital for enterprises ranging from the railways to the salt industry; expansion and improvement of the transport infrastructure benefited other economic sectors. Because collateral largely consisted of shares in the companies in whom it invested, the Crédit Mobilier not only had a lot riding on the viability of the companies, it was also notoriously short of liquid funds; as a result, it was dependent upon bond issuances for its available resources. Although state policies sometimes frustrated its operations, the Crédit Mobilier incarnated the Empire's encouragement of risky, though potentially profitable, speculations.

Nonetheless, after several years of a shaky economic picture, the 1850s ushered in a period of opulence, conspicuous consumption, and rampant materialism. Whereas standards of living, as measured by caloric intake and dietary diversity, were certainly improving for even the poorest segment of society, France continued to be plagued by disparities based on social class. In fact, those disparities might have been accentuated by an economy in which those with investitive resources had opportunities to maximize their wealth.[4] In spite of an improved economic picture, the plight of the Parisian working class remained precarious; the Prefect of the Seine, Baron Georges Haussmann, estimated that a slight rise in food prices would cause the capital's poor (estimated by Haussmann to be more than 70 percent of the population) to depend on public assistance.[5] While the material condition of the working class did not worsen during the Empire, it did not improve significantly either.

Haussmannization

Accentuating the problems facing urban workers was Haussmann's 1860 redevelopment of Paris. During the eighteenth century, visitors to Paris remarked upon the seeming incongruity of a city that, from a distance, appeared magnificent, but up close revealed squalor, poverty, and disorder.[6] Constrained by its medieval origins, Paris remained largely untouched until Louis-Philippe's Prefect of the Seine, comte de Rambuteau, initiated the drive to render Paris a more liveable city, promising to give Parisians 'water, air, and shade.' By the 1850s Paris was attracting legions of provincials, drawn to the capital's higher wages (offset, of course, by its higher cost of living). An ambitious, and almost pathologically opportunistic, functionary, Haussmann capitalized on the Emperor's passion for a make-over of Paris that would bear his indelible stamp. Haussmann was not motivated simply by cynical intentions. If the Paris confronted by Rambuteau was a fetid, dark, choking urban labyrinth, it had gotten far worse over the ensuing years, buckling under the weight of both an antiquated infrastructure and a growing population. Haussmann's plan was a radical expansion of Rambuteau's original project, unconstrained by the financial and spatial concerns that hamstrung his predecessor's proposed reforms.

Haussmann's renovations addressed Paris's most pressing problems. They called for the enlargement of Paris's city limits beyond the original tax gates, razing of many dilapidated buildings, beautification of public spaces, installation of more sewer and water pipes, and the construction of long rectilinear boulevards. Under Haussmann's direction Paris was completely transformed into a showcase. The traffic that previously choked its narrow streets now wended effortlessly through large boulevards, facilitating travel throughout the city and from one side of the Seine to the other. The sewer and water system was a technological breakthrough, even if the technology had been borrowed from the Roman Empire; at the Universal Exposition of 1867 (the forerunner to the World's Fair), it was celebrated as 'a subterranean second Paris.' Land devoted to parks increased by nearly 100-fold (including the magnificent Buttes Chaumont in working-class Belleville and the domestication of the Bois de Boulogne) while formerly privately maintained squares became open to the public. Spatially Paris absorbed an area of more than 9300 acres and an additional population of 351,189, overwhelmingly comprised of provincial and foreign wage workers, nearly all of it the *banlieue* (suburbs) northeast and east of Paris. Perhaps Haussmann's most compelling argument for incorporating the *banlieue* into Paris was to bring some semblance of order to an area known as 'a no-man's land beyond the civilized pale, marked by mud, squalor, and shantytowns.'[7]

Before Haussmann's appointment as Prefect, Napoléon III dedicated himself to the completion of two projects thought of, but never brought to fruition, by his uncle: construction of the market pavilions known as Les Halles and an extension to the Rue de Rivoli. Haussmann resumed these plans and expanded on them through two different networks of boulevards and major streets and avenues that facilitated intracity travel while opening Paris to increased light and air. The road-works cleared away many old, some might say distinctive, neighborhoods and commercial zones, to make way for opportunities for new construction. Whereas the Empire built a few structures, most notably the Paris Opera House, it left most of the construction to private developers who were blessed by tax exemptions and loans with favorable terms, while being restricted by regulations on height, architectural style, and exterior maintenance. In other words, the government's seemingly tight regulatory scheme, designed to produce a uniform and more attractive capital, did not extend to the interiors of buildings; rather dichotomously old tenements gave way to new tenements, the latter being distinguished only by more attractive exterior facades![8]

Demolition and construction projects also created more employment and encouraged even more migrations to Paris. While this helped to alleviate unemployment and was crucial to Paris's renovation, the additional workers further strained municipal resources. Paris's working class was a consideration only to the extent that the make-over would lead to greater control over the *banlieue* and greater difficulties for insurgents to erect barricades across the wide boulevards. In fact, one of the chief motivations for the transformation was to make Paris more hospitable to the bourgeoisie. Although some aspects of the renovation, for example, the sewer system, benefited all Parisians, they were offset by other consequences. Rents rose exponentially, driving the working population further away from central Paris and towards its periphery, increasing their commuting time while literally and figuratively shifting them to the margins of Parisian life. Paraphrasing Haussmann opponent Louis Lazare's account of a poor family's travails under Haussmannization, David Jordan writes:

> Originally residents of the Halles neighborhood [in central Paris] they were driven out by demolitions and were unable to return, because rents had doubled. The family moved out of the center of Paris to suburban Belleville, and their journey to work in the city was now lengthened. When Belleville was incorporated rents were raised, and they were forced still farther from the center.[9]

Criticism of Paris's renovation was slow to generate, but once commenced, it incorporated a variety of arguments that tied the general philosophy of the Empire in Haussmannization's Gordian knot. Liberal republicans characterized Haussmann's dictatorial approach as representative of the Empire's highly centralized, undemocratic structure. Others, including celebrated author Victor Hugo, condemned the government as being complicit in a 'spiv economy' that rewarded financial speculators while penalizing the public interest. Finally, revolutionary republicans decried the dispossession of the working class whose condition had, if anything, been worsened by being ghettoized in a suburban semicircle. Reflecting on the veracity of these criticisms, historian David Jordan states, 'The emotional energy of the Commune was already in place.'[10]

Proudhon and the Emergence of a Working-Class Identity

During the 1850s Pierre-Joseph Proudhon exercised perhaps the greatest influence on working-class political thought. Although Proudhon's esoteric, contradictory, unresolved, sometimes impractical, ideas generated a wide following in the middle of the nineteenth century, they defy tidy interpretation.[11] Even his statement, 'Property is theft' was misinterpreted as an attack on property *per se* rather than as a condemnation of unearned income. A product of peasant and provincial working-class stock, Proudhon is best remembered as an advocate of mutualism, a theory for social reorganization that called upon small producers to replace capitalist modes of production and exchange with a system based on bargaining and cooperation. Producers, whether individuals or groups, would freely enter into 'federative contracts,' assuming mutual obligations towards each other, without entirely surrendering their individuality.

Proudhon's mutualist scheme minimized the role of government and replaced the centralized state with a federalist political structure. Originally associated with the Girondins and counter-revolutionaries during the French Revolution, federalism witnessed a revival after the left's experiences during the Second Republic revealed that a centralized government, even a republican one, could be a repressive force. Whereas most federalists believed that a devolved political structure would increase democracy, protect regional diversity, and prevent authoritarianism, Proudhon simply saw federalism as the least interventionist form of government. For Proudhon, the relative merits of a centralized or decentralized governmental structure was not the extent of the problem; rather, in his estimation, the State, and its incorporation of 'natural groups into an unnatural entity,' was the real source of oppression.[12] Though ostensibly a socialist, Proudhon had long been at odds with Jacobin socialists like Louis Blanc, for whom an activist state was the necessary precondition for socialism's advent. Instead of laying the stress on communitarian equality, Proudhon's conception focused on the liberty of individuals willfully integrating into a collective whole and forging a social contract that 'is not an arrangement between man and government, or between man and polity, but between man and man.'[13] Though some would take the Hobbesian position that the withering away of the state would result in disorder, Proudhon would counter that there is no order when the state must continually resort to force.[14]

In contrast to his contemporaries in the socialist camp, Proudhon did not wax lyrical over the model provided by the French Revolution. Rather, Proudhon attributed 1848's failings to its emulation of the French Revolution. In both cases, Proudhon claimed, a cadre of revolutionaries, preoccupied by their own advancement within a transformed political landscape, limited the revolutions to political change, thwarting the resolution of social problems.[15] Reflecting upon these experiences, Proudhon was ambivalent over revolution as a vehicle for change. Though he believed the width of the social chasm mandated revolutionary change, Proudhon viewed revolution as an uncontrollable process that, in relying on coercion to achieve its results, obviates the unity and liberty at the core of the mutualist system.[16]

Moving from theory to practice, Proudhon's belief that all forms of government are inherently authoritarian led him to a brief flirtation with the Empire, misguidedly hoping that Napoléon III's quest for popular support might result in the initiation of progressive legislation. By 1857, however, Proudhon's view changed completely, and, until his death in 1865, he urged the working class to develop a distinct class identity separate from the bourgeoisie and to seek their own amelioration. Proudhon cautioned workers to abstain from voting, even for republicans, as participation in a bourgeois political system, be it imperial or republican, would be a tacit endorsement of that system.

Proudhon's ideas found particular resonance amongst a small, educated segment of the working class. Whether as students in night classes or autodidactic, these workers formed the core of a burgeoning working-class intelligentsia which sought to raise the class-consciousness of their fellow workers. Through working-class organizations, pamphlets, poems, songs, and plays, they indicated a Proudhonian sensibility by inculcating a sense of separateness and autonomy amongst their working-class constituency. That said, anecdotal evidence raises some questions as to the extent to which workers had personally imbibed Proudhon's works or had a very general familiarity with his ideas.[17] In fact, while Henri Tolain, a bronze engraver and one of the first working-class advocates, maintained his fidelity to mutualism, over the course of the 1860s most working-class activists departed from his prescriptions. Though they continued to acknowledge Proudhon's influence, they only preserved his advice that the working class must take the lead role in its own liberation.

Beginning in 1859, Napoléon III began a concerted effort to coopt the working class. Motivated by the loss of conservative Catholic support (after his 1859 abandonment of Pope Pius IX's temporal authority), Napoléon III's initial overtures were the issuance of an amnesty to all political prisoners and exiles, followed by his patronage of a worker delegation to the London International Exposition of 1862. In London, the Parisian delegates, led by Tolain, initiated discussions with their working-class counterparts in other European countries. Two years later these contacts led to the formation of the International Association of Workingmen ('the International') and the drafting of 'the Manifesto of the Sixty,' a declaraton reflective of the increasing autonomy of the French labor movement. Under the guidance of orthodox Proudhonians such as Tolain, Ernest Fribourg, and Charles Limousin, though, the French section of the International adopted a conciliatory stance condemning strikes and rejecting confrontational politics. In fact, many viewed the French section of the International in its early years as an ally of the Empire.[18]

'The International' and Working-Class Politicization

Whatever sycophancy the International was guilty of in the first half of the 1860s, its position changed, ironically, when the Empire extended it more liberties by repealing the 1791 Le Chapelier Law that forbade worker coalitions and strike activity (though still punishing threats of violence and interferences with the 'right to work'[19]). Beginning in 1865, French workers in a variety of industries from bookbinding to bronze works to coalmining organized strikes, demanding better working conditions, higher pay, and an equal bargaining position.

Taking advantage of the Empire's liberalism, the French labor movement was, after 1867, increasingly under the direction of a younger generation of workers who assumed a decidedly more militant posture in rejecting the Empire's largess as paternalistic. Eugène Varlin, a leader in the bookbinders' union, dismissed the Proudhonian position that workers eschew political solutions: 'political revolution and social revolution are intertwined and cannot do without each other.'[20] However, the more the International engaged in political activity, the more the Empire endeavored to eliminate it; nonetheless, with each successive campaign of repression, including its suppression in March 1868, the International gained more adherents, its ranks swelling to between 40,000 to 50,000 at Paris, and between 200,000 and 500,000 nationally.[21]

By the late 1860s, Varlin, a one-time mutualist, strayed from Proudhon's ideas, embracing collectivism, actively supporting the liberation of women workers, and encouraging workers to strike. Varlin's one remaining link to Proudhon's ideas was his disavowal of violent means. Napoléon III's carefully crafted facade of representing the 'nation' and no particular party or interest group cracked under the weight of more intense labor protests. In 1869, relations between the state and workers changed dramatically after the Empire called out the military against striking miners, first at la Ricamarie on 17 June, and then at Aubin on 8 October, resulting in 13 and 14 deaths respectively. As the dead became martyrs to the workers' cause, attitudes on both sides hardened. In outright defiance of the government, Varlin reorganized the International and, amongst the working class, both the International's prestige and its militancy were at their apex. As the state pursued, and received, one last series of judicial condemnations of leading Internationalists in July 1870, military hostilities between France and Prussia were about to commence. Within seven weeks, the Empire fell, the Internationalists were liberated, but the International faded from importance, overshadowed and subsumed by events between early September 1870 and late May 1871. Inasmuch as a number of Communards had been active in the International, it had little chance of surviving the repressive atmosphere that prevailed in post-Commune France. Blamed for having been the Commune's inspiration and feared as a potential source for future conflicts, the International was outlawed in both France and Spain while activists in the Commune were the targets of legal proceedings in Denmark, Austria-Hungary, and Germany.

Revolutionary Republicanism: Blanquists and Neo-Jacobins

Beaten, but not completely obliterated, republicanism limped through the 1850s to reemerge in the relatively relaxed political climate of the following decade as something akin to a loyal opposition. Having recognized the futility of their original strategy of urging abstention from elections, moderate republicans sought election to the Legislative Assembly. Being very much on the outside of Napoleonic political culture, republicans resisted their usual tendency towards political cannibalism and, instead, maintained the unity that proved illusive to them throughout the Second Republic. Republicans of all stripes, bourgeois and working class, liberals and socialists, centralists and decentralists coalesced around several fundamental republican ideals: anti-Bonapartism, to be sure, but more importantly, identification with the legacy of the French Revolution and attachment to its core ideals of liberty, fraternity, manhood suffrage, and anti-clericalism. With the accent squarely on political solutions, republicans largely shunted aside the more divisive social issue, emphasizing, instead, the unity necessary for arriving at the republic. As long as republicanism 'was contained by the imperatives of the political struggle against the Second Empire,' social and political republicans muted their differences and sought consensus.[22] Such unity, however, would not be enduring.

The 'social question,' though relegated to the back burner of republicanism, nevertheless persisted. The French Revolution, the historical experience that provided republicanism with its foundation and unified all republicans, also, on another level, drove a wedge between them. Although all republicans could find common ground around the most general principles of the Revolution, the Revolution was no ideological monolith. Rather, its legacy was readily divisible; 1793 provided a chronological fault line that, as under the Second Republic, separated political from social republicans.

During the second half of the 1860s, social republicanism became impregnated with revolutionary rhetoric. Historians have situated the revolutionary republicans in the Blanquist, Internationalist, or neo-Jacobin camps, but, in reality, these designations were no more than nuanced distinctions, and in some cases, reflected little more than personal animosities. For example, while imprisoned from 1861 to 1864, Auguste Blanqui, the unrepentant revolutionary, received visits from Georges Clemenceau, the future president of the Third Republic then a young doctor flirting with militant politics. Blanqui broke off contact with Clemenceau after learning that he had also been visiting Charles Delescluze, a *démoc-soc.*[23] While in prison, Blanqui became a magnet for students, journalists, and even some workers, many of whom had begun dabbling in the philosophical currents (e.g., mutualism and positivism) of the time. Assuming the role for a new generation of activists that Buonarroti had played for his cohort three decades previously, Blanqui's credibility was only enhanced when, as his prison term drew to a close in 1865, the authorities ordered him rearrested in the interest of public security.[24]

Whereas Blanqui's place in history has largely been confined to the role of inveterate conspirator, he was a substantive, if not always original, thinker. By the late 1860s, his writings amalgamated the principal currents of nineteenth-century French social and political thought – revolution, utopianism, republicanism, and communism. Characterizing revolutions as violent manifestations of social-class tension, Blanqui and his followers contributed an understanding of France's revolutionary history premised on social-class conflict. This represented a departure from previous conceptions of revolution as resulting from a national consensus against an economically and socially powerful minority. According to Blanqui, French history was littered with instances in which a revolutionary vanguard challenged the existing political order only to exit prematurely from the revolutionary stage, its work later subverted by opportunists. Blanqui insisted that, in order to ensure its control over the process it put in motion, the revolutionary elite needed to establish a Parisian dictatorship over the nation.[25]

The Blanquists located the origins of their revolutionary creed in the example of the Hébertists, followers of Jacques-René Hébert. A journalist whose extreme revolutionary views and vulgar prose were calculated to resonate with a *sans-culottes* audience, Hébert's place in the history of the Revolution was, at its most charitable, relegated to that of misguided idealist who sowed the seeds of class division. In 1864, one of Blanqui's most dedicated followers, Gustave Tridon, immortalized the Hébertists as representing the true ideals of the Revolution.

Consistent with the polemical nature of most publications on the French Revolution produced during the middle third of the nineteenth century, Tridon's *Les Hébertistes* represented yet another attempt at forging a tradition out of the Revolution's malleable past.[26] It made little difference that Tridon's idolatry of the Hébertists as harbingers of communism was totally misplaced and that nothing in Hébert's rhetoric evinced hostility to private property.[27] Less a historical tract than a political platform, *Les Hébertistes* conveyed the aspirations of Blanquism: an uprising by a committed cadre who maintain the revolutionary initiative. Exercising a dictatorship from Paris, the crucible of revolution, Blanqui's revolutionary elite would enlighten the unenlightened and regenerate France into an egalitarian, democratic, atheistic, fraternal and communist republic.

In retelling the story of the Hébertists, Tridon cast them as tragic heroes of the revolutionary saga, 'intellectuals . . . willing to share the suffering of the people,' beleaguered by adversaries masquarading as revolutionaries (the Girondins), and eliminated by rivals who had neither affinity nor empathy for the people (the Jacobins).[28] In fact, Hébert's adversarial relationship with Robespierre rendered him a particularly attractive historical standard bearer for the Blanquists. Blanqui's writings reveal an undisguised contempt for Robespierre. Although it is possible that there was a personal dimension to Blanqui's hostility (his father, a Girondin-sympathizing member of the Convention, barely survived the Terror), in all likelihood, Blanqui was unable to reconcile his material atheism with Robespierre's grounding of the First Republic on the deistic Festival of the Supreme Being.[29] Alone the Hébertists of Tridon's work exemplified, but were unable to bring to fruition, the Revolution's highest ideals.

The young intellectuals who formed the nucleus of Blanqui's disciples cast themselves as the inheritors of the Hébertist revolutionary tradition. By situating their movement in the Hébertist shadow, Blanquists claimed a piece of the Revolution for themselves. Association with the Revolution bestowed a sense of historical destiny to the Blanquists as their responses had transcendence over the immediate issues of the late 1860s.

The conspiratorial nature of Blanquism foreclosed any prospect of it becoming a mass movement. On the other hand, during the final two years of the Empire, neo-Jacobinism experienced a renaissance. Associated with such concepts as centralized government, revolutionary dictatorship, chauvanistic republican nationalism, and a controlled economy, Jacobinism had become, for conservatives, *la bête noire* of revolutionary excess. Though revolutionary republicans during the Second Republic routinely identified themselves as Jacobins, and were labeled as such by their opponents, their attachment was largely due to a mythologized understanding of Jacobinism as a beacon of republican socialism; in reality, neo-Jacobins so routinely strayed from its commanding eighteenth-century principles that Jacobinism had become little more than a convenient historical designation.[30]

Although some historians have gone to great lengths to draw strategic and doctrinal distinctions between Blanquists and neo-Jacobins[31] in the overall context of late Second Empire politics, the differences would have been barely perceptible at the time. The distrust neo-Jacobins, reconstructed *démoc-socs*, harbored towards the Blanquists appears to have been motivated more by historical considerations than by any substantive disputes. In other words, although they addressed contemporary issues, republicans were more bedeviled by their propensity to enrobe themselves symbolically in the vestments of their historical heroes and to revisit their disputes. In this case neo-Jacobins and Blanquists were less likely to view each other as revolutionary *confrères* than as latter day incarnations of Robespierre and Hébert, anachronistically resuming their conflict. Conversely, historians Alain Dalotel and Jean-Claude Freiermuth argue that substance lay behind these designations and that 'it was by virtue of these choices that people split themselves up into socialists or communists, idealists or materialists.'[32]

Above all, neo-Jacobins and Blanquists shared a similar perspective on the unavoidable inevitability of a violent contest for power, though as we have seen, Blanquism premised this on a sectarian *putsch*. Similar to the Blanquists, the neo-Jacobins also wove social and economic democracy into the weft of the fabric of their republic, crossing the warp of manhood suffrage. Neo-Jacobinism was not a political party, but rather a designation. As such, defining it by reference to anything approaching a party platform is nearly impossible. During the Second Empire, most neo-Jacobins rarely spoke or wrote in specific programatic terms, instead reiterating core republican values (manhood suffrage, secular and compulsory education), peppered with positions ranging from support for social welfare to substantial state intervention in the economy.

Some historians have characterized the Blanquists as anarchists committed to the elimination of the state, in contrast to the neo-Jacobins' support for a strong state, as evidence of a substantive difference between the two factions. The syllogism falls apart when one considers the contradictory evidence relative to the Blanquists' ultimate goal. It was Blanqui's hostile view of Robespierre, the symbol of Jacobin statism, rather than any identifiable expression of anarchistic rhetoric, that accounts for this confused interpretation.[33]

As it was, the neo-Jacobins were unambiguous in their advocacy of a strong centralized state emerging out of a revolution. Like the Blanquists, they too believed in the necessity of a period of dictatorship. While their activist and interventionist state was the antithesis of

Proudhonianism and bourgeois liberalism, their socialist convictions, though not well formulated, were not too far removed from the similarly ambiguous Blanquist communism.

Age, and its attendant frames of reference, best explain the differences between Blanquists and neo-Jacobins. Older than the Blanquists, and having actively participated in the Second Republic, neo-Jacobins, including Charles Delescluze, Félix Pyat, Charles Gambon, were less disillusioned by the ideals of 1848 than by how they had been betrayed. In contrast, the Blanquist leadership and support was centered amongst the students of the Latin Quarter. At once intellectually and viscerally appealing to students, Blanquism appeared as a romantic and adventurous alternative to other movements on the left. Students were drawn to Blanqui's stoic martyrdom and the seamlessness by which his life connected the French Revolution with nineteenth-century revolutions. In the estimation of many young intellectuals, the *démoc-socs* had squandered an opportunity in 1848 and lacked Blanqui's uncompromising verve, audacity, rationality, and stridency. Though Blanqui hoped, and expected, to attract working-class support, his efforts were largely unsuccessful as the Blanquist emphasis on atheism, direct action, and socialism did not resonate with workers.[34]

Liberalism Amid Turmoil: 1868–1870

The republican left's ability to disseminate its positions received a huge boost with the Empire's lifting of some restrictions on the press (11 May 1868) and the right to assemble (6 June 1868). Often cited as further evidence of the Empire's trend towards liberalization, the laws also encapsulated the limits to Napoléon III's liberalism. By maintaining restrictions on political and religious discussions, but permitting discussions of the social economy, the Empire hoped to direct the tone of working-class discourse away from its increasing infatuation with political solutions and to reestablish himself as the benefactor of organized labor.[35]

In promulgating reforms that gave a voice to his opposition, Napoléon III did not choose a very propitious moment. By the second half of the 1860s, the economic, diplomatic, and political buoyancy of the 1850s succumbed to the laws of gravity, reversing more than a decade of foreign policy successes, economic growth, and political stability. In 1867 Napoléon III was forced to order the evacuation of French troops from Mexico, ending a very costly six-year expedition whose goals or purposes were never formulated with any precision. In 1860, against the advice of French manufacturers, the Empire secretly negotiated a free-trade agreement with Britain. At the time, French manufacturing technology was significantly behind British standards; intent on modernizing and improving French production standards through free trade, Napoléon III disturbed France's traditional protective trade policies that shielded inefficient producers from foreign competition. Steadily over the course of the 1860s, the agreement contributed to an economic downturn in France as more efficiently manufactured British products flooded into France without a reciprocal flow. The 1867 collapse of the Crédit Mobilier Bank, the epitomy of the Bonapartist economic success of the 1850s, signaled economic disaster for the regime. Economic and foreign policy failures opened up the Empire to greater scrutiny by both its royalist and republican opponents. Republican candidates to the Corps Législatif, who had carried majorities at Paris, Marseilles, Lyon, Lille, Bordeaux, and Toulouse in 1863, nearly doubled their share of the urban vote in the 1869 election. More ominously, though, republicans unwilling to reconcile themselves to loyal opposition experienced the largest leap in support.

With the passage of the press and meetings laws, dissenters had an outlet for their opposition to the regime. Amongst the revolutionary republican press, Charles Delescluze's *Le Réveil* best exemplified the potential for reawakening the republican conscience. In November 1868 *Le Réveil* opened a subscription to erect a monument to Alphonse Baudin, heretofore an obscure Second Republic deputy who was killed on a Parisian barricade on 3 December 1851 while extolling workers to fight against Louis-Bonaparte's *coup d'état*. The imperial authorities chose to make an example of Delescluze, after a rally at Baudin's tomb turned violent. While Delescluze was convicted and sentenced to a six-month prison term, the trial pitted the regime against the liberty it claimed to represent. In the words of Dalotel and Freiermuth, by 'April 1870 the liberal Empire was very much the enemy of the very freedom it purported to establish.'[36] Though it was the central player in one of the pivotal domestic crises in the final years of the Empire, *Le Réveil*'s circulation was limited to 8000 copies. However, in mid-December 1869, Henri Rochefort, the iconoclastic scion of a prestigous noble family, launched *La Marseillaise*, a journal whose circulation exceeded 40,000. Uniting the various strands of revolutionary republican thought, *La Marseillaise* provided a journalistic forum for future Communards such as Arthur

Arnould, Gustave Cluseret, Gustave Flourens, Pascal Grousset, Paul Lafargue, Prosper Lissagaray, Benoît Malon, Jules Vallès, Eugène Varlin, and Eugène Vermersch to transcend the petty doctrinal squabbles in which revolutionary republicans were mired. Most notably, *La Marseillaise* printed the rhetoric at republican meetings.

Within months of the passage of the law on meetings, gatherings of between 800 and 3000 people proliferated throughout Paris. Throughout 1869 until May 1870, over 1000 meetings took place. While the majority stayed within the confines of the law while eschewing political questions, political questions were not completely ignored. Revolutionary republicans, in particular, routinely flouted the law and exposed themselves to prosecutions. Reflecting the spirit of *La Marseillaise*, they temporarily put a moratorium on their internecine conflicts and articulated and defined the ideals that would form the foundation for the Commune.

Whereas the parliamentary republican perspective dominated the press, revolutionary republican thought pervaded at the meetings. The discourse at the meetings can be broken down into the past, the present, and the future. More specifically, the past refers to the propensity of speakers to look back to the French Revolution and 1848 as either inspiration or pitfalls to avoid. As far as the present is concerned, contemporary topics such as elections to the Corps Législatif, the plebiscite on Napoléon III, the murder of journalist Victor Noir by the Emperor's cousin, were covered in the meetings. By far the most compelling rhetoric at the meetings was devoted to the future, and in particular, to revolution.

France's revolutionary tradition was never far from the surface at the political meetings. Fidelity to the French Revolution was hardly a litmus test for earning one's revolutionary republican credentials; nearly all republicans expressed their adhesion to the Revolution, seeing it as a fount of lost or as yet unrealized aspirations. The critical line of demarcation was over dates. To revolutionary republicans, the ideals of 1789, so dear to liberal and moderate republicans, were too tepid, too steeped in bourgeois principles. The true spirit of the Revolution, the one most worthy of emulation more than six decades later, was 1793. Although 1793 remained a potential flashpoint between neo-Hébertists and neo-Jacobins, as a whole speakers presented the Revolution as the progenitor of the modern revolutionary republican movement. This is not to say that fidelity to the Revolution was the equivalent of fidelity to accuracy. Speakers often mischaracterized the ideological stances of eighteenth-century Jacobins and the *sans-culottes*. Robespierre, Danton, Saint-Just were all transposed into communists; the *sans-culottes* nearly indistinct from the nineteenth-century proletariat. Ends justified means as speakers lauded the decisiveness, however violent, of crowds during the French Revolution whose idea of sovereignty was not limited to representative government.

Though bronze bas-relief plaques bearing Marat's likeness or emulations of Robespierre's fashion sense may have been more of a decorative fad, there was substance behind the choice of 1793. As Dalotel and Freiermuth remind us, declaring one's allegiance to 1793 was a means for circumventing the continued prohibition against political commentary. It was also understood to be a political testimonial in support of revolution. Although distinctions began to emerge between speakers when discussions turned to controversial figures like Hébert and Babeuf, by 1870, all revolutionary republicans accepted 1793 as their common heritage.[37]

If 1793 was the historical fault line that separated revolutionary from parliamentary republicans, June 1848 represented a tectonic schism of unbridgeable proportions. Having occurred within the lifetime of all participants in the meetings, 1848 was etched in the collective memory as the unfulfilled dream of a democratic and social republic. June 1848 revealed the folly of February's expectations that a republic could transcend class divisions. As republicans held on for dear life to what was left of the Second Republic, they subordinated social class for survival until the amalgamation of socialists and republicans during the 1860s revivified the political hues of social class conflict last seen in 1848. Social-class conflict moved to the center of the revolutionary republican universe, with bourgeois republicans, especially those connected to the collapse of the Second Republic, being lumped in with Legitimists, Orléanists, and Bonapartists as adversaries. In the 1869 campaign, speakers at revolutionary republican clubs urged the rejection of parliamentary republicans, reminding their audiences that these same individuals, responsible for repressing workers in June 1848, had since been coopted by Bonapartist liberalism.

While it is to be expected that revolutionary republicans would use the public meetings as a vehicle to lash out against the Empire, less predictable was the vehemence with which they expressed their hostility towards parliamentary republicans, whether moderate or radical. Militants vociferously attacked the 1869 candidacies of Marie, Garnier-Pagès, Jules Favre, and Eugène Cavaignac, all of whom were leaders of the republican parliamentary opposition to Napoléon III, but were com-promised by their conservatism during the Second Republic.[38] Although social democrats from 1848 (e.g., François Raspail) received strong support from the clubs, the rhetoric of 1860s revolutionary republi-canism had surpassed them. As June 1848 became the defining month of the Second Republic, 1848 became a cautionary tale for revolutionary republicans, made all the more imperative by a growing sense that the Empire was drawing to a close.

Political meetings also addressed contemporary events, distilling the issues of greatest pertinence to their audiences in the expectation of stimulating action. In fact, it was the responses generated at meetings to two events – the murder of journalist Victor Noir and the plebiscite on Napoléon III's liberal reforms – that led authorities to suspend the law of 6 June 1868. As already noted, the 1869 elections to the Corps Législatif dominated meetings during spring 1869, providing evidence of increasing social-class polarization.

On 10 January 1870, Prince Pierre Bonaparte, the Emperor's cousin, killed Victor Noir, a young editor on *La Marseillaise*. Two days later, a crowd estimated at between 80,000 and 200,000 turned up for Noir's funeral amid a highly charged atmosphere; a violent confrontation with government troops was only averted when Rochefort insisted that the cortege march to the western suburb of Neuilly rather than through central Paris where the troops awaited them. Nonetheless, while Noir's imperial killer received only a fine from a special court, Rochefort was charged with incitement and sentenced to six-months imprisonment. As the clubs rallied behind Rochefort, the government aggravated an already delicate situation, ordering the closure of clubs for one week and the arrest of numerous meeting organizers. The harsh treatment meted out to the cautious Rochefort led to a radicalization of discourse at the clubs as no accommodation with the Empire appeared possible.

Between January and March 1870 one of the most violent strikes of the period occurred at the Schneider mineworks at Le Creusot. One of the wealthiest men in France whose mineworks employed nearly 10,000 workers, Eugène Schneider also wielded considerable political influence as both a legislative deputy and board member of one of the major French railway lines (for which his mine works was a major supplier!) The Le Creusot strike, and the deadly strikes at La Ricamarie and Aubin the year before, brought the real world of labor–capital relations to the meetings in a way that abstract discussions of elections and socialism could not. Discussions of the strikes, collections of donations, and references to the martyrdom of the fallen fostered working-class solidarity while the violence at Le Creusot inspired revolutionary discourse. Ironically, the namesake of the 1864 law that legalized strikes, Émile Ollivier, a one-time republican who now headed the government, made the call for troops to repress the strike. Whereas the Empire's one-time paternalistic, palliative concessions to the working class encouraged workers to address labor activity in a non-political way, the Empire's violent defense of the interests of capital altered the dynamic; no longer could economic activity be bifurcated from political questions. Working-class activists, such as Eugène Varlin, understood that the solitary strike, shorn of linkage to larger political movements, was too limited. Varlin and others extolled attendees at meetings to view strikes as a weapon, but not the ends, of working-class activism. In other words, the working class had moved past the parochialism of labor issues.

Conceivably, strikes carried implications that transcended the narrowness of labor disputes. In the run-up to the 8 May 1870 plebiscite on the liberal Empire (increasingly appearing to be an oxymoron), orators addressed abstention from voting in terms of a strike. Revolutionary republicans argued at the clubs that even the act of casting a 'no' vote was tantamount to both a validation of the Empire's legitimacy in fixing the parameters of political debate and cession to the leadership provided by liberal and moderate opponents of the regime. Instead, revolutionary republicans urged their audiences to spoil their ballots with expressions of protest (e.g., 'long live the '93 consitution,' 'long live the social and democratic republic,' or just simply, 'shit') and thereby engage in the equivalent of a strike against the extant political process. On the other hand, clubbists were far from unified on this front; after the Empire directed a repression against advocates of abstention, the majority of speakers urged a 'no' vote as the least ambiguous sign of opposition to the Empire. Interestingly, both abstentionists and 'no' supporters believed they were at the forefront of a revolution; the former seeing no alternative to a violent confrontation, the latter hoping a majority vote against the Empire would produce a peaceful revolution limited to political change. The overwhelming majority won by the Empire in the plebiscite reaffirmed the revolutionary republican position that it was chimerical to believe that a revolution could ever be anything but violent and comprehensive in scope.[39]

Overshadowing discussions of the past and the present at the meetings were considerations of a future French republic. In spite of the judgment of at least one historian that, had it not been for the disastrous

Franco-Prussian War, 'there is no reason to doubt that the parliamentary Empire would have survived,'[40] clubbists seemed poised for its imminent collapse.[41] In fact, through discussions on a future revolution and the regenerated society it would produce, we see the Commune in chrysalis form, causing historian Alain Faure to conclude: 'The Commune was born during the Empire.'[42]

Anticipating the unity that would be needed to overcome both the Empire and bourgeois republicans, speakers urged revolutionaries to subordinate their doctrinal differences in favor of a unified commitment to very generally articulated socialist ideals. While revolutionary republican speakers at the clubs were unable to come to agreement on the feasibility of a post-revolution dictatorship or the extent to which privately owned property should be tolerated, they were unanimous in their call for the reorganization of society into 'social communes.' Perhaps in anticipation of different understandings of the Commune that would develop amongst the Communards, clubbists rarely got beyond the generalities of the idea. However, the very ambiguity of the Commune, and the fact that there were no precedents for organizing a republic as a confederation, allowed club activists wide latitude in formulating and conveying their conceptions of the Commune.

End of the Empire

The combination of the mandate he received from the May plebiscite, imprisonment or exile of club leaders in the repressive aftermath of the plebiscite, and the prohibition of public meetings appeared to offer Napoléon III a level of security he had not had since the early 1860s. Just over ten weeks later, however, France ill advisedly declared war on Prussia. Long anticipated, but until then avoided, the French declaration was further confirmation of Napoléon III's continued propensity for rash acts. Voices of sanity were drowned out amid baseless optimism that the Prussian army would collapse under the weight of a French offensive and diplomatic pressure by European states fearful of Prussia's growth. It was France, though, that was diplomatically isolated and a Prussian force that numbered over 800,000 easily outmatched its paltry army of 370,000 troops. By early August the French offensive had turned into a rout, and the Prussian army was fully ensconced on French soil.

In a premature gesture that was bound to fail, 300 Blanquists attacked the fire station at La Villette on 14 August, hoping to get their hands on its arsenal. Quickly routed by the local police force, the Blanquists descended into Belleville shouting, 'Long live the Republic! Death to the Prussians! To arms!' Their nationalistically tinged revolutionary cries went unheeded. Although he had attempted to temper the insurrectionary zeal of his young followers, much as he had urged caution in 1839, Blanqui had been unsuccessful. What Blanqui understood, but what was beyond the experiential ken of his disciples, was that revolutionary situations arise organically, and must be seized by its ever-vigilant vanguard. In the repression that followed, several Blanquists, including future Communard Émile Eudes, were tried, convicted, and sentenced to death; however, events less than three weeks later fortuitously saved Eudes. On 2 September, Napoléon III, his troops surrounded at Sedan, surrendered to the Prussians; two days later, at Paris, republicans of all varieties declared the fall of the Empire and proclaimed its replacement by a republic.

Conclusion

The French Revolution established the parameters of political culture in nineteenth-century France. The Revolution bequeathed the heritage of republicanism as a partible legacy that separated liberals from socialists, bourgeoisie from workers, reformers from revolutionaries, town from country. The Revolution's ideas and personalities were one part exemplar, one part commemorable event; they permeated and punctuated nineteenth-century discourse, ideology, and action, at times constraining republicans from accurately understanding the past or from creatively addressing contemporary problems. The stones set by the French Revolution, but reconfigured by nineteenth-century events, paved the road to the Commune.

Revolutionary republicanism in the nineteenth century functioned on two different levels: as an incessant quest to realize the egalitarian promise of the French Revolution and as a response to changes in the French political, economic, social, and cultural landscapes that were unimaginable at the time of the Revolution. The result of the French Revolution was to position the Parisian bourgeoisie and working class at opposite ends of the social axis, viewing each other with undisguised suspicion from vastly different existences. When locating a single republican consensus over fraternity, the least complicated, but most fundamental of the revolutionary triptych, proved illusory,[43] it was apparent that a social, political, and geographical chasm separated revolutionary republicans from most other shades of political opinion, including moderate republicans. As it turned out, the gulf dividing republicans was almost as unbridgeable, and nearly as violent, as the divide between monarchists and republicans.

Essentially, since the Revolution, politics had become more complicated as republicanism intersected with the social changes that emerged out of economic, demographic, ideological, and cultural transformations. The correspondence between brewing class conflict and the liberalized political climate of the late 1860s provided an opportunity for students, idealists, and labor activists to articulate an alternative revolutionary, though not always clear and consistent, vision of republicanism. However, this much was clear: the republican references and ideals to which they subscribed were fundamentally different from those of parliamentary and reformist republicans. If the rapid fall of the Second Empire made for an easy birth for the Third Republic, divisions that had developed over the decades within republicanism did not suggest an uncomplicated postpartum.

Chapter 2: Prelude to the Commune

It's always the same sham. These gentlemen believe they have the right to seize power in the name of the people.[1]

At a little past 10 a.m. on 5 September 1870 in a crowd at the Gare du Nord railway station, a fifty-one year old professor, Victor Desplats, looked longingly at a train heading towards Boulogne and carrying his loved ones: Clara, his young wife, and their three sons, Eugène, eleven years old, Lucien, two-and-a-half years old, and André, six months . . . . Desplats thought that he acted wisely. He believed the separation would last a few days, perhaps a few weeks at the most. The exile would, in fact, last twelve months and fourteen days.

Just the day before, on 4 September, Desplats had witnessed a frenzy of activity at Paris. At 10 a.m. rumors circulated that the French military had been defeated by the Prussians at Sedan. By 5:00 p.m. a crowd, that Desplats estimated at 30,000, marched in a peacefully and orderly fashion towards the Place de la Concorde and the Palais-Royale, the official residence of Emperor Louis-Napoléon. Within hours, Parisian republican deputies to the Corps Législatif, desirous of controlling a potentially explosive situation, formed a new government and officially proclaimed France to be a republic (republicans at Lyon and Marseille had done this several hours earlier). The mood was euphoric as republicans of different ideological orientations and generations celebrated yet another opportunity at forging a republic.

In spite of the absence of blood or gunfire in this profound transference of authority, Desplats felt very uneasy. He had a premonition of a Prussian invasion, war in the streets of Paris, and social conflict. With this in mind, Desplats felt it prudent to get his loved ones out of harm's

way until the crisis had subsided. Although Desplats was correct in presaging that the worst was yet to come, his expectation of a relatively
quick resolution of the crisis fell very wide of the mark.[2]

On 15 July 1870 the government of Napoléon III, enthusiastically
backed by the two chambers of the legislature, declared war on Prussia.
Overwhelmed by the chauvinistic nationalism of its colleagues, the
republican opposition in the legislature was unable to initiate a meaningful debate on the sagacity of such a declaration. Instead, France had
been lured into a war orchestrated by Prussian Chancellor Otto von
Bismarck. A couple of weeks earlier he had laid the groundwork by his
advancement of the candidacy of the Hohenzollern competitor for the
vacant Spanish throne. Fully aware of the good condition and state of
preparedness of Prussia's military and the commensurate decline of the
French military, Chancellor Bismarck had calculated that a successful
war against France would culminate in the geopolitical unification of
Germany.

In pursuit of this larger aim, and relating it to the succession to the
Spanish throne, Bismarck edited and then released to the press a
telegram sent by the King of Prussia. Calculated to be a 'red flag to the
Gallic bull,' the missive revealed the details of an acrimonious meeting
between the King and the French ambassador to Prussia, after which the
King stated his refusal to meet again with the ambassador over the
matter. France was thrown into a state of panic over the prospect of
being encircled by Prussia on the east and the south. The bellicosity of
opportunistic politicians and an overly zealous press had set the tone on
both sides of the Rhine; Bismarck exploited that mood and successfully
maneuvered France into declaring war while positioning Prussia in a
defensive posture against French aggression.

On 3 August, the French military had suffered its first big defeat; by 18
August, the Prussian army was entirely on French soil and France's
vaunted Army of the Rhine was completely blockaded; for France, the
combination of this circumstance and its inept military leadership and
strategy rendered the war virtually unwinnable. On 2 September,
Napoléon III entered into negotiations with Bismarck and, on the following day, formally surrendered to, and became a prisoner of, his
Prussian counterpart, King William I. Although the French public had
been informed of the various defeats, the idea of surrender was entirely
unconscionable.

As news of the surrender hit the Paris streets on 4 September, it provoked the series of events recounted by Desplats. Whereas Desplats saw a

bad omen, Victorine Brocher, an activist in the French section of the International Association of Workers, was elated. Brocher described the declaration of the republic as being the antidote to the surrender and of producing an intoxicating effect on the crowd that 'was so convinced that with the Republic, we would conquer the Prussians, that it was acclaimed with incomparable enthusiasm.'[3] However, the majority of the republican opposition in the legislature was not so enthusiastic about declaring a republic under such potentially volatile circumstances. In fact, it only had to look back a few weeks to 14 August when the first reports of mounting military defeats led some followers of professional revolutionary Auguste Blanqui on a half-hearted attempt at a republican revolution. Although that attempt ended in dismal failure, it did put moderate republicans, desirous of a seamless transition to republicanism, on notice regarding the historical association of French republics with revolution. This problem became thornier once the obvious comparisons were made between the circumstances attending the declaration of France's first republic in 1792 and the contemporary situation. Participants on 4 September could not help but view themselves as standing in the shadows of Jacobinism. Their nostalgic look back to France's First Republic provided them not only with inspiration for reversing military defeats, but, more troubling for republican moderates, the identification of Jacobinism with revolutionary government.

Jules Favre, a veteran of the Second Republic and leader of the republican opposition as a Parisian deputy to the Corps Législatif, had hoped for a parliamentary transition to a republic. The activity on 4 September prematurely pushed Favre to assume the reins of governmental power. Endeavoring to extinguish whatever revolutionary embers threatened to erupt into a general conflagration, Favre put together a provisional government drawn from the republican deputies elected from Paris, thus ensuring a government characterized by moderation, but also ostensibly confirming the leadership of the capital.

The core of the provisional government – known as the Government of National Defense (since its mandate was the expulsion of German troops from French soil) – was essentially comprised of liberal, constitutional republicans who were neither associated with the revolutionary left nor were advocates of a social republic. Some, like Favre, Emmanuel Arago, Louis-Antoine Garnier-Pagès, Adolphe Crémieux, had played prominent roles in 1848 and, in the eyes of the left, were forever associated with the lost promise of the Second Republic. Others, such as Jules Ferry, Ernest Picard, Jules Simon and Léon Gambetta, had cut their political teeth as part of the parliamentary republican opposition to Napoléon III. The naming of General Jules Trochu, the Governor of Paris, to the Government's presidency was both a recognition that the military crisis overshadowed all other issues as well as an effort at currying support from Orléanists. Trochu's appointment was balanced, though, by the inclusion of journalist Henri Rochefort (who had been liberated from prison literally minutes before) in the government. While Favre hoped to placate Orléanists with Trochu, the inclusion of Rochefort was not necessarily much of a gesture to social republicans; given the fact that Rochefort was a Parisian deputy, his exclusion from the Government would have been difficult to explain. That said, if Favre believed that a government of national unity required a voice from the left, Rochefort was a more palatable, and as a deputy for Paris, a more logical choice than such infamous revolutionary republicans as Gustave Flourens, Charles Delescluze, Auguste Blanqui and Jean-Baptiste Millière and, as a Parisian deputy, a more logical one.

The majority of the Government understood that its objective of attenuating the embryonic republic from revolutionary associations was not made any easier by the activities of 4 September. Perhaps more disconcerting was the prospect that the crowd which pushed for the declaration of the republic might ultimately determine its future orientation. Favre understood that the crowd's celebratory mood on 4 September and its failure to push for the inclusion of republican militants in the government was not to be confused with unqualified confidence in, and acceptance of, the personnel of the provisional government. The challenge for the Government was to maintain the left's support for its handling of the war effort while, at the same time, creating the conditions for an orderly, stable and secure republic.

While the republic was still in its chrysalis stage, all ideological differences that separated shades of republicanism and republicans from monarchists were subordinated to the nationalist cause. During the Empire, solidarity, rather than the internecine warfare that would soon become manifest, best characterized the republican movement as socialist and constitutional republicans coalesced against Bonapartism.[4] This same spirit of unity persisted during the first days after the fall of the Empire. For example, after Gustave Cluseret, an influential leader on the left, raised the specter of social-class conflict in the pages of the popular newspaper, La Marseillaise, he was personally threatened by a crowd from the working-class suburb of Belleville and the newspaper ceased publication altogether.[5]

Support for the Government from the left was conditional and temporary. In the long term, the republican left, with its emphasis on a social agenda and its references to 1793, was both ideologically and historically estranged from the moderates. During the Empire, the parliamentary republicans were little more than an opposition party, often in coalition with the Orléanists in the Corps Législatif. They limited their conception of the republic to a political form, and were careful not to advocate a corresponding social or cultural agenda that would require a period of revolutionary government.

By contrast, for the left, the transition to a republic was a transformative experience, reconnecting the nation with its history and providing it with a common identity. For the duration of the war, the left was willing to forgo its commitment to revolutionary republicanism. As Brocher's words indicate, Parisians enthusiastically believed that, as in 1793, the soldiers of republican France would fight with renewed vigor and commitment and, again, emerge victorious.[6] Desplats, though less sympathetic to the left, reflected the victorious sentiment that reigned at Paris during those first few weeks of the republic when, in his second letter to his wife, dated 10 September, he wrote, 'The war's character has changed today. This is the entire nation taking up arms. France cannot be conquered.'[7]

Those wielding authority did not share Desplats's unbridled optimism. Recognizing that the war was unwinnable and that its prolongation simply imperiled the stable social and political order they desired, the majority of the government favored surrender and immediate elections to a legislature. Favre also understood that, in spite of the peaceful transition from empire to republic, his government's legitimacy and longevity could still be determined on the streets of Paris.[8] With sentiment in the capital strongly opposed to a capitulation, an experienced politician like Favre was aware of the impracticality and impolicy of surrendering to the Prussians. However, Favre was also pulled by his desire to restore order and stability to France. Within a fortnight of having assumed power, the Government of National Defense was actively, though covertly, pursuing peace.

The prospects for peace were also made difficult by the establishment of quasi-rival sources of political authority. Throughout September, the number of National Guard battalions in Paris continued to grow. Formed in 1789 to safeguard the authority of the National Assembly from royal troops, the National Guard served, depending upon the extant political regime, as a loyal governmental militia or as the vigilant guardian of national (as opposed to royal) sovereignty.

The vicissitudes of the nineteenth-century French political landscape determined the National Guard's stature, while issues regarding its composition revealed simmering social-class conflict; this was especially the case when, at various times from its inception, eligibility to serve as a guardian of the nation's will was restricted to the bourgeoisie. Both of these points were exemplified during the last weeks of the summer of 1870. In August, Napoléon III succumbed to pressure and called for the formation of 60 National Guard battalions; all were to be comprised of the bourgeoisie.

Upon the fall of the Empire, the Government of National Defense formed an additional 60 battalions, again being careful to limit recruitment to bourgeois districts. By the end of September, though, there were 254 National Guard battalions comprised of some 360,000 men; nearly all of the newly formed battalions were constituted in working-class and artisanal districts. Although patriotic fervor, as measured by enlistement in the National Guard, was palpable in all Parisian districts (even the Baron de Rothschild served in the National Guard), few National Guardsmen volunteered to engage the enemy beyond the capital's walls.

While the National Guard was united in purpose, there was a huge enlistment disparity between different districts. Battalions were organized residentially and enrollment figures were much higher in the working-class and artisanal districts in the northern and eastern districts of the city.[9] Because most units remained in their own neighborhood, there was little prospect that the democratization of the National Guard would transcend an identity based on social class. Rather, the enlistment of artisans and workers had the effect of arming thousands of individuals whose trust of, and support for, the Government had its limits. Although this mass of armed workers and artisans remained largely loyal to the Government during the siege, it remained a potential source for conflict, particularly as rumors spread that the Government was entreating the enemy with peace overtures.

Administering Paris

The power vacuum following the fall of the Empire led to both a proliferation of impromptu neighborhood committees in Paris as well as to the strengthening of the administrative authority of the official *arrondissement* municipalities (whose functions under the Empire had been limited to those of a public registry office).

The day after the declaration of the republic, the Government nominated 20 mayors, one for each Parisian *arrondissement*. While all of those nominated possessed impeccable republican credentials, none had been activists in the revolutionary political clubs of the last years of the Empire. Officially given power over the Welfare Bureau (Bureaux de Bienfaisance) as the siege set in, the mayors' administrative responsibilities increased; the need to provide essential services during exigent circumstances often put the mayors at odds with both the Government and the Assistance Publique, a sort of umbrella unit for public assistance in Paris.[10]

Also in the wake of the Empire's collapse, a proliferation of impromptu neighborhood committees developed in Paris, ostensibly to organize the defense in each of Paris's 20 *arrondissements* and to make certain that basic necessities were being equitably distributed. It was out of these vigilance committees that the Central Committee of the Twenty *Arrondissements* germinated. Formed at the behest of a variety of political activists, including Internationalists and delegates from clubs, assemblies, and vigilance committees,[11] the Central Committee claimed to fill a role complementary to the Government of National Defense; whereas the latter was responsible for coordinating national policy, the former unofficially concerned itself with the day-to-day functioning of Paris, including public health, policing, and ensuring food distribution. In reality, though, the Central Committee was more of a pressure group than an administrative body.

The Central Committee's first communique, issued on 15 September, appeared to obfuscate the limits of its self-defined jurisdiction. In fact, the document was a veritable political program relative to the organization of public security, subsistence, the defense of Paris and the defense of France's other departements; while the Central Committee might not yet have had aspirations as a rival to the Government of National Defense, in attributing to itself a role similar to that played by the 1792 Paris Commune, the Central Committee exceeded its very limited mandate, revealing far more ambitious aspirations.

Although it was neither elected nor officially sanctioned, the Central Committee represented a first step towards Paris's revolutionary reconquest of its autonomy from the central government. Ever since the royal authority's defeat of Etienne Marcel, leader of Paris's powerful merchants, in 1358, Paris had suffered a steady withering away of its municipal liberties. One of the first acts of the French Revolution was the restoration of Paris's administrative autonomy. The perception that the

Paris Commune overstepped its jurisdiction and had been instrumental in the Terror led, in 1795, to the loss of Paris's right to self-government. A law passed in 1800 defined Paris's administrative status for more than a century: Paris was divided into *arrondissements* (12 of them until 1859 when the incorporation of the suburbs increased the number to 20); a mayor appointed by the central government assumed responsibility for the day-to-day affairs of each *arrondissement*.

The real administrative power at Paris was the Prefect of the Seine, also appointed by the government. Although in its early days, the Second Republic initially restored the rights of all municipalities, *arrondissements*, and departments in France to elect their own officials, the June 1848 revolution caused the conservative legislature to rethink the wisdom of affording this freedom to Paris. During the Second Empire, the 60 members of the municipal council of Paris (three representatives for each *arrondissement*) were all appointed for five-year terms by the emperor. During the final years of the Empire, republican militants became a little more strident in arguing for Parisian self-government.

Although one of the few demands of republican militants was the restoration of Paris's municipal liberties, the Government of National Defense initially continued the policy of appointing individuals to administer Paris. While the appointment of mayors to each *arrondissement* represented a first step towards municipal autonomy, it was not the same thing as municipal democracy. On 18 September, though, the Government issued a decree announcing that municipal elections would take place on 28 September.

At first blush it appears peculiar that a cause as seemingly banal as municipal liberties would generate such intense feelings. Paris's municipal liberties were elevated to an emotional plane that bitterly divided opponents from proponents by reference to a word which was inextricably linked to Parisian municipal liberties: Commune. In *Paris Libre*, Jacques Rougerie quotes a speaker at a bourgeois club as follows: 'the Versailles commune, the Rouen commune, the Marseille commune, doesn't bother anybody; but the Paris Commune! This is very different. Why? Because there is blood on this word.' The idea of the Paris Commune, especially in the context of the circumstances of September 1870, conjured up, for the right, the worst excesses of revolutionary dictatorship. For the left, on the other hand, the Commune represented a blueprint for both military victory and revolutionary energy. As long as the war remained the focal point, and the Government appeared committed to honor its promises of national defense and Parisian autonomy, there was little for the Government to fear from the left. This, however, was asking too much of men who desired order, stability, and moderation.

The announcement of elections coincided with a peace overture by Favre that the Prussians greeted with harsh demands. Favre's unsuccessful effort made it patently clear that there would be no swift conclusion to the war and, on 19 September, the 133-day Prussian siege of Paris commenced. All means of access and lines of communication into and out of Paris were destroyed by the Prussians while neighboring towns and villages were taken over by enemy troops. While Parisians demonstrated a cohesive determination to stand fast against the Prussians, Favre's attempts at negotiating a settlement strained relations between the Central Committee and the Government of National Defense. Behind the facade of organizing the defense of Paris, the Central Committee was a highly politicized body that maintained a close relationship with the Paris section of the International Association of Workers. Outside of some overlap in personnel between the two organizations, the Central Committee also shared space with the International on the second and third floors at 6 Place de la Corderie (now 14 Rue de la Corderie). On the other hand, in an effort at posturing itself as an advocate for the working class, the International distanced itself from an official connection with the Central Committee. Whereas the International was unabashedly opposed to the Government's moderate, bourgeois republicanism, the Central Committee staked out a less doctrinaire position; its increasingly hostile stance appeared to have developed as a response to the Government's handling of the war.

Rumors of a proposed capitulation provided the Central Committee with the pretext to question publicly the Government's determination to win the war, and thus its fitness to govern. Henceforward, the Central Committee no longer deferred to the Government on how best to manage national defense and, instead, increasingly challenged the Government's authority. For example, on 19 September, the Central Committee led a march of 230 militants to the Hôtel de Ville to protest against rumors of a French capitulation. More ominously, on 22 September, the Central Committee published a new manifesto that was more explicit in prognosticating that, once constituted, the Commune will 'revolutionarily defeat the enemy.' To which enemy, though, was this manifesto making reference? The document's words are somewhat vague on this point; surely, in the context of the siege, it was a reference to the Prussians. The manifesto, though, concluded with an allusion to 'the success or the downfall of the political and social principles of the Revolution.'

On the other hand, it was not axiomatic that a Paris Commune elected by manhood suffrage would mirror the views of the Central Committee. Nonetheless, under the circumstances that existed at the end of September, the Government was not at all inclined to run the risk of bestowing electoral legitimacy on a Commune that, by most indicators, looked back to 1792–3 for inspiration. Consequently, using the pretext of the unsettled military situation, the Government made plans to postpone both the municipal elections whose results it feared, as well as the national elections that it hoped would diminish the influence Paris had thus far exercised over the government. When the adjournment of elections was announced on 25 September, the Central Committee responded by organizing electoral meetings, virtually ignoring the Government's decision. The increasing militancy of the Central Committee and its prospects for developing links with working-class National Guard battalions was epitomized by socialist teacher Gustave Lefrançais: 'It has been said that the [National Guard] battalion chiefs should not involve themselves in political matters, that they should, instead, apply themselves to national defense: wrong! Politics has a very powerful influence over national defense and the one cannot be separated from the other.' The following day, 26 September, 140 heads of National Guard battalions marched in protest against the cancellation of elections to the Paris Commune. When elections were eventually held, in the middle of the siege, on 5 November, less than 50 percent of the eligible voters turned out to vote, a reflection, perhaps, of an electorate (in at least the 'popular' *arrondissements*) that had become cynical regarding the relationship between the constituted Parisian authority and the Government, and especially distrustful of the latter.[12]

Federalism and Communalism

Paris was neither the only, nor the first, French city that would declared a commune. Beginning with the news of the first military defeats in August 1870, revolutionaries at Lyon and Marseille, two of the major cities to have rejected the May 1870 plebiscite on the Empire, temporarily denied Napoléon III's authority and established short-lived communes.[13] On 4 September, news of Napoléon III's surrender prompted republicans at Lyon and Marseille to declare the republic hours before Paris had proclaimed it, and to set up communal authorities to administer both cities. Neither of those early experiments in municipal autonomy, launched primarily at the instigation of internationalists, succeeded. They were, on the other hand, the first evidence of a vibrant communal movement in the provinces ready to occupy the political void left by war, but equally drawing inspiration from federalist currents and the articulation of revolutionary republicanism, as both were mediated by particular local conditions.

Fearing that the collapse of the Empire could signal the internal disintegration of the newly declared republic, the Government of National Defense established a Delegation at Tours to maintain the unity of the French state and to prevent the annexation of any French territory by the Prussian invaders.[14] Declarations of a Committee of Public Safety at Lyon and a Revolutionary Committee at Marseille during the first week of September 1870 prompted the Tours Delegation to preempt any manifestations of municipal autonomy. In dispatching Paul Challemel-Lacour to Lyon and Henri Esquiros to Marseille, Léon Gambetta, the Government's interior minister and representative of radical (not revolutionary!) republicanism, expected nothing less than complete fidelity to the Tours Delegation from his provincial emissaries. When faced with the prospects of municipal revolution, Challemel-Lacour and Esquiros proved to be of different political temperaments.

In mid-September, Mikhail Bakunin, the legendary revolutionary Russian anarchist whose advocacy of federalism (though as a precondition to the dissolution of the state) rendered him popular with Lyonnais and Marseillais sections of the International arrived at Lyon. Although Jeanne Gaillard has disputed the impact of Bakunin on the situation at Lyon,[15] other historians have credited him with providing inspiration to Lyonnais revolutionaries.[16] On 18 September, a few days after Bakunin's arrival, his supporters, in combination with members of revolutionary committees in 13 other southeast departments, created the League of the Midi for the National Defense of the Republic. Though ostensibly formed to coordinate and consolidate the region's defenses against the Prussians, the League's articulation of a federalist-socialist agenda (including regional political liberties, a surtax on the rich, confiscation of property belonging to traitors, purges of the military and civil administration, separation of church and state) was a response to its popular base of support and evinced wider political aspirations.[17] The Tours Delegation's initial toleration of the League turned to suspicion and antipathy after events during the autumn of 1870 cast doubts upon the Delegation's ability to control the League. In particular, Gambetta came to see the League as either inspiring or working in cooperation with recently declared revolutionary municipal councils and as a harbinger of a future decentralized socialist republic.

Lyon, whose silk workers' political consciousness imbued the city with a rich revolutionary past, became the first municipality to raise the revolutionary communal curtain in 1870. On 28 September, thousands of workers dependent on the city's defensive public works projects protested in front of the Hôtel de Ville against a reduction in both the length of their workday and their daily wage. Protest morphed into insurgency when insurgents, led by Bakunin, endeavored to channel economic conflict into political protest. Temporarily seizing control of the Hôtel de Ville from the moderate republican municipal council elected only a fortnight before, they expected to be supported by National Guard battalions from the historic center of revolutionary Lyon, the Croix-Rousse district; instead, they were routed by those whom they expected to be their natural allies.[18]

At Marseille, political militants learned from the experiences of the Lyonnais in avoiding a premature leap into revolutionary politics. Whereas Bakunin and his cohorts had endeavored to craft a revolutionary commune at Lyon out of economic grievances, Marseillais militants grounded their efforts in patriotism. Unlike Challemel-Lacour, the Government's representative at Lyon, who had steadfastly opposed any hint of federalism, Esquiros, at Marseille, supported the League of the Midi, a position that caused him to lose favor with Gambetta; by mid-October, he had been forced to tender his resignation as the Government's representative to the region. Already agitated by Esquiros's removal, news of General Bazaine's capitulation at Metz at the end of October created a combustible situation at Marseille. In response to calls for provincial autonomy issued at a rally by the charismatic Marseillais internationalist André Bastelica calling for provincial autonomy, Marseillais militants seized control of the municipality on 31 October, ousted the Gambettist-oriented city council, and declared a revolutionary municipal commune under the military leadership of Gustave Cluseret. Within a day, however, the newly arrived Gambetta-allied prefect had reestablished order, largely with the consent of Bastelica who feared that a split between radical and revolutionary republicans would undermine the military defense of the region. The results of municipal elections on 13 November confirmed what the rapid disintegration of the revolution had made manifest: under the existent circumstances, and as long as the Government appeared committed to national defense, preservation of republican unity overshadowed decentralist and socialist aspirations.

The International, which exercised a profound influence over Lyonnais workers during the last years of the Empire, was chastened by the defeat of the Lyon Commune on 28 September.[19] News of massive casualties suffered by Lyonnais troops at the battle of Nuits St-Georges (35 kilometers south of Dijon) on 18 December provided one final opportunity for Lyonnais militants to challenge the Government over its conduct of the war. A day of recriminations on 20 December ended with the execution of Antoine Arnaud, a National Guard battalion commander who had assisted in the repression of the 28 September uprising. According to Moissonnier, the killing of Arnaud, a master silk weaver, Freemason, and democratic republican, resulted from a collective 'psychosis of treason' stemming from the equivocal attitude of the bourgeois administration.[20]

Arnaud's murder also highlighted recent changes in the Lyonnais social and political landscape resulting from the decline of the silk industry and an urban renovation similar to the Haussmannization of Paris. As Lyon's working population shifted from artisanal Croix-Rousse, ground zero for the insurrections of 1831 and 1834, to the industrial suburb of La Guillotière, on the south bank of the Rhône River, the city experienced a tectonic shift in its revolutionary geography; the more proletarianized workers at La Guillotière became what Croix-Roussian silk workers had once been.[21] Arnaud's murder also had a sobering effect on the revolutionary movement at Lyon. Gambetta personally attended his funeral, exploited the suicidal nature of republican fratricide, and rallied all but the most committed revolutionaries to the Government. The February elections to the National Assembly appeared to confirm Lyonnais antipathy towards revolutionary republicanism as the elected delegation from the city was comprised exclusively of individuals who had allied themselves with the Government.[22]

A Divided Government

The Government itself was geographically divided, with a skeletal delegation sitting at Tours, approximately 150 kilometers from Paris. Removed from the political pressures at Paris, eager to restore order and stability to France, and desirous of strengthening its own position lest Parisian militants leave their indelible imprint on the embryonic republic, the Tours delegation pushed for elections to a National Assembly to be held on 15 October. As the Government knew, an announcement on national elections would also engender demands for municipal elections at Paris.

In an effort at bringing the Tours delegation to heel, on 7 October the Government dispatched the ever-flamboyant, though somewhat reluctant, Gambetta via hot-air balloon to Tours. The choice of Gambetta reflected, in part, the dual perspectives of the majority on the Government towards Gambetta. On one level, they wanted to rid themselves of a colleague whom they perceived to be grandiloquent, dictatorial, opportunistic, and a potential demagogue. Once the siege began, conflicts and recriminations, based partly on personality and partly on ideology and percolating beneath the surface of consensus since 4 September, became public. Gambetta was a lightening rod for conflict; although his departure for Tours was designed to bring the Tours delegation in line with the Government's position, his very public support for all-out war raised Gambetta's stature amongst Parisians and threatened to undermine credibility for the armistice sought by Favre. On another level, though, because of the above attributes, Gambetta was also best suited for ending the pretensions of the Tours delegation and for accomplishing the other part of his mission – the recruitment of provincials to defend Paris.

Beginning in late September 1870, balloons were being used for postal delivery, reconnaissance, and delivery of munitions. At the time of Gambetta's flight, there were only seven balloons in Paris, most of them patched together with paste and paper. Even in the most propitious circumstances, hot-air ballooning carried a large element of risk; Gambetta's journey, for its time, was nearly the equivalent of early space travel – but without the teams of scientists on earth to grapple with technical difficulties – and required of aeronauts an equal measure of courage.[23] Although the construction of balloons had improved since the launching of de Montgolfier's first one in 1783, travelers were still subject to discomforts and uncertainties, most notably exposure to the elements and unpredictable wind velocity and direction.

Perhaps no flight better revealed the perils of ballooning than that of the *Ville d'Orléans*, a balloon carrying a crew of two, sacks of mail, and a crucial dispatch from Trochu to Gambetta regarding a secret plan for lifting the siege. Launched from the Gare du Nord at midnight on 24

November (so its flight would be protected by cover of darkness), the *Ville d'Orléans* got caught in fog that virtually eliminated all visibility. For the first six hours of the flight the crew heard, but was unable to visually ascertain the source of, loud noises beneath them. The break of dawn revealed that the immense forest, over which they assumed they were flying, was, in reality, the sea. As the balloon began a perilous descent towards the water, the crew jettisoned much of its cargo, including the crucial military dispatches. The now lightened balloon rose to an altitude of around 4800 meters. Freezing, panic stricken, and clueless as to its location, at around 3:30 p.m. the crew spotted a forest and prepared to descend. Leaping some 200 meters from the basket of the balloon onto fresh snow, the two crewmembers discovered that they had landed in Norway, 1246 kilometers from Paris! Miraculously the sacks of dispatches jettisoned by the crew were later found by fishermen; by the time they were turned over to the French, it was too late to effectuate Trochu's plan.[24]

Gambetta faced the usual discomforts and vicissitudes of balloon travel: exposure to the elements, unpredictable wind felocity, sudden changes of wind direction, the uncertainty of reaching one's intended destination, unreliable navigational tools, but added into the mix in autumn 1871 was the threat of being shot down by, or landing amidst, Prussian troops. Whatever apprehension the balloonists experienced prior to take off appeared to fade once they were 2000 meters above ground. Aloft, travelers were not only largely impervious to Prussian bullets, but also felt a sense of security and familiarity as the serene and bucolic countryside came into view, an eerie contradistinction with the chaos and fear in Paris. The 65 hot-air balloon flights that departed Paris during the siege were crucial in combatting the growing sense amongst Parisians of their isolation from the rest of the nation.[25]

Arriving at Tours, Gambetta declared that national elections would not take place while France was at war. As far as the military situation was concerned, Gambetta, under authority of his new role of Minister of War and the Interior, found the army in complete disarray and losing critical towns to the Prussians. All of this culminated in the 'treason' of Marshall Bazaine who, in contradiction of government orders, surrendered Metz on 27 October. When revealed by journalist Félix Pyat, a left-wing *quarante-huitard* who had been active in the International, the Government issued a denial, while Pyat, falsely characterized as a Prussian agent, became a target of abuse.

On 28 October, news arrived that French forces had won their first victory since the siege began. French General Carey de Bellemare, resentful of Trochu's lethargic leadership, took it upon himself to lead a battalion of *francs-tireurs*[26] in recapturing Le Bourget. Bellemare, himself, came to make the announcement to Paris. Trochu was unimpressed. While he was embarrassed by Bellemare's victory, Trochu also believed Le Bourget to be so strategically inconsequential that it was not worth the cost of life that would have been required to defend it. While most military historians agree that even a successful defense of Le Bourget would have been a Pyrrhic victory, at the end of October 1870 it conjured up comparisons to the victory at Valmy on 20 September 1792. In a letter dated 30 October, Desplats referred to Le Bourget as 'a critical position' which would serve as a springboard for further French advances 'a little at a time until Paris is unblocked and France will be saved.'[27] On 20 September 1792, a largely inexperienced, undisciplined French army defeated the Prussians, thus preserving the Revolution and ushering in the official declaration of the First Republic the following day. There would be no similar heroics in 1870 as Bellemare returned to Le Bourget without the reinforcements he sought. The following day, the Prussians, at the cost of 1200 French lives, retook Le Bourget.

On 30 October, the Government made the announcements that both Le Bourget and Metz had fallen to the Prussians. For those favoring a 'war to the distance,' news of the defeats could not have come at a less propitious moment. Adolphe Thiers, whose political career could be characterized as reflecting either raw ambition or adaptability (it ranged from Interior Minister under Louis-Philippe to promoter of Louis-Napoléon's presidential campaign in 1848 to liberal opponent of resurrected Bonapartism), arrived at Tours on 21 October after futile attempts to drum up support for France in Russia, Austria, and the United Kingdom. Unsuccessful in his foreign efforts, Thiers, ever the high priest of order in France, clashed with Gambetta over Thiers's desire to surrender. Despite being no more successful in persuading Gambetta than he was in appealing to the other European powers, Thiers, nonetheless, met with the Prussian chancellor, Otto von Bismarck, on 30 October to work on an armistice. Arriving in Paris later in the day, Thiers's demand for an immediate meeting of a National Assembly and the conclusion of an armistice was agreed to by Favre, Trochu, and Picard. A rump of the Government, led by Rochefort and Arago, opposed the armistice and, in the process, unveiled a deep governmental division over the most fundamental of issues. That evening the Government issued the announcements on Le Bourget, Metz, and the armistice.

'On people's faces you see anguish over Bazaine's surrender [at Metz], a kind of fury over yesterday's setback at Le Bourget, and at the same time an angry and heroically impulsive determination not to make peace.'[28] In the newspaper *Le Réveil*, Charles Delescluze posed the following questions: 'Imbeciles or traitors? If the Government which is today seated at the Hôtel de Ville remains in place, what will become of Paris? Of France? Of the republic?' Beginning at ten o'clock on the morning of 31 October, Paris was in an agitated state. By afternoon a crowd invaded the Hôtel de Ville, the first sign that France was in the midst of a revolution. United in their distrust of the Government and their desire for a Paris Commune, the revolutionaries had different ideas relative to the next move after the seizure of power. This equivocation allowed the Government to marshal its forces and, by four o'clock the following morning, after promising to hold elections and to amnesty all who participated, Trochu, Favre, and company were back at the Hôtel de Ville.

The insurrection of 31 October was the only serious uprising against the Government during the siege. Whatever prospects for success it might have had in its first hours, it was ultimately the victim of the spontaneity which, ironically, was also responsible for its initial success. The individuals who might have given some coordination to the uprising – Blanqui, Flourens, Delescluze – were merely swept along by events that were not of their making and over which they had only marginal control. The insurrection did have some important consequences.

That the uprising was not comprised exclusively of working-class or socialist National Guard battalions revealed that skepticism towards the Government cut across class lines. It also split the Government. In fact, bourgeois battalions of the National Guard only appeared in defense of the Government when the arrival of Blanqui and Flourens appeared to detract a manifestation against the inept handling of the war into an opportunity for a social revolution. When, on 1 November, the Government reneged on its amnesty agreement and decided, instead, to pursue those it held responsible for the insurrection, Prefect of Police Edmond Adam, General Tamasier, Commander of the National Guard, and Rochefort, the one left-wing member of the Government, resigned their positions.

Although it initially rescinded the order for elections, the Government realized that its legitimacy depended upon the public being given some outlet for political expression. Rather than an election, plebiscites, the preferred electoral form of the Bonapartes, were held on 3 November, limiting voters to a choice between confidence in, or disapproval of, the Government and the military. On the other hand, elections to a Paris Commune were not allowed and Paris was limited to the election of mayors for each *arrondissement*. The Government won an overwhelming vote of confidence in the election, seemingly indicating a broad base of support.

A different conclusion, though, could be drawn from the results of the mayoral elections that led to the nullification of three elections where the victors had been arrested for activities on 31 October; some of the adjoints in other *arrondissements* had been active members in the International. Reflecting upon the 31 October uprising, Karl Marx opined that had the insurrection been successful, the character of the war would have changed and France would have been spared the civil war that followed. While it is questionable whether a change of policy or personnel could have altered the complexion of a war so thoroughly dominated by Prussia, over the ensuing weeks the Government was unable to disassociate the emphasis on order and stability it represented from the national defeat for which it was responsible. Furthermore, as Taithe has suggested, during the siege each *arrondissement* acted as a more or less autonomous geopolitical unit. Responsibility for the daily needs of their inhabitants devolved to the *arrondissements*, which also had the added benefit of being less constrained than the Government by budgetary concerns; as a result, whatever interventionist measures were undertaken during the siege came at the behest of each *arrondissement*. Consequently, according to Taithe, Parisians developed inversely pro-portionate relationships in how they viewed the performances of the *arrondissements* and the Government during the siege; whereas the latter's incompetent prosecution of the war had created the messy con-ditions under which Parisians endured for 133 days, the former had acted as best it could to mitigate the severity of those conditions.[29]

During the first week of November, Thiers again endeavored to secure an armistice with Bismarck. In the highly charged atmosphere that still persisted in Paris, the Government would have been hard pressed to agree to any terms that might have been interpreted as a capitulation. Unable to conclude the armistice, Trochu announced on 5 November that the Government 'owed it to the country, "if not to triumph, at least to succumb gloriously after having fought valiantly."'[30] With the excep-tion of one more victory at Coulmiers (west of Orléans) upon which, characteristically, the victorious French commander failed to capitalize, the war was over for France.

Paris Besieged

Surrounded by the Prussian army since the middle of September, the effects of Paris's isolation from the rest of France were about to get worse as the Prussians were determined to starve Paris into submission. At the start of the siege, Paris assumed an almost festive-like mood.[31] Beginning with his letter dated 23 September, Desplats's daily correspondence to his wife notes that, in spite of the near incessant thundering of cannon fire, Paris remained calm. Even after the mood in Paris became decidedly mournful following a very bloody battle on Friday, 30 September, in a letter dated 2 October Desplats noted: 'All is calm around Paris and in the interior. The population strolls as it would on a Feast Day.'[32] Similarly, Edmond Goncourt wrote that '[g]ay and joyous, Paris streams out to all her gates for a promenade, as giddy as though she were going to Longchamp for the races.'[33]

Through the first six weeks or so of the siege, Paris maintained contact with the world outside its ramparts through mail carried by the aforementioned hot-air balloons and via carrier pigeons. During the 1860s René Dagron invented the process of microphotography, a close forerunner to today's microfilm. Documents would be reduced in size so that a single pigeon could carry something like 40,000 dispatches on a flight. The equipment for reducing the messages was set up in Tours and once the dispatches reached Paris, they could be magnified. During the siege, 302 pigeons were sent off with 59 actually reaching Paris. The arrival of pigeons raised spirits in Paris, giving the besieged inhabitants a sense of being less isolated. But, as with nearly all aspects of the siege, as the days grew shorter with the onset of winter, the pigeons became a less reliable mode of communication; by November, their infrequent arrivals contributed to the growing despair.[34]

However, the festive mood would not endure for long. Although Parisians of all classes coalesced around a common purpose and their shared hardship, the extent to which one was willing to endure privation was clearly a function of social class. All was not equal during the siege; privation was relative and the threat of starvation did not prove to be the great equalizer.[35] While the well off, accustomed as they were to the conspicuous consumption of the Second Empire, groused about ersatz meat dishes and food rendered boring by the absence of seasonings, the poor subsisted on a diet of bread of questionable consistency, sugar, and wine.[36]

As late as mid-December, Peter's, an upscale restaurant located just off the Boulevard des Italiens in the second *arrondissement*, served a menu in honor of the mayor of the third *arrondissement*, of:

Butter, Celery, Sardines, Olives
Sago soup with Bordeaux wine
Salmon à la Berzélius
Escalloped Elephant Meat, scallion sauce
Vegetable Salad à la Raspail
Apples, Pears, Biscuits[37]

At the conclusion of the siege, Goncourt and 13 other men of letters presented Brébant, proprietor of Vachette, a popular restaurant at the time, with a medal thanking him for having fed them once a fortnight 'in a city of two million besieged souls.'[38] Early in the siege voices on the left, such as Blanqui, called for mandatory rationing, arguing that if the war was a truly national effort, all must equally endure the crisis through sacrifice. In fact, as Kranzberg has noted, one of the most astonishing aspects of the siege was the fact that the working and artisanal classes did not rise up against the culinary disparity. Instead, he notes that they bore their condition with great equanimity, adjusting their behavior to fit the circumstances and maintaining a very positivist belief in science's prospects for solving hunger.[39]

Buoyed by the expectation in October that an armistice was about to be concluded and endeavoring to remain faithful to its belief in a market economy, the Government resisted most measures at controlling the economy. Given the Government's control over grain stocks, it was logical that bread could easily be rationed; while a Maximum (price control) reminiscent of 1793 was instituted on 23 September, it was not until January, when fear of popular upheaval took precedence over *laissez-faire* economic principles, that grain was finally requisitioned and rationed at 300 grams per adult. Beginning in mid-October, the Government established regulations on meat rations, but, unlike grain, the supply of meat could not be controlled; thus consumers were armed with meaningless ration cards while, in reality, being abandoned to the vicissitudes of an unforgiving market.[40] On 6 December, Henry Labouchere, a besieged correspondent for the London *Daily Mail*, wrote that 'rations, consisting alternately of horse and salt fish, are still distributed, but they are hardly sufficient to keep body and soul together. Unless we make up our minds to kill our artillery horses, we shall soon come to the end of our supply.'[41]

Whatever reticence the Government might have had about regulating the economy (e.g., rationing, establishing price controls) was not shared by the municipal authorities who were free to be proactive and innovative in grappling with the subsistence problems in their respective *arrondissements*.[42] By December, the mayors in several *arrondissements* created forerunners to soup kitchens, distributing around 190,000 meager rations per day. The poor also made up for caloric deficiencies by increasing their consumption of wine, in abundance throughout the siege, even if the quality likely suffered. This, though, may have led to other problems as the amount of alcohol consumed tripled during the siege and, when food supplies were at their shortest, was likely consumed on empty stomachs.[43]

While food may not have been very plentiful at Paris during the siege, its scarcity spawned a veritable cottage industry of stories of necessity and dearth as having encouraged creative culinary skills. At the start of the siege Trochu estimated that Paris had the means to sustain itself for 80 days. From the first days of the siege, Parisians with the means and foresight to do so stockpiled foodstuffs; at that time, it was anticipated that the siege would not last more than a few weeks, at most. The 40,000 cows, 250,000 sheep, and stock of grain listed on an official government census was sufficient until the beginning of October when it became increasingly rare to find conventional meats. Horsemeat, consumption of which had only been introduced during the 1860s as the meat of the poor, became the substitute for beef. As the ersatz beef, the price of horsemeat also began to climb, putting it out of the reach of the working class. Academics and government officials had an array of other creative recipes for staving off hunger, including amongst other things, rehydrating the dried albumin used in textile printing as an egg substitute![44]

By October, whatever social stigmas previously inhibited the well-to-do from buying horsemeat were abandoned amid its packaging in the accouterments of *haute cuisine*. At the commencement of the siege, there were 100,000 horses at Paris; at the end only one-third of that number remained. Towards mid-November, signs began to appear advertising dog and cat butchers, with cats being advertised as 'gutter rabbits.' It has been estimated that over 25,000 cats were eaten during the siege, often boiled and seasoned with pistachios, olives, pimentos, and cornichons. During the second to last week of November, a rat market opened up at the Place de l'Hôtel de Ville, with rats selling for 10–15 sous, or one-third to one-half of a National Guardsman's daily salary. The rats were almost assuredly destined for the infamous *salami de rat*.[45]

By the end of December, the authorities were no longer able to sustain the animals at the Jardin des Plantes, the Paris zoo. As a result, the animals in the zoo were executed, their carcasses sold to elite butcher shops and their meat ultimately purchased at exorbitant prices by the bourgeoisie for New Year's dinners or, as we saw with the example of Peter's, by restaurants for special occasions.[46] The slaughter of the zoo's animals might have been a necessary act to forestall the suffering of starving animals, but it is doubtful whether their meat was necessary to stave off starvation; rather, it appears as though those who consumed the meat did so for its novelty value. In the words of Labouchere, elephant meat is 'tough, coarse, and oily, and I do not recommend English families to eat elephant as long as they can get beef or mutton.'[47] Spang asserts that the ability of the elite to remain *bon vivants* even under the most trying of circumstances represented, to them, a victory over Prussian efforts to starve them into submission.[48] However, it is equally true that, given the inaccessibility of such fare to Parisian workers, it also signified a victory of the bourgeoisie over their fellow inhabitants and a reification of their privileged position within the social hierarchy.

At the end of the siege, rumors circulated about the existence of stockpiles of food. Some suggested that the forts surrounding Paris were veritable storehouses of food that were accessible to the authorities until they were surrendered to the Prussians as part of the armistice of 28 January. Whether or not the forts contained food, these rumors, in highlighting governmental neglect of Paris, added another dimension to the perception that France lost the war through governmental incompetence or indifference. Adding to the sense that the Government acted indifferently towards the starving population was the emergence of 'a sudden rush of hidden foods to the market stalls' once the armistice was announced.[49]

The winter of 1870–1 was one of the coldest on record for the nineteenth century. During November the weather took a decided turn for the worse. By December, the freezing conditions at Paris were almost a cruel irony. The average temperature in December for the previous half-century had been 3.54°; during December 1870 the average temperature was 1.07° with the Celsius reaching 0° or above on only nine days.

Aggravating the cold conditions (and making cooking nearly impossible) was a fuel shortage that, beginning in November, caused the price of wood and coal to quadruple. On 26 December, Goncourt wrote that the combination of cold weather and lack of fuel for cooking caused Parisians to uproot trees, trellises, and wooden fences from the Bois de

Boulogne to the Champs-Élysées; Goncourt concluded that '[i]f this terrible winter weather goes on, all the trees in Paris will go down to satisfy people's urgent need of fuel.'[50] Brocher noted that because much of the wood was green and damp, it simply smoked, forcing cooks to heat their food outdoors where the slightest wind extinguished the fire.[51] The lack of fuel also rendered Paris a dark city, as the gas and oil used to illuminate the 'city of lights' had to be strictly regulated.[52]

Needless to say, conditions during the siege caused the Parisian infrastructure to buckle. Rains throughout November and December caused flooding and, with sanitation not at a premium, diseases flourished. The blend of flour, straw, and rice in bread led to an increase in enteritis in children, while the entire population was exposed to the ravages of smallpox, typhoid, and pneumonia. The death rate rose considerably, especially amongst the very young and the aged. Infant mortality for those born just before or during the siege hovered at around 90 percent. The combined death toll at Paris over the previous five years for the first week of October was 754; by the end of the first week of October 1870, 1483 had perished. It should be remembered that the weather was not yet a factor in early October. When, during the siege's eighteenth week (14–21 January) the weather conditions were at their worst, the weekly death toll rose to 4444. While lack of sanitation, poor nutrition, and miserable weather were directly responsible for many deaths, Goncourt noted the psychological impact of living conditions during the siege. Alluding to 'the grief, displacment, homesickness' on a population of refugees from 'the sunny corners in the Paris region,' Goncourt cited the example of five deaths amongst the 25 refugees in Paris from Croissy-Beaubourg.[53]

During the Empire, Paris was renowned for its vibrant nightlife. Needless to say, the siege altered that. Besieged residents found greater consolation staying in bed for longer hours, going to sleep earlier, arising later, in order to mitigate 'somewhat the effects of the hunger and cold.' Paris's theatres had closed after 4 September, but the Théâtre-Français reopened on 25 October, followed by the Comédie-Française. Theatrical performances (and musical concerts), however, reflected the mood of a besieged and struggling city as productions were spartan and light fare, judged inappropriate under the circumstances, gave way to more somber and grave pieces; rather than providing an escape, the theatres tended to reaffirm life outside their walls. With the exception of a celebration of Molière's 244th birthday on 15 January, all theatrical productions were halted by the end of December, as the lack of fuel made staging nearly impossible. Rather, entertainment in the besieged capital tended to be limited to activities that revolved around the siege: promenades to the fortifications that ringed the city, viewing the enemy through telescopes located at the highest forts, spectatorship at launchings of the hot-air balloons, and the bizarre practice of weekly weigh-ins 'to see how many pounds one had lost on his siege diet.'[54] In addition, attendance at political clubs – most of which were located in Montmartre, Belleville, and the Latin Quarter – increased, especially after the closure of the theatres. Although acknowledging that the government had no option relative to the theatres, Molinari, an editor of the liberal newspaper *Journal des Débats*, questioned whether closing the theatres was worth the price of a resurgence of the revolutionary socialism spawned by the clubs.[55]

In a letter written on New Year's Eve, Desplats summed up the physical condition of Paris:

> This is no longer an elegant city, noisy and full of life. Only a portion of the boutiques are open; the streets are silent and nearly deserted. The petrol, which has replaced gas, casts a pallid color on the houses, accompanied by a revolting odor. Around Paris the ruins pile up! Destroyed or burned villas, demolished houses, chopped trees, the routes littered with branches and barricades![56]

Commencing on 5 January, Prussian projectiles fell on Paris at the rate of 300-400 per day. Rather than demoralizing Paris (as the Prussians believed it would), the bombardment intensified Paris's resolve not to surrender. In fact, even those newspapers that had been most receptive to an armistice adopted a more determined position as the war was brought directly to the Parisian populace. Although the left had been relatively dormant (though not completely inactive) after the check of the 31 October uprising and ensuing elections, it publicly reemerged on 6 January by placarding Paris with a 'second red poster.' The poster, produced by the Delegation of Twenty *Arrondissements* (formerly the Central Committee; the name change presaging the establishment of a Paris Commune) commenced with the usual rhetorical attack on the Government's handling of the war and betrayal of republican principles before progressing to a reminder (as though this was necessary) of what Parisians had endured over the preceding 17 weeks. The poster concluded by demanding that the Government voluntarily relinquish its authority to the people of Paris 'who would never accept this misery and this shame' while there 'is still time for decisive measures to be taken to permit workers to live, and to fight.' The poster failed to produce the desired effect; there was neither a relinquishment of authority by the Government nor a massive uprising against the Government.

For the next week or so, the Government was in a tenuous position; knowing that with each further day of besiegement, the prospects of revolution were that much closer, it was also keenly aware that the only way to end the siege was to surrender. A surrender also enhanced the prospects of revolution. The Government's response was to give the impression that it was still committed to victory and receptive to the claims that the National Guard was more determined to realize this goal than was the regular army. Consequently, amid great fanfare on 18 January, 84,000 National Guardsmen assembled on the slopes of Mont-Valérien in order to mount an assault to retake Versailles the following day.

As should have been obvious to all but the most blindly optimistic Parisians, the sortie was a disaster. Military leadership, displaying unparalleled bad judgement throughout the war, was even more wanting at Buzenval on 19 January; the attack, which began in the morning, was over by 6:00 p.m. with the French forces, characteristically, in full retreat. The front line of attack featured National Guard battalions from bourgeois districts mixed in with the regular army; and they suffered the bulk of the casualties. Some used this as propaganda to discredit battalions from working-class districts as being too faint-hearted to fight.[57] On another level, it has also been suggested that, in the knowledge that the inexperienced National Guard would be overmatched, the Government accepted the 'limited carnage' as necessary for persuading the Parisian bourgeoisie that further resistance was futile. As with its conduct of the war, the Government miscalculated the extent to which hostility towards its conduct of the war united all shades of the French population.

At a meeting comprised of National Guard delegates, militants from the political clubs and the Vigilance Committees (the base-level committee in each *arrondissement* from which Central Committee members were selected) on the night of 21 January agreed to assemble at the Hôtel de Ville the following morning in order to denounce the anticipated capitulation and to demand an all-out war. After having liberated Flourens (who had been arrested in early December for his participation in the 31 October uprising), a few hundred activists, later joined by National Guard units from the outlying *arrondissements*, marched to the Hôtel de Ville where they held a noisy demonstration. The Government, having gotten advanced notice of the demonstration and desirous of avoiding a potentially more serious version of 31 October, took the precaution of moving to the Louvre, its call to bourgeois National Guard battalions to defend order against sedition having gone unheeded. This left the defense of the Hôtel de Ville in the hands of the Breton *mobiles*, who had little understanding or patience for Parisian militants. Whether or not ordered to do so, the *mobiles* began firing and after a half-hour around 30 of the protesters were dead, including Théodore Sapia, a popular Blanquist and member of the Central Committee of Twenty *Arrondissements*.

Capitulation and National Elections

It has been suggested that the Government provoked the incident on 22 January in order to accomplish its twin aims: repression of the left and capitulation to the Prussians. In the aftermath of 22 January, the Government stepped up its persecution of the left by arresting republicans, closing political clubs, and forbidding the publication of 17 newspapers. As for the armistice, for several days after the uprising, Favre met with Bismarck at Versailles to hammer out the French surrender. In spite of promises to Gambetta that any armistice would only apply to Paris, a full armistice was announced on 28 January. Although Gambetta was inclined to expose Favre's duplicity and Bismarck's efforts at manipulating France's domestic politics, his fear that this would play into the hands of socialists led to his acceptance of the armistice.

The terms of the armistice were, essentially, unchanged since the last attempt back in November. French forts were disarmed, all but one unit of the regular army disarmed, a triumphal march through Paris by the Prussian army, and the payment of a war indemnity by the city of Paris of 200 million francs. The one army unit to which the armistice did not apply – the Army of the East – had not gotten word of its exclusion. Wanting to eliminate any threat from the east, the Prussians had insisted – and Favre agreed – to its exclusion from the cessation of hostilities. While the Army of the East believed the war was over, the Prussians knew otherwise and chased the humiliated 80,000–90,000 soldiers from that unit into Switzerland where they were promptly disarmed and interned until the final ratification of the peace treaty.[58]

When on 28 January 1871 the official governmental organ published details of the armistice, the siege of Paris was over – nearly four and one-half months after it had commenced. Much had occurred from the day that Napoléon III officially surrendered at Sedan and the Republic was declared at the Hôtel de Ville. France's tempestuous political culture virtually assured that the third attempt at a republic would be no less difficult than the first two attempts. The republican tradition was far from a monolith and the irreconcilability of revolutionary and moderate republicans ensured that any changeover to a republic was just foreplay before the main event – the struggle for the soul of the republic. Throughout the autumn/early winter of 1870, the stakes were beyond the mere theoretical as republicans alternated between the facade of cooperation and the more genuine feelings of contempt. As the latter won out over the former, attitudes hardened on both sides. However, for revolutionary republicans, their marginalization and repression during the siege were indistinguishable and inseparable from the losses inflicted on the French nation. To the extent that revolutionary republicans perceived themselves as the heirs to the traditions of the Revolution's heritage, comparisons between 1870–1 and 1792–3 were striking. 'In 1792, our fathers conquered Europe, without bread, without uniforms, without shoes,' read an article in *Le Réveil*, 'in 1871, with an arsenal full of arms and ammunition and only fighting against Prussia, we capitulate.'[59]

With the war essentially over and the siege lifted, the Government, under pressure from Bismarck, prepared to normalize the republic by holding elections to the National Assembly on 8 February. The election was the first opportunity since the fall of the Empire for the nation to express itself on its future political direction. While it was also a referendum on the Government's performance and conduct of the national defense, outside of Paris the Government turned the election into a referendum on Paris's behavior. Playing on the traditional suspicions of the provinces towards Paris, the government blurred the line between the patriotism demonstrated at Paris during the war and the capital's historic expressions of militant republicanism, depicting the former as a subterfuge for the political machinations of extremists. In the process, an experiential and ideological divide had now replaced the siege, formerly the barrier that isolated Paris from the rest of France. From Brocher's perspective, provincials viewed the end of the war as providing them with an opportunity to exploit, rather than give thanks to the Parisians.

these countryfolk are cowards, [sic] they sell the littlest thing at a huge price to the franc-tireurs, but through terror, give all they have to the

Prussians. A peasant demanded that a franc-tireur I know, who left his family to defend his country, pay him one franc for a glass of water.'[60]

The elections were held under anything but normal circumstances.

Only ten days separated the announcement of elections and the actual voting. Furthermore, over 500,000 soldiers were disenfranchised by virtue of either having been captured by the Prussians or having fled to either Belgium or Switzerland. The Prussians were still on French soil, and in those parts of the country they occupied voting was determined by Prussian military commanders. In those areas not occupied by the Prussians, governmental prefects worked in conjunction with the press to sustain candidates favorable to the armistice, regardless of whether they were monarchists, bonapartists, or moderate republicans. In spite of Gambetta's efforts to disqualify the candidatures of individuals who held significant positions in either the Second Empire or France's monarchies, out of 675 deputies elected to the National Assembly, 400 were monarchists; as it did in 1848, this created the specter of a republic dominated by legislators antagonistic to that form of government. The election result confirmed a stark difference in political sensibilities born out of the respective political evolutions and experiences over the past five months that separated Paris from rural France. For peasant voters, habitually deferential to their social superiors and hostile to making any further sacrifices on behalf of Paris, the choice was clear. For Parisians, having suffered and sacrificed on behalf of national honor only to see those sacrifices nullified by a shameless surrender, the choice, though entirely different, was equally clear. Adolphe Thiers's candidacy underscored this point. In spite of his prestige, Thiers finished twentieth out of the 43 deputies elected at Paris; Thiers, though, finished at the top of the electoral list in 26 other constituencies. By contrast, Gambetta, who finished third at Paris, did not finish first in any constituencies and was elected in only nine other districts.[61] Whereas Favre finished thirty-fourth at Paris and Trochu chose not to stand there, the Parisian delegation was headed by a combination of social reformers, socialists, and supporters of all-out war against Prussia.

Based on his overall vote count, Thiers was named as chief executive of the government which, initially, was seated at Bordeaux. In his memoirs, Thiers noted that, 'When I was put in charge, I was immediately preoccupied with two tasks: concluding the peace and making Paris submissive.' At the end of February, Thiers concluded the armistice by formally surrendering to Bismarck, an act overwhelmingly ratified by the

Assembly. The surrender inextricably intertwined the issues of nationalism and ideology; the monarchists in the Assembly solidly stood behind a termination of hostilities, even if this meant France having to cede Alsace and a portion of the Lorraine. Not only did this act transform the status of the Rhine River from being a natural boundary between Germany and France to becoming Germany's stream, it also changed the citizenship of more than 1.6 million French men and women. By contrast, though, the Assembly was capable of extreme demonstrations of chauvinism as witnessed by its refusal to validate the election of Garibaldi, elected in four constituencies, on the grounds that he was a foreigner, and thus negating one of France's republican traditions of allowing the election of anyone who had rendered public service to France. In response to the capitulation and its overwhelming ratification in the Assembly, six Parisian deputies, including Victor Hugo, Pyat, and Rochefort, all resigned their seats.

An Unbridgeable Chasm

The results of the election demonstrated the existence of a wide gulf separating Paris and a few other large cities from the provinces. Not only had Paris had an entirely different experience from the rest of the country over the past four months, but, after the armistice, the social class complexion of Paris became more decidedly working class and petit bourgeois, as those who were able to leave Paris did so; this included between 50,000 and 140,000 National Guardsmen, principally from the bourgeois districts. The remaining Parisian National Guardsmen originated almost entirely from popular districts. On 15 February, 3000 Parisian National Guard activists held a meeting at which they developed preliminary sketches for a Republican Federation of the Parisian National Guard battalions under the umbrella of an executive commission, the Central Committee of the National Guard, to which each *arrondissement* would elect three delegates without regard to rank.

Organized along strict democratic and federated lines, the National Guard and its Central Committee exemplified 'the spirit of the democratic republic'[62] and challenged the military's historic resistance to democratic ideals. Although the Central Committee's organization was sufficiently radical, the broad mandate it ascribed to itself in its organizing statute – safeguarding the Republic and defending the nation – was too ambiguous for most activists in the International; with the exception of bookbinder, Eugène Varlin, most internationalists remained aloof towards the Central Committee.[63]

The results of elections to the Central Committee could not have done much to assuage the concerns of internationalists; although those elected were politically on the left, only a handful of the 38 – and all concentrated in the peripheral *arrondissements* – could properly be classified as working class.[64] Within days of its formation, the Central Committee assumed the role of the unofficial power in Paris, refusing to succumb to the authority of the Assembly, but in the same measure, refusing to place itself in a revolutionary posture. The first two issues to which the Central Committee had to respond were the parade of the Prussian army through central Paris and the disarming of the National Guard. As the triumphal march of the Prussian army through central Paris approached, the Central Committee initially decided to resist it by force.

In anticipation of the Prussian occupation of the capital the Central Committee took a crucial step that, two and one-half weeks later, would prove decisive: it secured 400 cannons, built in Paris by funds collected through public subscription during the siege and carelessly left behind by the Government. The Central Committee relocated the cannons to working-class and artisanal districts like Montmartre, Belleville, the Place des Vosges, and the Place d'Italie. With respect to the march by the Prussian army, after much debate the Central Committee settled on a non-confrontational approach.[65] One poster, in particular, produced on 28 February by 29 heretofore unknown worker delegates to the Central Committee, anticipated that the Assembly and the Prussians might now be working collusively to instigate conflict in Paris in order to carry out a blood bath. On the twenty-third anniversary of the declaration of the Second Republic, this poster drew upon the experiences of June, 1848, in cautioning that: '[a]ny attack will unleash on the people the fury of the enemies of the Revolution, drowning social demands in a river of blood. We remember the lugubrious days of June.'[66]

Meanwhile the Assembly adopted a series of measures that, whether or not by design, increased tensions between it and Paris. Whether or not Thiers was bent on provoking Paris to revolt, the first actions of the Assembly widened an already substantial chasm between Paris and the provincial representatives. Many contemporaries and historians have contended that, in the aftermath of the elections, Thiers and the Assembly made it their mission to render Paris impotent. The first laws passed by the Assembly reflected either a precipitous, albeit insensitive, move towards ending the siege mentality, or, more likely, an effort at directly provoking Paris to revolt. Thiers's testimony before the parliamentary inquest into 18 March, seem to confirm that the latter was the case: 'After signing the peace treaty, I soon saw that we would have to sustain a terrible struggle against the people of all sorts accumulated at Paris.' During the first two weeks of March, the Assembly passed laws ending moratoriums on the sale of goods left at the State pawnshop, the *Monts de Piété* (7 March) and on rent and overdue bills (10 March). In fact, even though Paris was a long way from experiencing economic recovery, rents and payments on bills accrued since the siege became due within four months. A final measure, the decision on a permanent site for the Assembly was particularly contentious: the adoption of Versailles, beginning on 20 March, as the meeting place of the Assembly especially so. In pressing for Versailles, Thiers wanted to shield the Assembly from the growing radical movements in the capital, yet remain close enough to subdue it should an expected uprising materialize. In the event of this, Thiers, after having capitulated to the foreign enemy, expected to emerge a hero who not only ended the war, but also saved France from disorder. The choice of Versailles also carried with it innuendoes that, ultimately, the royalist-led Assembly would restore the monarchy.

By mid-March, the Assembly had banned six popular leftist newspapers, four of which had a print run of 200,000 copies. Included among the six was *Le Mot d'Ordre*, published by former Government member Henri Rochefort. Deprived of newspapers which contradicted the official reports, Paris was placarded with an endless stream of anonymously produced posters which, in some respects, were more vitriolic than the banned papers. Finally, several leaders of the 31 October uprising (including Blanqui and Flourens) were condemned, *in absentia*, to death.

For nearly a week after the federation of the National Guard, the mood at Paris vacillated between euphoric and threatened. For all the festiveness that accompanied the belief that Paris had recaptured its autonomy, also came the realization that independence could be violently fleeting. On 6 March, Desplats wrote: 'On the surface, Paris is calm, but is agitated at its depths . . ..' The next day he dismissed the news being spread in provincial papers that anarchy was reigning at Paris, but noted that the provincial view was causing alarm at Paris. As a supporter of order and moderation, Desplats expressed the hope that the Assembly would come to Paris and reaffirm that 'the form of government will be the Republic; without this, a formidable insurrection will be inevitable, not only at Paris, but in all the large cities.'[67]

Rather than trying to defuse the situation, in the two weeks between the departure of the Prussian troops and 18 March Thiers appeared determined to provoke Paris into a fight.[68] The overarching issue was the cannons; after all, without the cannons, Paris would be rendered impotent and would be in no position to challenge the Assembly. During the first two weeks of March, at least two forays to confiscate the cannons at the Place des Vosges were unsuccessful. Negotiations were underway between representatives of the Central Committee and a variety of Parisian deputies to the Assembly, including Georges Clemenceau, deputy to the Assembly as well as mayor of Montmartre (and future Premier of France during the First World War), for the relinquishment of the cannons on 10 March. That, however, was the same day that the moratoriums on rent and bills were annulled by the Assembly and the day that General Joseph Vinoy, Commander of the Army of Paris and Thiers's ideological soul mate, announced plans to suspend the publication of the six newspapers. We can never be certain whether the Central Committee would have turned over the cannons, but whatever prospects there were for a peaceful resolution of the crisis were sabotaged by intemperate actions, thus fueling the suspicion that Thiers was more motivated to negotiate with Prussians than Parisians. Mistaking the capital's tranquility for complacency, and striving to inform the Assembly at its first Versailles sitting that Paris had been disarmed, Thiers decided, as he would later testify, 'to risk all' in securing the cannons.

Even though previous attempts at confiscating the cannons had focused on the ones at Place des Vosges, the bigger threat to the Assembly were the cannons at Belleville (twentieth *arrondissement*) and Montmartre (eighteenth *arrondissement*), working-class districts known for their militancy. Consequently, it was to the latter spot that Versailles dispatched troops on the morning of Saturday, 18 March. The military operation, which commenced at 3:00 a.m., proved to be a disaster. Under the command of General Claude Lecomte, the 6000 strong force, comprised of *mobiles* and the hated gendarmes, easily overran the National Guard contingent guarding the cannons; though the one National Guard casualty died a few days later, his statement that he was 'glad ... to have lived to see the Revolution,' provided the Commune with its first martyr.[69] Arriving at Montmartre at around 5:30 a.m., the troops appeared to have had a successful mission; however, they did not have a sufficient number of horses with which to haul away the cannons. By 8:00 a.m., the inhabitants of Montmartre had awakened to the spectacle of troops and three posters issued by Thiers which, anticipating a successful mission at disarming Paris, referred to the Central Committee as 'an occult committee' and stated that those who obstructed the surrender of the cannons to the Prussians at the end of February would be classified as criminals. In spite of the efforts of Clemenceau, as mayor of the eighteenth *arrondissement*, to gain control over the situation, the crowd at Montmartre – comprised of men, women, and children of the district – were too agitated. Upon the arrival of the National Guard and the appeal of the women to the troops, 'Will you fire on us? On your brothers? Our husbands? Our children?,' the two sides embraced and fraternized, the troops completely ignoring Lecomte's imploration to fire on the crowd. Over the next hours, beginning with the seizure of Lecomte by the crowd, the failed military operation at Montmartre touched off a series of events which dramatically altered the stakes. By 10:30 a.m., when it was apparent that the government's calls to the bourgeois National Guard battalions had gone unheeded, Vinoy gave the order to evacuate the Right Bank of the Seine.

Yet, in spite of the extraordinary activity, 18 March was also a typical Saturday full of families engaged in the routine of weekend shopping. The surreal nature of the day was underscored between 12:00 midday and 2:50 p.m. when Paris enjoyed a respite from revolution. This interlude was, in part, motivated by a show of respect for the funeral procession of Charles Hugo, son of the venerated author. By 3:00 p.m., news that the government had lost control of various spots on the Left Bank, coupled with increasingly boisterous processions of National Guardsmen shouting revolutionary slogans, put the government on notice that further resistance would be futile. It was at this point that Thiers departed the Invalides and, escorted by some gendarmes, rode up the rue de l'Université and headed for Versailles, giving the order for a complete withdrawal of the army from the capital. In making this fateful decision, Thiers drew upon his memories of 24 February 1848 when he advised Louis-Philippe to leave the capital, regroup, and return sometime later with a more formidable force, rather than resist a more powerful revolutionary force; Louis-Philippe did not take the advice. In his memoirs, Thiers wrote: 'I was not successful on 24 February, but on this day [18 March], I triumphed over all objections.'[70] As the evacuation was taking place, Lecomte's future grew more perilous. By most accounts, the National Guard endeavored to maintain custody of

Lecomte, lest he be torn to shreds by the crowd or, as some suspected, liberated by Clemenceau. At 5:00 p.m., some veterans of the June 1848 revolution recognized General Clément-Thomas, dressed in civilian clothes. A moderate republican, Clément-Thomas was, nonetheless, indelibly identified as one of the commanders responsible for the deaths of workers in that revolution. Seized by the crowd, Clément-Thomas was taken to the same location where the National Guard had earlier escorted Lecomte, for his protection. That location was now besieged by a large crowd which included Lecomte's own troops. In spite of the efforts of an overwhelmed National Guard contingent to fend off the crowd and to assure it that a court martial would be summoned to adjudicate their fates, the two generals were taken from their custodians and summarily executed by a crowd that included army troops formerly under Lecomte's command.

What had started off as a defense against an ill-prepared attempt to disarm Paris had blossomed into a full-scale insurrection. By evening, the government had ceded Paris to the insurgents, but Jules Ferry, mayor of Paris, was determined to hold out against the insurrection; at 6:00 p.m., though, the troops protecting the Hôtel de Ville abandoned their posts, and by 10:00 p.m. Ferry was also leaving Paris. In spite of the momentous nature of the events on 18 March, Goncourt's journal entry for that date conveys almost a sense of insouciance in Paris towards the revolutionary activity, an attitude born, perhaps, out of the frequency of insurgency at the capital: 'I have dinner at the Frères Provençaux to the deafening sound of patriotic shouts, and I am completely surprised when I leave the restaurant to bump into people standing in line for the Palais Royal Theatre.'[71] A revolution, completely improvised and spun from a series of mishaps, had succeeded. The war, however, was about to begin.

Chapter 3: The Commmune

The men of the Commune would have become the saviors of the morrow if they had been able to realize their ideal.[1]

Paris Separates

On Sunday, 19 March, victorious Paris debated its next step. The Central Committee occupied the Hôtel de Ville, but was unwilling to assume the revolutionary task with which it was confronted. The Central Committee was in the throes of an identity crisis. Of the various bodies that could provide Paris with the leadership it required after 18 March, the Central Committee was the most logical choice. In spite of other differences, the one bond uniting all Parisians was their shared experiences during the siege; the National Guard reflected the Parisian determination to stand fast against the Prussian army well past the point when victory was beyond reach. As the most visible symbol of Paris's resistance to the Prussians and to its Government's capitulation, the National Guard was less an overtly political body than were the Vigilance Committees. Even though ideology and patriotism intersected at the war's conclusion and the National Guard could not escape being imbued with the political discourse of the day, its majority strove to remain above the political passions and dampen any revolutionary embers. That's not to say, though, that prominent members of the National Guard were ideologically vacant before the siege and the capitulation; from Adolphe Assi, a veteran of Garibaldi's 'Red Shirts' and activist in the strike against the Schneider works at Le Creusot in January 1870, to Eugène Varlin, bookbinder and internationalist whose ideas evolved from early Proudhonian influences into political militancy, the Central Committee contained a large contingent of individuals well known for their political activism. In the final analysis did the Central Committee's hesitation at capitalizing on its victory at Paris by marching on Versailles doom, as historian Jacques Rougerie has suggested, a revolution that was nearly unavoidable?[2]

The decisions made during those first days after 18 March ultimately determined the course of events for the next ten weeks. At every possible occurrence, those in authority avoided the adoption of a confrontational posture *vis-à-vis* the Government. For example, on 18 March, the National Guard took no action to stop the exodus of Thiers, Favre, Picard, and others to Versailles. More significantly, though, the Central Committee publicly rejected calls for a military action against Versailles being openly made around the Hôtel de Ville.[3] Potentially the biggest blunder, though, was a military decision. As the government left Paris, so too were the forts surrounding the city evacuated. Though the Commune seized all the forts south of Paris (Issy, Vanves, Montrouge, Bicêtre, and Ivry), they neglected to occupy the fort at Mont-Valérien. Located in the west, Mont-Valérien was, arguably, the most strategic fort and post-mortems on the Commune often point to the Commune's failure to seize it as a critical mistake that determined the civil war: Charles Ernest Lullier, named commander-in-chief of the National Guard on 18 March, hesitated to occupy Mont-Valérien after the fort's commander allegedly promised to remain neutral in a war between Paris and Versailles. Lullier was promptly relieved of his command.[4] This move cost the Commune control over the fort, and as events would later prove, gave the Versaillais a staging ground for the invasion of Paris.

Some (principally Blanquists and internationalists) spoke of the need to maintain the revolutionary initiative by seizing the Government ministries and preparing for civil war. On a more extreme note, Louise Michel, teacher and head of the female complement to the eighteenth *arrondissement* Vigilance Committee, floated a plan to assassinate Thiers at Versailles to fellow activists Théophile Ferré and Raoul Rigault. Michel might have been motivated by the romantic image of tyrannicide as a revolutionary act, executing justice in the name of the people; attempted assassins of Louis-Philippe under the July Monarchy employed such a defense, claiming to follow in the tradition of the regicides who voted for Louis XVI's execution. Mindful that, in the wake of the execution of the two generals, provincial opinion was unlikely to be sympathetic to Paris, Ferré and Rigault resisted the idea.[5]

A number of reasons have been advanced for the Central Committee's hesitancy. Based on the discussions engaged in by the Central

Committee on 19 March, the majority either did not believe that a revolution had occurred or were unwilling to assume so big a responsibility. From a purely logistical standpoint, a military venture might have changed the course of events. In contrast to the 200,000 National Guardsmen at Paris, the force at Versailles numbered between 12,000 and 20,000 dispirited troops. Fears that a march on Versailles would spur the Prussian military to intervene against revolutionaries on behalf of the 'forces of order' appear to have been unfounded and there is little evidence that, provided the Central Committee abided by the peace treaty, Bismarck would have interceded in an internal French conflict. Surprised by the rapidity of events, seeing its mandate in terms of municipal autonomy, and hesitant to assume the reins of power by revolutionary means, the Central Committee confirmed the authority of the mayors of the 20 Paris *arrondissements* and entered into discussions with them for the organization of elections. Reflecting on the decision to hold elections, Michel wrote: 'Legality, universal suffrage . . . as usual these kinds of scruples arose, and they are fatal to any Revolution.'[6] At the Central Committee, Edouard Moreau[7] expressed the optimistic belief that if Paris limited itself to the pursuit of municipal rights, there was a decent chance the provinces would imitate Paris's example.[8] At a meeting of *arrondissement* mayors, Parisian deputies to the Assembly, and National Guard battalion leaders held on the evening of 19 March, heretofore political militants such as Benoît Malon, and Jean-Baptiste Millière argued that the Versailles Assembly and, for that matter, the rest of France would be more likely to accept the legitimacy of Paris's demands if these were expressed through a legally constituted authority, such as the mayors or a democratically elected body. It was clear that in the immediate aftermath of 18 March, the majority of those in authority at Paris did not view the events of that date as a revolutionary *journée*, but instead as a defensive measure. Consequently, in the expectation that the Versailles Assembly would be more disposed to negotiate with an elected body, the Central Committee called for elections to be held to the Paris Commune on 22 March. Until a democratically elected body could be constituted, the Central Committee recognized that it would have to assume some governmental functions, this included an agreement with Baron Rothschild whereby the Paris Government would have a credit account at the Bank of France in return for a promise not to take over the bank.

Regardless of the modesty of the aims expressed from Paris and the generally tepid steps taken, reconciliation with Paris had no place in

Thiers's universe. First, what occurred on 18 March had been a personal humiliation for Thiers. Ever since being named chief executive to the Republic, Thiers had made the pacification of Paris his chief goal. Only two days before the Assembly was to have its first sitting at Versailles, a location personally chosen by Thiers for its proximity to Paris, he had been forced to flee the capital. Second, reconciliation carried too dear a price for Thiers. Never a committed republican, Thiers only grudgingly accepted the Second Republic in Februay 1850; when faced with the prospect of another empire, he referred to the republic as the regime 'which divides us the least.' In 1870, Thiers had no intention of presiding over a republic imbued with leftist, let alone revolutionary, principles.

Given Thiers's own predilections and the inclinations of the majority of the Assembly, there was virtually no chance for a *rapprochement* between Versailles and Paris, even if the latter limited its demands to municipal liberties. For the affluent, Paris was teetering on the precipice of that most unbridgeable of nineteenth-century divides: class warfare. Goncourt, for example, believed it impractical to institute a republic in a land where 'evil, petty passions' dominate. 'To them *Liberty, Equality, Fraternity* mean only the enslavement or death of the upper class.' As Central Committee proclamations rolled off the presses, Goncourt contemptuously noted that Paris's fate was now in the hands of unknowns and, in the case of Charles Lullier, an epileptic and alcoholic, was being run by 'the notoriously mad.' Based on Lullier's decision at Mont-Valérien, it is doubtful that many Communards would have disagreed with Goncourt's assessment. Regarding the correlation between experience and competency, political activist and socialist teacher Gustave Lefrançais took a diametrically opposite view. For Lefrançais, the past months were hardly a testimonial to the correspondence between renown and effective leadership and Lefrançais rhetorically asked: 'Weren't those who organized the Commune on the night of 10 August 1792 and forced the Convention to proclaim the fall of the monarchy equally unknown?'[9] The exodus of Thiers, Favre, and other members of the Government for Versailles was followed by a more general departure of the bourgeoisie for Versailles, raising its population from 40,000 to 250,000 and engendering a huge accommodation problem.[10]

Within Paris, conflict developed between the Central Committee and the mayors of the bourgeois *arrondissements* over the legality of municipal elections not sanctioned by the Assembly. The mayors insisted that, until Versailles decided the future of Paris's government, they should take over at the Hôtel de Ville. While the Central Committee had rejected a revolutionary course of action, it could not countenance what amounted to a surrender of Paris's newly gained autonomy back to the Assembly. The schism between the mayors and the Central Committee grew on 21 March when the former organized a demonstration by around 500 marchers who called themselves the 'Friends of Order' through the bourgeois first and second *arrondissements*. Virulently opposed to the Central Committee, the 'Friends of Order' called for a boycott of elections to the Commune. On the following day, the National Guard met with force a larger demonstration by the 'Friends of Order,' designed to lead to a confrontation at the Hôtel de Ville; when the dust cleared, 12 demonstrators and one National Guardsman were dead. In light of the violence and the breakdown of trust between the Central Committee and the mayors, the elections were postponed until 26 March. Malvina Blanchecotte, celebrated author and poet, was uncertain who fired the first shots on 22 March, but she understood the day's significance: 'Again, the blood flows, the civil war is on. Paris is filled with consternation . . ..'[11]

At its first meetings at Versailles, the monarchist majority of the Assembly demonstrated little desire to placate Paris or to search for any means of reconciliation. The monarchists, though, were not the only intransigents against Paris. Attributing more determined leadership to the National Guard than that provided by the Central Committee, republicans like Favre conjured up images of Parisian troops poised to enter Versailles and wreak violence on the Assembly; so bellicose were Favre's remarks that Thiers was forced to clarify that the government had no plans to march on Paris.[12] Even the proposals by the Parisian mayors and deputies, more moderate than what was being called for at Paris, were rejected by the conservative majority at the Assembly. The Assembly's intransigent attitude produced two contradictory results: it both invigorated the opposition to the Central Committee at Paris[13] and caused a coalescence of more extremist organizations around it. Immediately at issue were the impending Paris elections; at its core was the authority of the Central Committee to authorize such elections. One last ditch effort by the mayors to delay the elections by a few more days failed and, on Saturday 25 March, the mayors agreed that the elections could go forward on the following day. In the final analysis, it would appear that the mayors' acquiescence was really a moot issue; the elections would have been held regardless of their position. As any chance of a negotiated settlement between Versailles and Paris was lost, the mayors understood that nothing could be gained from continued resistance to the elections; their support appeared to indicate the slim possibility that moderation might prevail at the ballot box. The most important impact of the mayors' decision was to bestow a semblance of legality on the elections and legitimacy for its results.

The elections were held amid a festive atmosphere on 26 March. According to the poet Catulle Mendès, queuing electors shared the public space with street performers, street merchants, women dressed for spring and inquiring children belying the monumental step upon which Paris was embarking. Mendès further noted:

> Paris finds itself obliged to choose between, on the one hand, a regular government which it wants to accept, but whose faults render obedience to it impossible and, on the other hand, an illegitimate authority, also guilty, but whose demands often represent the aspirations of the majority of republicans.[14]

Only seven days separated the calling of elections from the actual voting day. In terminating its own mandate, the Central Committee did not endorse any specific candidates or lists of individuals. On the other hand, its election-day proclamation encouraged Parisians to:

> defy both the ambitious and new-comers . . .. Defy, as well, blow hards who are incapable of taking action . . .. Avoid those whom fortune has favored too much because those who possess a fortune are rarely inclined to consider the worker as a brother . . .. Finally, seek men of sincere convictions, men of the people, resolute, active, of sound reason and a recognized honesty.[15]

Fittingly, the *Journal Officiel de la Commune* published the first of a two-day installment, taken from Edgar Quinet's *La Révolution*, of an excerpt on the insurrectionary Paris Commune's role in the overthrow of the monarchy on 10 August 1792.

The turnout on 26 March was little different from previous elections. From a registration list of 485,569, established for the final plebiscite of the Empire in February 1870, less than half (229,167) of the ballots were cast. However, deaths and migrations because of the war, the siege, and the capitulation took their toll on the Paris population and at least one historian has estimated that at least 160,000 of those registered during the Empire were no longer in Paris on 26 March 1871; the large exodus would appear to be validated by Thiers himself, who estimated that

100,000 Parisians heeded his call to flee the capital between 18 and 25 March. If Thiers is accurate, the proportion of eligible voters who turned out for the election to the Paris Commune was probably larger than those who voted in the municipal election on 3 November 1870 and the national election on 8 February 1871 when the figure was around 300,000. Ninety-three seats were up for grabs in the elections to the Commune, with one representative elected for every 20,000 residents per *arrondissement*. On the basis of this proportional representation scheme, the more working-class *arrondissements* received the larger number of representatives (e.g., the eighteenth and nineteenth *arrondissements* each elected seven to the Commune). Predictably, voting was heavier in the popular districts (those inhabited by the petite bourgeoisie and working class) than in bourgeois districts (first, second, ninth, and sixteenth).[16]

Those winning election to the Commune were overwhelmingly identified with the left. Nine were Blanquists, disciples of Auguste Blanqui[17]; 14 were members of the Central Committee; 17 can be classified as militant-activists in the International; 11 were socialists, involved in worker politics; four were 'old beards,' veterans of the Second Republic.[18] The election of 15 candidates aligned with the Paris mayors appears to undercut Thiers's claim that 'the friends of order' abstained from voting; within days of the election, though, all 15 resigned their seats.

One of the most striking features of the election was the three-fold increase of support since the February elections for candidates supported by the Vigilance Committee; it would be rash, however, to conclude that this reflected an ideological affinity with the program of the left as much as it demonstrated republican lack of confidence in the Thiers government and the legislative majority at Versailles.[19] In fact, during the campaign, platitudinous expressions about revolutionary change characterized nearly all of the placards and posters, but few contained anything approaching a specific program. That said, the broad principles outlined in these statements contributed to the impression that, in a century characterized by extreme political polarization, the declaration of the Commune constituted a new link in France's revolutionary chain.

On 28 March, at the Hôtel de Ville (symbolically decked out in both tricolors and red flags for the occasion) an enthusiastic crowd, estimated as numbering anywhere from 20,000 to 200,000, heard the declaration of the Paris Commune 'in the name of the people.' Commenting on that day supporters of, and detractors from, the Commune, agreed that the Commune's mandate would not be limited to matters of municipal

1 'Hommes et Martyrs de la Commune' (Men and martyrs of the Commune)
Source: © Photothèque des musées de la ville de Paris, France.

jurisdiction. In fact, Tirard, the conservative mayor of the bourgeois second *arrondissement*, who was elected to both the Assembly and the Commune, in announcing why he would sit in the Assembly rather than on the Commune, opined that the Commune was transgressing the limits of its mandate as a municipal authority by seeking to act as a national body.[20] Gustave Lefrançais, who at 45 years old was one of the oldest Communards, described the day as one of the 'great and beautiful days of our revolutionary history' and proclaimed that a 'new social era' had commenced.[21] In *le Cri du Peuple*, Jules Vallès waxed lyrical about 'the buzz of this revolution, calm and beautiful as a blue river . . . ' before adopting a more fatalistic tone: 'Whatever happens, whether we are conquered and die tomorrow, our generation is consoled! We have settled twenty years of defeats and distress.'[22] From the other end of the spectrum, Edmond Goncourt rejected any suggestion that the Commune was limited to the goal of administrative decentralization, and instead characterized it as the fruition of long anticipated class warfare: 'Decentralization, indeed! What is happening is very simply the conquest of France by the workers and the enslavement under their despotism of the nobles, the middle class, and the peasants. The government is leaving the hands of those who have, to go into the hands of those who have not . . ..'[23]

Though elements associated with the left were dominant on the Commune, the French left was hardly a monolith. Perhaps nothing epitomizes this better than the respective views of Communards towards the breadth of their jurisdiction. Although administrative issues are not often very stimulating, in the case of the Commune, it was central to its identity as either a municipal or a national revolution. As early as its first few meetings, the Commune appeared divided over the extent of its mandate. As he turned over the presidency of the Commune, on 29 March, to Lefrançais, Charles Beslay, who at 75 was the oldest Communard, distinguished – to great applause – the respective jurisdictions of the Commune, the department, and the National Assembly, warning his fellow Communards not to usurp the latter's authority.[24] Although the presidency was largely a ceremonial position, the replacement of Beslay, bourgeois, liberal, and a close associate of Proudhon, with Lefrançais, considered to be a militant socialist (or, to some, a communist), signaled the direction in which the Commune was headed.

While its first acts (prolongation of rent control and a moratorium on the sale of items deposited at the *monts-de-piété*) were direct responses to the residual impact of the siege, they were also calculated retorts to the punitive legislation voted earlier by the National Assembly. The Commune quickly followed these measures with other directives abolishing military conscription (though, paradoxically, replacing it with compulsory service in the politically more acceptable National Guard) and a declaration ordering public employees to ignore instructions emanating from Versailles.[25] At its second meeting, the Commune filled the administrative void by establishing commissions with responsibility for Finances, War, Justice, Welfare, Public Service, Education, General Security, Foreign Relations, and Labor and Exchange. As should be readily obvious, these commissions clearly exceeded the limitations of a conventional municipal mandate, and, in replicating governmental ministries, positioned the Commune as a rival national authority.

Following Paris's Lead? Provincial Communes

On 22 March, militant National Guard battalions at Lyon seized control of the Hôtel de Ville and established the first provincial commune to follow Paris's lead. Over the next few days, Marseille, Toulouse, Saint-Etienne, Limoges, Narbonne, and Le Creusot would follow suit. With the military defeat of the Marseille and Limoges communes on 4 April, no independent communes existed outside of Paris. The following will take a comprehensive look at the factors that motivated the declarations of provincial communes and conclude by examining why their lifespans were so brief.

As with the revolutions of 1830 and 1848, provincial revolutionary aftershocks followed the fall of the Second Empire. Even though revolutionary republicans led them, under the circumstances prevailing in autumn 1870, the aftershocks appeared less as ideological expressions than as protests against ineffective political and military leadership. While the inglorious conclusion to the war engendered hostility, it was not until Paris's declaration of autonomy in March that decentralization and socialism combined in revolutionary ways in the French provinces.

In his comparative study of Paris, Lyon, and Marseille, Louis Greenberg described the goal of the communalist movement in 1871 as 'a republic of republicans, based on extended freedom for the department, the commune, and the individual.'[26] In minimizing the impact of ideology, revolutionary *mentalité*, and tradition on the development of the Paris Commune, Greenberg simplistically grounded provincial support for the Paris Commune on an understanding that it stood for a decentralized, federal republic. With the exception of a brief period during the French Revolution, centralized authority had historically been monopolized by conservative forces and employed to frustrate democratic and social objectives. Consequently, if understood as more than simply a geopolitical shift in authority, decentralization also encompassed the dialectic on the nature of republicanism that divided its political and social wings. As Gaillard noted, 'there was no contradiction between the program advanced by Parisian socialists and that of provincial republicans.'[27]

The variegated provincial responses to the Paris Commune were partly based on perceptions of whether Paris or Versailles represented the true spirit of republicanism, but, as Ronald Aminzade has found, were also conditioned on local realities of cooperation and conflict between liberal, radical, and socialist strands of republicanism.[28]

More recently, Raymond Huard suggested that the prospect for a given city following Paris's lead in March 1871 was a function of the interplay between four factors: the experience of the municipality during the repression of republicanism at the time of the 1851 *coup d'état*; the political autonomy of the working class; the relationship between republicans and their adversaries; and the extent to which militant republicanism enrooted itself during the final years of the Empire and/or its expression in extragovernmental organizations (e.g., League of the Midi) formed during the war.[29] Huard's paradigm, employed in a case study of Nîmes' failure to proclaim a commune, nuanced the correlation drawn by Gaillard between a democratic-socialist tradition during the Second Republic and the resumption of revolutionary republican activity in 1870–1. In fact, according to Huard, the experiences with repression in December 1851 produced a chilling effect on its victims and foreclosed their willingness to travel down that same path in 1870–1. In addition, rather than emboldening militant republicans at Nîmes, their minority status in a heavily monarchist region actually inhibited and intimidated them. As instructive as any point raised by Huard is his insistence on a connection between working-class politicization and communalism; though Nîmes had a large working-class population, it was in a state of transition and lacked class-based cohesion. In establishing the existence of republican militantism and working-class politicization as the parameters of communalism in 1871, Huard underscores both the revolutionary and socialist natures of provincial communes. Case studies of provincial communes substantiate Huard's model and call into question much of Greenberg's thesis.[30]

Regardless of all other considerations, none of the successfully declared provincial communes lasted more than two weeks. In all cases they faced formidable opposition, whether military or propagandistic and lacked Paris's pervasive and historical revolutionary élan. Furthermore, the provincial communes bore a symbiotic relationship to each other; for example, news of the proclamation of the commune at Lyon mobilized revolutionaries at Saint-Etienne; on the other hand, the obverse was also true as the defeat of the Lyon commune discouraged the stéphanoise communards.[31]

If the goal of the communal movement was the establishment of municipal liberties, most municipalities did not have the same sense of urgency as Paris; in most cases, they had elected councils. On the other hand, the idea of launching a revolution while the foreign enemy was still on French soil, and after elections had been held, proved too problematic for all but the most militant of republicans. Though the full range of strange bedfellows opposed to the Empire cast themselves in decentralization's glow during the 1860s, upon the fall of the Empire communalism assumed decidedly leftist hues as a militant movement equally opposed to imperial centralization and conservative parliamentarianism.[32] Ultimately, the intersection of social class conflict, obscure objectives, and ill-defined missions undermined the efforts of provincial revolutionaries as much as the superiority of the military forces they faced.

The day after the Communards lost their first military sortie against Versailles, forces sympathetic to the Paris Commune controlled not one municipality in France. The absence of provincial support presented Paris with a logistical nightmare. Throughout April and May, the Paris Commune launched appeals to the provinces, understanding that the adhesion of other municipalities and departments was indispensable to its success. Though countless missives reaffirmed that Paris had no dictatorial aspirations, and that it only represented the ideal of a republic forged by the unification and free association of independent and autonomous communes, it failed to stir the provinces. In a declaration written by Jules Vallès and Charles Delescluze, and published in the *Journel Officiel de la Commune* on 20 April, the Commune delineated a series of rights each commune would reserve to itself.

These appeals failed to stir all but the most isolated pockets of support. Although supporters in more than 50 towns and cities 'paraded, carried red flags, booed the National Assembly, applauded and wrote on behalf of the Paris Commune, read and posted its proclamations, addresses, and petitions,' Paris remained isolated. In the end, regardless of the depths of their convictions and the passion with which they defended the Paris Commune, provincial revolutionaries lacked military resources and political influence to do anything 'but make noise.'[33] That said, provincials did nothing to assist in the repression of the Commune, either, and most appeared more desirous of a peaceful, negotiated settlement.[34]

As Huard's and Aminzade's works inform us, provincial communes are barometers of working-class politicization in the late nineteenth century. However, they also reveal the limitations of their political consciousness and their inability to translate political mobilization into a coherent and sustainable program. As rudderless movements navigating revolutionary waters the ephemerality of provincial communes appears to have been almost predetermined. Lacking a definite sense of purpose, largely isolated from each other and Paris, and riven by class and sectarian divisions, the advent of provincial communes was more remarkable than the inevitability of their demise.

The Commencement of Hostilities

Seeking to make good on his promise that 'order would be reestablished at Paris,' Thiers launched the Versaillais offensive on the morning of Palm Sunday, 2 April. National Guard batallions loyal to the Commune (known as the *fédérés*) occupied Courbevoie, ten kilometers west of the Arc de Triomphe, and commanded the route to Versailles, a fact which, according to Lissagaray, 'made the rurals very anxious.' Although Desplats was oblivious that the war had commenced ('All is perfectly peaceful, a lot of noise, a lot of movement of National Guards in our area'[35]), Lissagaray's account paints a picture of the city bordering on the edge of panic as it confronts, again, within a few months of the siege, the horrors of war:

> No one believed in an attack, so completely did all, since the 28th, live in an atmosphere of confidence . . . .. When the news, the ambulance-carriages, arrived; when the word was spoken, 'The siege is recommencing!' an explosion of horror shook all quarters. An affrighted hive, such was Paris.[36]

By contrast, Goncourt's account reveals a different type of uncertainty upon first hearing that the civil war had broken out. Goncourt's reactions turned from initial fears that Versailles had lost the skirmish ('Alas, if Versailles has the least setback, Versailles is lost!') to jubilation upon reading that the *fédérés* had been defeated. Nonetheless, Goncourt could not help but marvel at how Parisians 'have become accustomed to living to the sound of cannons and have acquired such insouciance that I see gardners quietly laying turf alongside workmen who are resetting gates with all the calm of former springs.'[37]

The Commune was not prepared for a war. Whereas prior French revolutions overthrew the existing power structure and did not have to contend with a rival source of authority, the situation in 1871 was far more complicated. Neither Versailles nor Paris could really count on the loyalty of an army that was largely decimated after being defeated by Prussia. In any event, the commencement of armed hostilities on 2 April forced both sides into hasty organizations of their armies.

Three Communards with some military experience – Émile Eudes, Émile Duval, and Jules Bergeret – advocated that the Commune should act in kind. Drawing upon a wellspring of popular indignation (which, according to Lefrançais, transcended social-class lines), they expressed confidence in the superior size of the Commune's National Guard-dominated forces in countering the hesitations of Lefrançais, Félix Pyat, Gustave Tridon, and Edouard Vaillant, who urged prudence. In his memoirs, Lefrançais wrote that in spite of having 'nearly 200,000 men in arms,' the Commune was not prepared for a precipitously organized military engagement. In fact, Lefrançais noted that while there was an abundance of enthusiasm, the situation was not analagous to that attending the victory on 18 March.[38]

As it turned out, the military offensive of 3 April was a rash act. Counting on the army either to surrender or defect (as it had on 18 March), the Commune's military had not developed a strategy. The resulting defeat portended consequences that extended beyond the immediate battles. On the one hand, two generals, Duval and Gustave Flourens, a National Guard general, were both killed. Flourens, the 32-year-old son of a professor at the Collège de France, was a mixture of erudition, idealism, and audacity; he also exemplified the international revolutionary so prominent on the Commune. The holder of degrees in both letters and science, Flourens had been a professor at the Collège de France (from which he had been fired for incorporating his atheistic, materialistic, and anti-bonapartist views in his natural history course). He participated in the Cretan uprising against the Ottoman Empire in 1866 before returning to France and involving himself in revolutionary republican activities (these included his efforts at provoking an insurrection during Victor Noir's funeral and his participation in the 31 October 1870 uprising). With a death sentence hanging over his head after his escape from prison on 21 January, Flourens was elected to the Commune in two *arrondissements*. When the offensive of 3 April went horribly wrong, Flourens's troops accused him of ineptitude and left him to the caprices of the Versaillais troops who promptly split open Flourens's head with a blow from a saber. Flourens's brutal death (and the inglorious transportation of his corpse to Versailles in a dung cart where it sat for four days before being released to his mother for burial at Père Lachaise cemetery) reminds us that, regardless of its detractors' accusations, the Commune did not have a monopoly on wanton acts of cruelty.[39]

The events of 2–3 April made it imperative that both sides develop a stronger, more disciplined military structure. The Commune appointed Gustave Cluseret as its Delegate of War. Cluseret possessed impeccable military credentials; in addition, though, he was ideologically committed to the Commune. A graduate of the military academy at Saint-Cyr, Cluseret fought on behalf of the Government in June 1848 and was wounded in the Crimean War. In the first half of the 1860s, Cluseret developed a reputation for adventurism in fighting on behalf of the liberation of the oppressed, first in Garibaldi's expedition of the Thousand in 1860, and then being appointed to the rank of general of the Union Army in the American Civil War. During the last years of the Empire, Cluseret became active in revolutionary republican journalism and organizations (including the International). On the surface, the mixture of idealism and military training in Cluseret's résumé would appear to have been the perfect combination for the head of the Commune's military. To the extent that part of the Commune's mandate entailed the exorcism of France's authoritarian traditions, idealism was bound to conflict with the realities of warfare and military dictates.

Versailles had its own military difficulties, though of a decidedly different nature. On one level, it was largely dependent upon the regular army, a significant portion of which was being held captive by the Prussians. Second, given the actions of his troops on 18 March, Thiers was wary of the republican sympathies of many of his soldiers. One of the biggest challenges facing the Versaillais political and military leadership was in combatting the sense that the only forces willing to fight for Versailles were anti-republican ones. In fact, few trained officers were sympathetic to the ideals of French republicanism. Many of those who were so committed joined the Commune less out of ideology than out of hostility to the elitism and nepotism that characterized the promotional system within the French military.[40] In fact, the absence of officers with an affinity to republicanism risked neutralizing the impression Versailles was trying to cultivate of the Commune as being well beyond the mainstream of French republicanism. Thiers's first move, the appointment of Marshal de MacMahon to head the Army of Versailles confirmed these suspicions. A descendant of Irish Jacobite exiles who never lost a penchant for the royal prerogative, authoritarianism, and an ossified social order, MacMahon epitomized the antithesis of republicanism. The appointment of such an unabashed Legitimist, especially one whose leadership in the Franco-Prussian War had been so ineffectual, appeared to offer a strong impression of a royalist campaign against republican Paris. Similarly, Espivent de la Villeboisnet, the commander who led the violent repression of the Marseille commune in April, was an ultracatholic conservative and son of *émigrés* during the French Revolution for whom republicanism, let alone the variety represented by the communal movement, was anathema.[41]

In his study of the military defeat of the Commune, Robert Tombs explained why, in spite of the urgings of a number of its generals, Versailles adopted a cautious military strategy, rather than choosing a quick foray into Paris. If nothing else, the débâcle of 18 March informed Versailles of the precariousness of its troops' loyalty. Given a little more time, Versailles would be able to compensate for the neutrality toward, or even sympathy for, the Commune among its lower officer ranks and soldiers by effectively spinning its own definition of the Commune's objectives and the character of individual Communards.

> [T]his 'Versailles view' may be summarized under three broad headings. Each constituted a different argument against the Commune, showing it not as an equally legitimate government but as an impossible and criminal regime necessitating repression, if necessary by armed force. The first theme was that of order against disorder; the second, of nation against faction; the third, of liberty against tyranny.[42]

The military engagements during those first days of April changed the entire complexion of the conflict. According to Victorine Brocher, 'Since 5 April, the nights given to sleep were rare.'[43] The Commune's inability to capitalize on the numerical superiority of its troops and the impressions the sortie provided of leadership in disarray and an absence of discipline dimmed the confidence and support of all but those most committed to the Communard cause.[44] According to Émile Maury, a quartermaster-sargeant in the 204th batallion of the National Guard, the National Guard suffered daily defections until all that remained were 'the needy, the fanatical, and the bizarre.'[45] On 6 May, the *Journal Officiel de la Commune* itemized, by legion and rank, the number of available *fédérés* (after subtracting those who were indisposed from the active numbers) as being 169,558. However, that figure included the vast majority of *fédérés* who accepted rations but did not report for duty; in fact, throughout April, the more realistic estimate of officers and troops ranged between 25,000 to 30,000, and dropped even lower in May. According to Lissagaray, barely 6000 troops guarded the western approaches to the city in mid-May. 'At bastions 36 to 70, precisely at the point of attack, there were not twenty artillerymen; the sentinels were absent.'[46] Whereas many were caught up in the enthusiasm that prevailed at Paris after 18 March, the results of the first engagements dimmed their fervor.

In mid-April, one of Cluseret's reforms called for the introduction of a form of conscription whereby all men between the ages 19 and 40 were to report for National Guard duty if so ordered. Though the call went out, Communard Benoît Malon, for one, doubted that it generated more than 1000 extra troops.[47] For those looking to back a winner, or at least to avoid the retribution that awaited the loser, the Commune did not look to be the horse upon which to place a wager. Furthermore, victories emboldened the Versailles troops with a belief in their own invincibility. The Commune would win the occasional victory, but the final outcome was all but decided.[48]

Many of the Communards' problems stemmed from their lack of governmental and military experience. The Communards were notorious at underutilizing the substantial armaments at their disposal.[49] Further, their antimilitaristic spirit hampered the discipline and resolute decision making called for by the times.[50] In fact, during the crucial month of May, when the Commune most needed to sing with one voice, its political and military leadership was most noted for their unharmonious notes.

French Republicanism and the Commune: Between Opposition and Conciliation

The Commune stood no chance of gaining the adhesion of the provinces to its cause. As we have seen, communes formed in other

French cities lasted barely more than a week, and were too preoccupied with their own survival to offer anything but moral support to Paris. Though the lines separating the monarchist government and legislature at Versailles and the revolutionary republican government at Paris appeared to be very clear, French republicans were conflicted over whether to support the Commune. For some, the Commune represented a revolt against one of the foundations of republicanism: a legally elected assembly. The integrity of the Third Republic hinged on respect for a legally constituted Government. This was true even though the majority of that Government was hostile to the republic under which it had been elected. Beyond this, the Commune was fraught with too many ambiguities. When Communards used the language of social-class oppression, they conjured up the social divisions that a republic, premised on manhood suffrage, was meant to heal. When Communards spoke of municipal liberties, their ideas appeared to represent a repudiation of the integrated national unity that was the historical soul of French republicanism and the legacy of the French Revolution. Nine Parisian deputies, including Louis Blanc and Edgar Quinet, drafted a declaration, published in several Versailles newspapers, that was condemnatory of the Commune and urged no compromise with it:

> However legitimate the demand for full and entire communal liberties for Paris and the other cities of France, it is not legitimate to revolt against universal suffrage . . .. Though the excesses of centralization are bad, the autonomy of the Commune, pushed to the destruction of national unity contructed over several centuries, is worse still. To work to the dismemberment of France is to repudiate the traditions of the French Revolution.[51]

While many republicans might have been ideologically closer to the position of the Commune than to that of the Versailles Government, they eschewed the resort to violence against a legally constituted Government and, perhaps most significantly, the ends being pursued by the revolution.

That said, a number of prominent republicans endeavored to mediate the dispute and arrive at a peaceful reconciliation between Paris and Versailles. On 20 and 21 March, Clemenceau and Jean-Baptiste Millière endeavored to negotiate a settlement between Paris and Versailles. Their efforts were undermined by the bellicosity of politicians at Versailles and the 'Friends of Order' at Paris. An indefatigable socialist republican who was elected to the National Assembly in February, Millière maintained a commitment to a peaceful resolution until the outbreak of hostilities removed his illusions of a peaceful reconciliation. On 25 March, six Parisian deputies (Clemenceau, Schoelcher, Floquet, Greppo, Lockroy, and Tolain) made one final attempt at a negotiated settlement before war broke out. By this time, Thiers had already made the determination to rebuild his army and pursue a military solution. Once the war against Paris started on Palm Sunday, Millière, Lockroy, and Floquet resigned their seats in the Assembly.

Following the battles during the first week of April, several other groups launched attempts at conciliation that were, *ab initio*, futile. As Versailles and Paris locked themselves into increasingly intractable positions and as the recriminations freely flowed, any reconciliation short of total capitulation by one side, was a non-starter. Operating as the Republican Union for the Rights of Paris ('Republican Union'), Clemenceau and a group of Parisian mayors and deputies urged recognition of Paris's rights to a freely elected municipal government as a first step towards peace. Even the most intractable Communards (e.g., Pyat) gave positive responses to the efforts at conciliation. Given that Thiers regularly referred to the Communards as criminals, it is hardly surprising that none of these meetings between 10 April and 20 May produced positive results.[52]

In late April, Millière provided the impetus behind the Republican Alliance of Departments. Comprised of Parisians originally from the provinces, the Republican Alliance strove to encourage compatriots from their native departments to put pressure on Versailles to stop the war against Paris. As with all other efforts, this one failed.[53] Also at the beginning of May, efforts were made to coordinate the various initiatives of departments and provincial cities to mediate the conflict. Organizers called for a congress of French cities, but on 7 May Thiers prohibited the convocation of such a meeting. Nonetheless, on 14 May 70 delegates representing 16 departments met at Lyon to urge a compromise whereby new elections would be held for both the National Assembly and the Paris Commune. Within one week of this meeting, the Versaillais had entered Paris.

On 21 April, a delegation of Freemasons, long-time advocates of republicanism, met with Thiers to try to put an end to the hostilities. Disappointed by the response they received from him and believing that Thiers had no interest in a peaceful settlement, a large majority of Freemasons manifested their adherence to the Commune in a procession consisting of some 10,000 members on 29 April. Within days, Freemasons would be killed as they defended the Commune from behind barricades capped by the banners of their various lodges.

With its army camped outside of Paris since September and the progress of peace negotiations taking place at Brussels seemingly resting on the resolution of the Versailles–Paris conflict, Prussia also had a vested stake in the conflict. Although the Prussians managed to resist direct intervention in the civil war, a Communard victory was clearly not in their interests. First, it would carry with it the potential of a resumption of hostilities against the Prussians. Recall that the Commune germinated, in part, out of the sense of betrayal and outrage that followed the capitulation to Prussia.

Whereas the Commune's association with municipal liberties, decentralization, and a socialist agenda alienated critical constituencies, its rejection of the peace terms allowed it to recover some support. Resonant with the rhetoric of nationalism, it reflected that enigmatic ability of French revolutionaries to imbue their discourse with broad nationalist strokes. In other words, of all the arguments Paris had at its disposal, the nationalist appeal was the most likely to generate support outside of Paris. For the Prussians, this message, and the possibility of its resonance, also carried the very real risk of an abnegation of the armistice and terms that ended the Franco-Prussian War. Beyond this, to the extent that the Commune was a socialist revolution led by a number of individuals who served their political apprenticeships in the International, a victory by the Communards could signal a clarion call to socialist revolutionaries throughout Europe to challenge existent regimes. By mid-May, Prussian Chancellor Otto von Bismarck no longer revealed any trace of neutrality, referring to the Communards as 'a pack of thieves.'

The German military and diplomatic corps maintained a neutral stance throughout April, all the while hoping to influence an ensuing settlement. Both the Commune and the Versaillais wanted Prussia to remain neutral, fearing both the impressions and the future consequences of such intervention. From its side, the Commune reassured the Prussians of its respect for the armistice, going as far as to offer 500 million francs in exchange for Prussian neutrality and an evacuation of the Department of the Seine. Thiers rejected an offer by the Prussians at the end of March for a joint invasion of Paris. From Thiers's perspective, any arrangement that allowed the Prussians to serve as power brokers would jeopardize the legitimacy of his regime. Already compromised by charges of not having been fully committed to the defense of France, the last impression Thiers wanted to give was of his Government's complicity with France's historic enemy.

Although it was not in Thiers's interest to rely on direct intervention by the Prussians, he was receptive to their logistical assistance. Until Thiers's representative at Brussels finalized the peace settlement from the Franco-Prussian War, Prussia continued to hold around 310,000 French prisoners of war, including officers and experienced soldiers. Perhaps the only obstacle Versailles faced to launching a crushing offensive against Paris was a paucity of troops. Prussia's *quid pro quo* for the liberation of French troops held by Prussia was Thiers's signature on the peace treaty. On 10 May Thiers signed, and on 18 May the Assembly ratified, the treaty ending the Franco-Prussian War. On 20 May, Prussia began liberating 30,000 prisoners of war at a time. The following day, Sunday, 21 May, the Versaillais were in Paris.[54]

In the final analysis, Versailles, and Thiers in particular, was responsible for the failure of a negotiated settlement of the conflict. While it is true that the monarchist-dominated Assembly adopted a belligerent, uncompromising posture towards Paris, Philip Nord has described Thiers's stance towards the various conciliators as 'rude and duplicitous, breaking appointments and keeping hopes alive even as he prepared the Commune's final destruction.'[55] For Thiers, who, since the July Monarchy, had made a political career out of repressing and stifling the political left, obliterating the Commune would be a fitting climax.

Three Crucial Weeks in May

On 30 April, the Commune temporarily lost control of the fort at Issy. Though it recaptured it on the following day, blame for the defeat, but not credit for the fort's recapture, settled on Cluseret. The Commune stripped Cluseret of his position, imprisoned him, and replaced him as Delegate of War with Louis Nathaniel Rossel. Descended from a republican, Protestant family with roots in the military, Rossel rose to the rank of captain during the Franco-Prussian War and achieved renown for having accused several officers of treason. In contrast to Cluseret's ideological affinity with the Commune, it was Rossel's ardent sense of patriotism, rather than political considerations, that influenced his support for the Commune.

Rossel's appointment as Delegate of War on 1 May corresponded with the Commune's consolidation of executive authority in a five-member Committee of Public Safety. The creation of the Committee bitterly divided the Commune. Supporters of the move argued everything from the historical precedent set by the 1793–4 Committee to the need for more efficient and effective decision making. Opponents, on the other hand, charged that the Commune was reverting to a dictatorship, eschewing one of its principal *raisons d'être*, and attaching itself to an anachronistic past.

Neither the appointment of Rossel nor the creation of the Committee of Public Safety could save the Commune. On 8 May, the Commune lost Issy for the last time. The following day, Rossel resigned his position, citing poor discipline and endless deliberations, bordering on paralysis, by the governing bodies. In fact, the pervasive mood in Paris was that neither the military nor the political leadership was taking a proactive approach to the growing crisis. During May, many Parisians delusionally convinced themselves that a negotiated settlement would end the crisis, or failing this, that the Versaillais would never attack the city. Others, such as the participants at some political clubs, like the Club des Prolétaires for instance, frequently railed against the inertia of the revolutionary authorities.[56]

After Rossel's resignation, the Commune's military operations were in a shambles. Having lost two trained military leaders within a fortnight, it had no militarily experienced candidates for the, by now, critical position of Delegate of War. Given the severity of the circumstances, the appointment of Charles Delescluze to the post appears curious. To the extent that neither Cluseret nor Rossel had proved effective, the Commune believed that a respected politician like Delescluze could provide the defenses with a much-needed boost.[57] With Blanqui in captivity, Delescluze was the next best thing to a revolutionary republican icon. A combattant on behalf of the republic in 1830 (though after *les trois glorieuses*) and a member of secret societies during the July Monarchy, Delescluze was a *démoc-soc* during the Second Republic. Delescluze's stints, between 1849 and 1870, in France's most notorious prisons for political detainees – Belle-Île, Corsica, Cayenne – rivaled that of Blanqui. Unlike Blanqui, Delescluze never developed a cadre of followers; neither a theoretician nor a man of action, Delescluze instead maintained an almost unflinching, if not anachronistic, affinity for the Jacobins of the 1790s. Parisians elected him to the National Assembly in February 1871, but Delescluze resigned his seat in favor of his election to a place on the Commune. Delescluze, though, was no military tactician, and with the fall of Issy, it would only be a short time before the Versaillais entered Paris.

Compounding the loss of Issy were accusations and recriminations. The Commune was beginning to haemorrhage at a most inopportune time. Cluseret and Rossel were arrested, along with several officers who had been responsible for the defense of Issy. Over the next week, the Versaillais gained control of Vanves, Longchamp, and Bourg-la-Reine. One of the most sanguinary and destructive weeks in the history of any city was about to commence.

Outside of marking the final act of the Paris Commune, the Bloody Week became the defining moment of the Commune. For defenders of the Commune, it signified the ruthless brutality of the bourgeoisie; for the Commune's detractors, it was the culmination of the Commune's criminality as Parisians torched their own city, depriving future generations of much of its historical patrimony. In fact, to this day the controversies surrounding the Commune are so intense and unsettled that it is either avoided or minimalized in the history curriculum in French schools. Because the accounts of the Commune's last weeks are so varied there are no means for apportioning, with any certainty, responsibility for the destruction and atrocities committed during May.

While it is incontrovertible that the Commune ordered the destruction of monuments, less clear is whether these acts can be characterized as criminal. On 27 April, a divided Commune decreed the demolition of a chapel that had been built to memorialize General Jean-Baptiste Bréa, on the site of a former restaurant where insurgents in June, 1848 executed him. The Commune coupled this measure with one pardoning the man convicted of killing Bréa. Later, the Commune ordered the destruction of the Expiatory Chapel built during the Restoration as a gesture of national penitence for the execution of Louis XVI. Though the Commune realized neither project, each act was no less political than the ones that led to the construction of the chapels in the first place.

Less symbolically, but more pragmatically, on 11 May, the Commune ordered the demolition of Thiers's house on Place Saint-Georges and the confiscation of his art collection. From the perspective of its adversaries, the Commune had acted criminally, abrogated whatever claims it might have had to being a legitimate government, and evinced an antipathy towards the sanctity of private property. The Commune issued its order at the moment when the Versaillais constructed an enormous battery just south of Mont-Valérien that, the Commune accurately speculated, would be used to escalate the bombardment of Paris (which, the day before, Thiers had denied).[58] As Communard Arthur Arnould reasoned, when he first proposed on 26 April the demolition of Thiers's house, Thiers's personal loss would be a form of poetic justice, albeit a pale one in comparison to the losses his orders would inflict on Parisians.[59] The following day, the Commune decided that the bronze works, books, and historical documents would be entrusted to scholars and artists who would preserve them as part of the national patrimony.[60] Though no one else in Paris received compensation for their property losses during the repression of the Commune, the National Assembly awarded Thiers the generous indemnity of 1,053,000 francs (though less than the 1.6 million francs he had sought).[61]

No act of demolition stirred emotions more than the toppling of the Vendôme Column on 16 May. As the name would suggest, the Column was a vertical, phallic structure, originally constructed in 1810 to pay homage to French military prowess and imperial authority. By all accounts toppling the massive structure was an engineering feat, but it was, in the estimation of the Communards, critical to the revolutionary reconfiguration and reconquest of the Parisian public space, its architectural landscape, and its commemorative authority. Perhaps more than any event during the Commune, the Vendôme affair embodied the chasm separating the meaning of nation and the nationalist sensibilities at Versailles and Paris. For conservatives at Versailles, particularly military officers poised to lead their troops into Paris, the collapse of the Column was tantamount to a personal assault on their most deeply held national convictions.

The Bloody Week

The immediate prelude to the final act of the Commune began on 20 May when the Versaillais began a relentless bombardment of Paris. *Fédérés* responded by abandoning key positions in the west of the city from Porte de Passy to Porte d'Auteuil to Porte de Saint Cloud, opening up a breach through which the Versaillais had easy entry into the city. In what turned out to be its last meeting, held while the Versaillais were literally at the gates of the city, the Communards mired themselves in debate over whether Cluseret was guilty of a dereliction of duty at the end of April![62] This irrelevant exercise was only concluded when Alfred Billioray, a member of the Committee of Public Safety, related the con-

tents of a dispatch from Communard General Jaroslaw Dombrowski that
the Versaillais had entered Paris from the Porte de Saint Cloud. As
members of the Commune departed the Hôtel de Ville at 8:00 p.m.,
their faces revealed to a contingent of journalists eager for news the
gravity of the situation.[63]

The following day confirmed the worst fears of the most pessimistic of
Communards. Both Edward Malet, the second secretary at the British
Embassy, and United States Ambassador E. B. Washburne, awoke at
their neighboring embassies on the sunny morning of 22 May to the
sight of the tricolor, rather than the red flag of the Commune, flying
over the Arc de Triomphe.[64] In his diary entry of 22 May, Goncourt
gloated over the 'demoralization and discouragement' amongst the
fédérés.[65]

By the evening of 22 May, the Versaillais were in control of a significant portion of central Paris. Writing to his wife, Desplats related his
efforts to leave Paris, but found the south and west blocked by the
Versaillais and the north and east by the Prussians (thus raising questions relative to Prussia's overt participation in the Commune's repression). Desplats described the efficiency by which the Versaillais rapidly
became masters of the capital:

> Throughout Monday afternoon the army made real progress,
> advancing on both sides of the Seine, spreading out on the Champs-
> Elysées, occupying the Palace of Industry, the faubourg Saint-Honoré,
> the Madeleine, the boulevards Malesherbes, Haussman, the Church of
> the Trinity, etc. And then, on the other side of the water, Grenelle,
> Faubourg Saint-Germain, where the shells put the Ministry of Finances
> and of the Admiralty on fire.[66]

Devoid of much of a strategy for protecting their city, the Communards
instead relied on barricades and a utopian, though delusional, view of
social-class solidarity. Placards in Paris made appeals to the imagined
shared class backgrounds and aspirations of the combattants on both
sides of the barricades, some urging the Versaillais to 'do as your
brothers of 18 March,'[67] others warning of ominous consequences
should they act like the military did in June 1848 and December 1851.[68]

Much as the Communards hoped for a reprise of 18 March, circumstances had changed since that date. First, the Communard success on
18 March largely resulted from a number of unpredictable variables:
poor planning by the Versaillais, the element of surprise as Montmartre

awakened, the resonance of an emotional appeal. Second, by May, the Germans had released many of their prisoners of war. On one level, between mid-April and mid-May, a number of officers, experienced by their engagements in June 1848, in the Crimea, in Italy, in Algeria, in Mexico, augmented the Versaillais military leadership, bringing with them a greater sense of discipline and obedience.[69] On another level, the Versailles military was more selective in choosing the troops to deploy in its reconquest of Paris. Rather than the 'rural hordes' that the Communards expected to materialize against them (and which conservatives at Versailles, initially, boasted would efface the Commune), the vast majority of volunteers who answered Versailles's call for troops came from the Île-de-France. Thiers was also at least moderately successful in recruiting disaffected Parisian National Guardsmen; thus he was able to deprive the Commune of a claim that it represented the republic against the reactionaries at Versailles and their army of provincial 'yokels.'[70]

Both the Communards and the reactionary element at Versailles had mistakenly reduced the conflict to a historical oversimplification: Paris versus the provinces. Each side had something to gain from this approach; for the Commune, it symbolized enlightened Paris against provincial ignorance, for reactionaries, it was a further example of Paris's dictatorial aspirations. In 1871, the provincial view of the conflict was more complex and nuanced; Tombs argues that through a combination of lassitude and distrust on both sides, most provincials wanted a negotiated, rather than a violent, end to the war. In the face of provincial ambivalence towards Versailles, the Communards modified their position, launching appeals for provincial support. At the same time, though, in their calls for republican unity, the Communards never abandoned their reliance on the 'Chouan myth' of rural hordes determined to destroy the republic.[71]

By the evening of 22 May, most defenders of the Commune dropped back into their neighborhoods and abandoned whatever chance might once have existed for winning the war. The Commune's desperation could be read in the communiqués issued by the Committee of Public Safety, the Commune, and the Central Committee of the National Guard. That these three bodies, with undefined jurisdictional boundaries, had never coordinated their efforts reveals in part the Communards' share of the responsibility for their demise. In other words, as their city verged on the precipice of collapse, the Communards remained committed to, if not victimized by, their obsession with debate and rhetoric.

Once the enemy was inside Paris, it would only be a short time before the Paris Commune's defeat. In his memoirs of the Commune, Gaston Da Costa, the Commune's 21-year-old substitute public prosecutor, speculated that Thiers purposely stopped short of an easy conquest of Paris either to provoke the Communards to engage in the week-long atrocities for which history would villify them or as a pretext for rendering Paris impotent.[72] While it is true that the 110,000 Versailles troops moved ploddingly through the city, it has also been suggested that fears of mines, snipers, and other potential hazards behind barricades, as well as fatigue, dictated their pace.[73]

Within a fortnight of having recaptured Issy, the Versaillais had 110,000 soldiers in Paris. By contrast, though they had been on notice for quite some time that a Versaillais invasion of Paris was inevitable, neither the Commune nor the Committee of Public Safety nor the Central Committee of National Guardsmen was able to mobilize much of a defense. Instead, with the Versaillais literally beating down the last defenses of Paris's ramparts, the Commune was reduced to a frantic 48-hour period of intense barricade building. Since early April, the Commune had anticipated that barricades would ultimately be its best defense. On 12 April, the newly formed Commission of Barricades issued very precise specifications on the form and size of defensive barricades. Napoléon Gaillard, though, appointed by Rossel to oversee barricade construction, was more consumed with his *chef d'œuvre*, a barricade he had built at Place de la Concorde, than with ensuring a steady and secure network of barricades to protect the city.[74] Consequently, most of the 500-600 barricades constructed in haste between 22 and 23 May were barely two meters high, and were composed of cobblestones, public benches, barrels, and any metal that could be found. Few were armed with cannons or rapid-fire guns.[75]

Delescluze understood that once the Versaillais had entered Paris, the Commune could not win the war. On the other hand, he believed that if Parisians redoubled their efforts and engaged the Versaillais in guerrilla warfare tactics from behind the barricades, Paris might be able to resist long enough to negotiate a peaceful settlement. By 24 May, Delescluze no longer deluded himself over the prospects of realizing even these modest goals; the barricades were notoriously understaffed and those defending them had neither reinforcements nor ammunition nor food.[76]

On 25 May, Delescluze and a contingent of Communards made one last ditch effort to persuade the Prussians to mediate an end to the con-

2 Barricade at the Rue Royale, Place de la Concorde; Madeleine is in the background
Source: © Photothèque des musées de la ville de Paris, France.

flict. *Fédérés* guarding the Porte de Vincennes, believed instead that the Communards were trying to flee Paris 'after having gotten us into this mess.' After writing to his sister that he 'can't bear to submit to another defeat after so many others,' Delescluze walked to the barricade at Place du Château d'Eau (now Place de la République), one of the few barricades still under heavy contention. Dressed in his familiar black hat, coat, trousers, and red scarf tied around his waist, Delescluze arrived at around 8:00 p.m., mounted the barricade, and stoically met his death. For Delescluze the barricade, the symbol of a nineteenth-century revolutionary tradition, was the fitting end to the cause to which he had devoted, and ultimately given, his life.[77]

The Bloody Week's death toll was not limited to combatants or individuals like Delescluze who placed themselves in combat situations. The Versaillais were especially ruthless in executing their prisoners or indiscriminantly killing those they suspected of aiding or abetting their enemy.

Ever since the beginning of the war, both sides grappled with the issue of hostages and captured enemy combatants. As early as 4 April, reports revealed that Joseph Vinoy, commander-in-chief of the Versailles army,

3 Young victims of the Versaillais: two dead children
Source: © Photothèque des musées de la ville de Paris, France.

had given the order to shoot prisoners taken by his troops; as the source of this report was a pro-Versailles newspaper, this was not Communard propaganda.[78] According to Lissagaray, 'the savagery of the Versaillese [sic], the assassination of the prisoners, of Flourens and Duval, had excited the most calm.'[79] On 5 April, the Commune issued a decree which, in substance, stated that anyone suspected of complicity with Versailles would be brought before a jury and, if found guilty, would be defined, and held, as a hostage; further, for every one Communard executed by Versailles, three hostages would be executed by the Commune.

The Commune had hoped to use the hostages, and in particular its 'A-list' hostage, Monsignor Georges Darboy, archbishop of Paris, as a bargaining chip to secure Blanqui's liberation. Thiers refused repeated offers by the Commune to swap Darboy for Blanqui, including one final offer to exchange all 74 hostages held by the Commune for Blanqui, reasoning that Blanqui's value to the Commune would be the equivalent of a military unit, whereas Darboy was of only marginal significance to the Versaillais. In spite of grounding itself in the tradition of revolutionary secularism, the Commune had no personal animus towards

Darboy. Communards mistakenly calculated that Versailles placed greater value on his safety. Darboy, however, was a liberal member of the clergy opposed to the doctrine of papal infallibility, and with few genuine friends amongst the conservatives at Versailles. As we will see, he had greater significance to the anti-Communards in death than in life.

Despite incessant reports of Communard prisoners of war at Versailles being massacred, the Commune exercised restraint. Once the Versaillais entered Paris, though, the hostage situation reached a critical point; the *fédérés* clamored for retribution. During the evening of 23 May, Raoul Rigault, the Commune's public prosecutor, personally went to the Sainte-Pélagie Prison and ordered the execution of moderate republican journalist Gustave Chaudey and, for good measure, three gendarmes. Chaudey first entered politics in 1848, largely at the behest of Alphonse Lamartine. After spending a few years in exile in Switzerland following Napoléon III's *coup d'état*, Chaudey returned to France and became Proudhon's most trusted disciple. With the fall of the Empire, he allied himself with moderate republicans like Jules Ferry (who named him deputy-mayor of Paris). Chaudey had few friends amongst the Communards, least of all Rigault who was standing near his friend Sapia when the latter was killed on 22 January, an act for which Rigault held Chaudey personally responsible.[80]

From there, matters rapidly spun out of the Commune's control and, faced with the brutality of the Versaillais troops, the likelihood of their own deaths, and, lest we forget, Thiers's steadfast refusal of a negotiated end to the stand-off, frustrated *fédérés*, devoid of accountability, carried out a series of reprisals. On the following day, 24 May, a crowd of National Guardsmen, seeking vengeance for the Commune's imminent collapse, demanded the execution of Charles de Beaufort, a National Guard commander whose aristocratic affectations and questionable leadership had raised suspicions amongst the *fédérés*. Although Delescluze, amongst others, pleaded for de Beaufort's life, the crowd summarily executed him.

Later in the evening, a crowd of *fédérés* turned its attention to Darboy and several other clerics being held at the La Roquette prison. Although he initially vacillated, Théophile Ferré, a member of the Commune's General Security Commission, signed the order that turned Darboy and five other hostages, all clerics, over to their executioners. At roughly 8:30 that night, *fédérés* executed the six hostages. The news inspired revulsion amongst both Versaillais and Communards, alike. Jules Vallès and

Delescluze, bitterly divided three weeks ago over the creation of the Committee of Public Safety, despaired over how a revolution that had promised the dawning of a new era had deteriorated into an orgy of destruction and death.[81] For the Versaillais, Darboy's execution was a bit more complex. On one level, most of the monarchists in the Versailles Assembly had no love for Darboy's liberalism; on another level, the murder of a cleric, and a reform-minded one at that, allowed them to define the Communards as gratuitous murderers unfit for the authority they had assumed over the past ten weeks. In fact, over the next three days, summary executions would continue. At the end of the Bloody Week, somewhere between 63 and 107 hostages and prisoners held by the Commune would be executed by crowds acting on their own volition.[82]

As unsavory as the atrocities committed in the name of the Commune were, they pale in comparison to those perpetrated by the Versaillais. Neither the troops nor their commanders received precise directions from Versailles relative to the treatment of those suspected to be enemy combatants. On the other hand, Versailles had established a precedent for the treatment of hostages back in the first days of April with Vinoy's policy of killing prisoners of war and even deserters from the French army.

In order to handle the thousands of cases of individuals arrested during the Bloody Week, Versailles authorized its commanding officers to establish and supervise *ad hoc* military courts that would expeditiously make a preliminary determination of guilt, innocence, or the need for further proceedings. These tribunals operated without any procedural guidelines and the hearings were more akin to fishing expeditions to uncover evidence of wrongdoing than resulting from any actual information of criminal malfeasance. General Valentin, appointed by Versailles as Prefect of Police, summed up the prevailing juridical philosophy at Versailles towards Parisians: 'The simple fact of having stayed in Paris under the Commune is a crime. Everyone there is to blame, and if I had my way everyone would be punished.'[83] Those found guilty were sentenced to death, the sentence being carried out immediately at Champ de Mars, École Militaire, Place Vendôme, La Roquette, Petit Luxembourg, Châtelet, Buttes-Chaumont, Père Lachaise, and at a site near Gare du Nord. Verdicts of 'not proven' resulted in the accused being bound over for a further determination at Versailles. Very few, if any, were set free.[84]

Even more egregious than the military tribunals (whose authority, after all, carried a pretense of legality) were the executions summarily carried out by military units without even a hint of a procedural safe-guard. In the words of the Abbé Vildieu, vicar of Saint-Roch, 'The soldiers from Versailles often had little pity for the insurgents; they killed 300 who had taken refuge at the Madeleine.' Although some of the Versailles military units were comprised of individuals who bore excessive animus towards the Communards (e.g., the Volunteers of the Seine, Volunteers of the West), few executions were the random acts of rogue soldiers. The Versailles army was extremely well disciplined and remained under the firm control of its commanders.[85]

Public revulsion over this policy became a huge embarrasssment for the Versaillais; in spite of MacMahon's claims to have issued orders limiting the homicidal zealotry of the troops and officers under his command, the record is somewhat unsettled as to whether, when, or how sweepingly MacMahon ordered his generals not to execute any prisoners. Summary executions continued into at least the second week of June, laying open to question how high up the chain of command went the knowledge of atrocities.[86]

At the start of the Bloody Week, MacMahon's order regarding the treatment of prisoners appears to have been either rescinded or simply disregarded.[87] Thousands of prisoners were rounded up in Paris and taken to various public spaces – Parc Monceau, Place Vendôme, and École Militaire – before ostensibly being sent to Versailles or having their cases heard by kangaroo courts run by the military. However, wide discretion over the fates of the prisoners was accorded the commanding officers with some, such as the Marquis de Galliffet, an aristocrat known for his brutality and disdain for anything associated with republicanism, being notorious for their caprice. In fact, at one point, Galliffet ordered that 111 prisoners be summarily executed because their white hair indicated to Galliffet that they had probably been participants in the 1848 revolution.[88]

Recently, 'brutalization theory' has been advanced as an explanation for the intensity of violence exercised in repressing the Commune.[89] 'Brutalization theory' holds that violence is self-perpetuating and accustoms a society in the throes of a violent conflict to 'a heightened indifference to human life.'[90] This indifference manifests itself in the dehumanization of one's adversaries, justifying, in the process, the most brutally egregious acts. In his application of brutalization theory to the Commune, Bertrand Taithe focuses on the correspondence of a political culture punctuated, since the French Revolution, by violent conflict and the experiences of a society at war between July 1870 and January 1871.

The present study suggests a more expansive approach to the functioning of brutalization and considers the imperialist backgrounds of the generals most frequently implicated as having either overtly or tacitly encouraged the brutal reprisals against the Commune. In addition, a propaganda campaign that applied familiar tropes of savagery and bestiality to the Communards conditioned the Versailles troops to view their adversaries as invaders and threats to the nation.[91]

In a very recent article about the Bloody Week, Robert Tombs wrote that the Bloody Week represented the confluence of two currents: 'an ideological disposition of politicians, military chiefs, and intellectuals towards the acceptance of violence; and, as well, an organization of butchery by the "ordinary men" of the French army, who did not necessarily share the beliefs of their superior officers.' In addition, Tombs cited the impact of the Franco-Prussian War in forging a climate of fear and anger, providing a pretext for the suspension of civil liberties, arming the nation, and, most importantly, in the nation's defeat, creating a sense of national decline (and, with the belief that the Commune represented decentralization, national dismemberment). For conservatives (and even many republicans), the Commune represented something so abhorrent that those defending it could not even be considered suitable for inclusion within a civilized community. According to Tombs, though, the slaughter that occurred during the Bloody Week was not inevitable; instead, the generals in charge of subduing the Commune made a calculated choice to eviscerate the Communards.[92]

Generals MacMahon, Galliffet, Vinoy, and Ernest-Louis-Octave Courtot de Cissey were veterans of France's military campaigns in Algeria and Mexico.[93] French military atrocities against the indigenous peoples of both countries have been well documented.[94] A colonial *mentalité* that judged colonials according to their assimiliability to French values, compliance to French objectives, and adaptability to French rule underpinned the acts of cruelty in Algeria and Mexico. While liberal and Orientalist currents in 1860s France led to a more positive view of Algerians, as Patricia Lorcin has observed, even 'pro-Arab sentiments were inevitably subordinated to the received ideas of a European heritage. In Algeria passive resistance to French methods led to further denigration of the Arab.'[95] In other words, as with the working class in France, tolerance of the indigenous people of the colonial world was limited to French perceptions of their adaptability and compliability to the ideals represented by the French state.[96]

The French military dehumanized those who resisted French control as intractable obstacles to civilization, whose very existence threatened to return society to a primordial state. Characterized as such, brutality was, if not the only, at least an acceptable means for controlling and subduing the indigenous peoples. In 1871 the generals again confronted an enemy who, in their view, stood in oppostion to their conceptions of the basic tenets of civil society. Having internalized conventional conceptions of Arabs in Algeria and Communards at Paris as uncivilized hordes incapable of reasonable and rational behavior, the French military's barbarous behavior became a self-fulfilling prophecy justifying the imposition of their authority and the stability of the political, social, and cultural order to which they subscribed.

Certain profiled groups were more likely to receive harsh treatment: men in National Guard uniforms; foreigners (especially Poles, Italians, and Germans); individuals – especially women and the working class – suspected of having been in contact with gunpowder or kerosene (being in possession of an empty bottle was sufficient); those suspected of aiding or abetting the Commune. This last category included doctors who helped the wounded, employees of the Parisian administration, and those with the misfortune of having been mistaken for members of the Commune. [97]

4   National Guardsmen killed by the Versaillais
     Source: © Photothèque des musées de la ville de Paris, France.

In particular, the Versaillais reserved a particular hatred for elected Communards. Although Rigault was killed on 24 May for having shouted, 'Long live the Commune,' rather than because his killers were able to identify him, in other cases, the Versaillais subjected the Communards to especially brutal treatment. For example, though Jean-Baptiste Millière was not a member of the Commune (he was an elected member of the Assembly who resigned his seat in April after the Versailles offensive), the Versaillais pegged him as a Commune sympathizer. Arrested on 26 May, he was taken to the Panthéon where he was shot in the knees, and ordered 'to seek pardon from society for all the evil he had caused.' Instead, Millière shouted, 'Long live the Republic! Long live the people! Long live humanity!' whereupon he received a fatal, point-blank shot to the head.

Recognized by a priest on Rue Lafayette as he disconsolately wandered through Paris on the last day of the Bloody Week, Eugène Varlin was dragged along the streets of Montmartre to the Rue des Rosiers (now part of Sacre-Cœur Cathedral), where the Commune had its origins on 18 March. As soldiers mercilessly beat him along the one-hour march through the streets, residents of the district, potential one-time supporters of the Commune, their bitterness and fury now concentrated on Varlin, stoned him until he was 'one mass of blood, of mangled flesh, the eye protruding from the orbit.' After being shot, the soldiers looted Varlin of all his possessions before pummeling his body until the corpse was dismembered. At the end of their lives, Varlin and Delescluze, separated by a generation and not always in agreement over their visions for the Commune, were unified by their shared embodiments of revolutionary idealism and virtue. 'It is to Varlin and Delescluze that this story should be dedicated,' wrote Lissagaray, 'if there was room in the frontpiece for any other name than that of Paris.'[98]

The final barricade of the Commune located on the northwestern fringe of Belleville fell a few hours after Varlin's death. The killings, however, lasted until 15 June – more than two weeks after the fall of the Commune – while the police investigations into individuals who might have had a remote connection to the Commune lasted until a few years later. No exact figures exist for the number of Communards who perished. MacMahon gave an estimate of 17,000. Historian Jacques Rougerie believes the number to be at least twice as high. Basing his estimate on a comparison of Paris's population in 1870 and 1872, while taking into account a whole host of variables relative to migrations, returns, and deaths from the Franco-Prussian War and Commune,

5   Last battles – Père-Lachaise cemetery (27 May 1871)
     Source: © Photothèque des musées de la ville de Paris, France.

Rougerie concludes that a plausible figure would be over 30,000 dead. By contrast, Versaillais losses – those killed in battle, as hostages, and disappearances – amounted to less than 1200![99]

French school textbooks written during the half-century after the Commune presented a grim picture of the Commune. In excoriating the Commune for its absence of decency, they focused on Darboy's death (to the neglect of the tens of thousands of slaughtered Parisians) and the loss of property from the fires that raged throughout Paris. Missing from nearly every textbook was any discussion of Versaillais atrocities, including the military's policy of exterminating suspected insurgents. During the week of 22–28 May, fires engulfed a large section of Paris, consuming many of its most famous landmarks. In all probability, the initial fires – including the ones which destroyed the Ministry of Finance and the suburb of Neuilly and which hit the Palais Bourbon, statues at Place de la Concorde, and the Palais du Luxembourg – resulted from missiles fired into Paris by the Versaillais.

Parisians also started a large number of the fires, sometimes to cover their retreat, sometimes out of malice, sometimes out of desperation. Between 23 and 26 May, supporters of the Commune torched the

6 Destruction on Rue de Rivoli
Source: © Photothèque des musées de la ville de Paris, France.

Tuileries Palace, the Hôtel de Ville, the Louvre, the Palais of the Legion of Honor, the Prefecture of Police, Palais de Justice, the Porte-Saint-Martin and Lyric theatres, the docks at La Villette, and the Palais Royal. On the other hand, had it not been for the quick response of some Communards, a number of other buildings and the priceless documents stored within, including the National Archives, Notre-Dame Cathedral, la Sainte-Chapelle, the Mazarin Library, would have been lost. That said, France lost a large chunk of its historical and cultural patrimony as fire destroyed hundreds of thousands of books, manuscripts, maps, and other documents. The fires left an indelible impression on those who were in Paris at the time; in the words of Marie Colombier, an actress and courtesan, 'The light became so bright that it lit up the whole terrace: a fearful apotheosis . . .. After eighteen hundred years, a crime as terrible, as fearfully radiant as the sack of Rome, blazed out under the starry calm of heaven: Paris was burning.'[100] While numerous accounts testify to the fear inspired by the fires, the truth, though, is that the breadth of the fires may have been more apocryphal than real.

As Paris burned and then smoldered, commentators reviled the Communards for torching their own city. Rather than seeing the fires as part of a defensive strategy, the result of accident, or caused by the Versaillais bombardment, journalists and politicians characterized them as blatantly malicious acts by the have-nots, those who, by nature, are only capable of destroying, but not constructing. Typical was the account by W. P. Fetridge, a nineteenth-century travel writer from the United States:

> The burning of Paris had long been premeditated by the Commune as a last resource, and every preparation had been made to ensure its success.
>
> . . .
>
> These designs were not due, as one would like to believe, to the sudden inspiration of madmen, drunk with whiskey, powder and despair. No! It is certain, unhappily for the honor of human nature, that these projects of destruction, dictated by a true sentiment of social hatred, formed a part of the plan of resistance of the Commune and the Central Committee, and were, above all, entertained by the members of the Committee of Public Safety.[101]

By any measure, the deliberate torching of the city, for reasons other than defense, lacked rationality. After all, once the war ended and order was restored, workers would need employment and a habitable Paris; torched, it would provide neither. Sometime during the Bloody Week, the press began to identify women and children as the instigators of the fires. Before long, the myth of the *pétroleuse* – literally, 'female arsonist,' but conventionally used as a reference to women who were accused of having indiscriminantly torched Paris – developed and women's culpability for burning down Paris became resonant with conventional views on gender. Initial stories claimed that women were being paid by the Commune to light the fires. However, within a short time, journalists and commentators rejected that rationale in favor of arguments rooted in the essence of gender and, in particular, womanhood, a subject to which we will turn in Chapter 5.

According to Rougerie, in addition to the indeterminate number they killed, the military pursued investigations of 46,835 individuals. Of this number, 30,940 were never brought to trial. All told over a four-year period (though convictions were still being handed down as late as 1878!), 2445 were acquitted, 13,450 convicted by the 26 specially con-

7　Photomontage of the trial of Communards before the Council of War
Source: © Photothèque des musées de la ville de Paris, France.

vened *Conseils de Guerre*, this included all 3313 defendants tried *in absentia.*

Death during the Bloody Week carried the consolation of being spared the indignities and humiliations suffered by those taken prisoner. Bourgeois preconceptions of the working class as subhumans became self-justifications for the treatment meted out to them. Nearly all the prisoners were marched to Versailles where crowds viewed them with both anthropological curiosity and unconcealed contempt. Quoting the daily newspaper *Le Siècle*, Lissagaray wrote of bourgeois women striking the prisoners with umbrellas, a '[f]rightful retrogression of human nature, all the more hideous in that it contrasted with the elegance of the costume!' The prisoners – men, women, and children, alike – were either housed in fetid conditions impenetrable to light and fresh air or, at the roofless camp at Satory, exposed to alternations between intense heat and cold and rain. Amid mud, filth, acrid stenches, and lack of sanitation (where prisoners were forced to drink from ponds where others had cleansed their bloody wounds), disease and delirium flourished; the absence of doctors meant that no medical care was forthcoming. The

8 Photomontage of female prisoners at Satory; Louise Michel is second from the right, standing
Source: © Photothèque des musées de la ville de Paris, France.

few instances of humane behavior towards the prisoners were more notable as deviations from, rather than examples of, the norm.[102]

Because the *Conseils* were extraordinary tribunals, there was some variance between the *Conseils* and their application of the ordinary rules of criminal procedure; the Third Council of War was particularly scandalous in disregarding the defendants' legal rights. Few of the *Conseils* afforded the defendants with effective legal counsel and their rights to call witness were routinely ignored. The *Conseils* meted out relatively harsh sentences. While the majority received prison sentences, the charges against them were relatively minor. These included individuals who made seditious statements, demonstrated in public spaces, or carried a red flag. Serman cites the example of Pierre Malardier, a National Assembly member in 1849, who was handed a 15-year sentence for having assisted in pro-Commune rallies in the Nièvre. Although only 95 were sentenced to death this has to be put in context. First, 251 were sentenced to forced labor, 4586 to deportation. Second, given the scale of deaths during the Bloody Week, the government feared the prospect of generating sympathy for the Communards. Consequently, unlike the indiscriminate deaths that occurred on Parisian streets, the one area in which the tribunals assumed a posture of probity was in its selectivity in handing down death sentences.

The Fourth Council of War rejected Louise Michel's request of a death sentence, in spite of her admission to a variety of offenses (including arson and, possibly, the assassinations of Generals Lecomte and Thomas). Nearly all who were found guilty had been implicated in murders or fires, though in most cases the evidence was flimsy, and, in the case of Michel's admission to being part of the assassinations, complicated to the point of being incomprehensible. Others, like Ferré and Rossel were held responsible for deaths that allegedly occurred at their behest. One of the more egregiously disproportionate death sentences was passed at Marseille where a Council of War sentenced to death Gaston Crémieux, a one-time ally of Gambetta, for a variety of offenses related to his role in animating and leading the commune at Marseille. More of a conciliator than an insurgent (his efforts at negotiating an end to the Marseille commune were rebuffed by Espivent de la Villeboisnet), Crémieux's actions differed little from other provincial communards, none of whom received death sentences. Crémieux's biographer has insinuated that antisemitism was the motivation behind the harsh treatment meted out to Crémieux, who was Jewish.[103]

On 23 March 1872, the National Assembly passed a law ordering the deportation to New Caledonia of the 4,586 Communards sentenced to hard labor or deportation. The first boatload left Brest on 3 May for a journey that lasted just under five months. Between the roughness of the open sea, the conditions in which the prisoners were kept, the spread of diseases, and the climate, the journey to New Caledonia was excruciatingly difficult. Between 2 and 5 percent of the deportees died en route.

In the estimation of French politicians, New Caledonia was an ideal location. A French possession since 1853, and a penal colony since 1863, New Caledonia was, at the time, the most remote holding of the French Empire. From the beginning, the French intended it to be the equivalent of what Australia was for the British: a distant penal colony where, incidentally, a civil colony could be established.[104] Government officials viewed the Communards as incorrigible, recidivist savages, unfit for, and incapable of adapting to, a civilized society. Once placed in the wilds of New Caledonia, the Communards could, if properly reconditioned, become productive and virtuous members of a community. That community, though, would not be France.

Theorists reasoned that, once thrust in New Caledonia, the Communards would become 'emissaries of civilization,' their inclination towards anti-social behavior mediated by the need to conform to a moral order that, coincidentally, bore an uncanny resemblance to the bourgeois order. In addition, in comparison to the indigenous population of New Caledonia, the Communards were at least grounded in Western ideals of civilization. Captivity, confinement, and a relentless diet of morality lessons would, in conjunction with nature, transform the Communards into paragons of French virtue. They would naturally conform to, and see the wisdom of, the values against which they were more accustomed to revolting. In the end, they would serve as agents of France's cultural largess, spreading it to the tribes of their new home.[105]

The results were far more mixed than the expectations. Most of the Communards simply devoted themselves to survival and to normalizing their lives. To this end, they constructed straw bungalows, planted vegetables, opened a school and a hospital, built roads, and even started a theatre. There were a couple of escape attempts; while one group perished in a shipwreck, the other group (which included journalist Henri Rochefort) successfully made it to Europe.

Exile in New Caledonia was chock full of complexities especially over the thorny issue of race and class. On one level, the more the Communards identified with the French colonial administration, the more complete would be their rehabilitation and new identity as purveyors of the French *status quo*. On another level, Communards readily saw similarities between their repression at the hands of the French Government and the treatment of the Kanaks. Many Communards, most notably Louise Michel, established solidarity with the Kanaks. There were numerous instances of social interactions between Kanaks and Communards and a couple of examples where Communards married Kanaks. The Kanak revolt against French colonial rule in 1878 divided the Communard community. Intellectually, in their debates and in their press, the Communards considered the larger issues of the revolt: whether civilization can coexist with the exigencies of civilization. Some Communards chose to identify with the Kanaks' struggle (e.g., Michel), seeing in it, and the characterizations of the Kanaks as savages, a reprise of their own battle against the 'forces of order.' Others viewed the Kanaks' revolt as an opportunity to cast off the cloak of alterity that they had been forced to assume. In the process, their atonement would result in the reclamation of their place, as French citizens, in the evolutionary hierarchy, while situating the Kanaks in a subordinate position.[106]

Those Communards tried *in absentia* had managed to escape the repression by fleeing the country. Large contingents of Communards obtained refuge in Switzerland, Belgium, and Great Britain, with smaller numbers in the Netherlands, Spain, Luxembourg, Italy, the United States, Argentina, and Chile. Most Commuards settled in francophone countries. As refugees, most Communards experienced economic difficulties in exile; while manual workers might have had an easier time than intellectuals and professionals in some countries where their skills were in demand, in other countries, most notably non-francophone ones, professionals found work giving French classes.[107]

With the most liberal policy on political asylum in Europe, Britain was a particularly attractive destination for fleeing Communards. Since an 1843 extradition treaty between Britain and France did not cover political crimes, Britain could ignore its asylum law provided it followed the French Government's characterization of the Communards as common criminals. The British judiciary's granting of political refugee status to the Communards and the general outpouring of sympathy from the British public, led the French to retaliate by sending hundreds of banished Communards, most of them dependent on welfare, to Britain.[108]

Although Germany and Austria were the only countries to declare the Communards *persona non grata*, the only other state that came close to heeding Jules Favre's demand not to grant asylum to fugitive Communards was Belgium. A scandal developed there on 25 May when, in response to the Belgian foreign minister's refusal to allow Communards into Belgium, Victor Hugo, resident at Brussels since 21 March, defied this order and offered his home to refugee Communards. Conservative Belgians stoned Hugo's home, and alternately shouted for his skin or his deportation to the penal colony at Cayenne. Hugo left Belgium for Luxembourg, but eventually Belgian liberals succeeded in softening the Government's position on refugees. While in self-imposed exile, the Communards developed communities and provided each other with moral and material sustenance.[109] In addition, the exiles remained politically active, devoting part of their energy to rehabilitating and justifying the Commune, and another part to developing strategies for the empowerment of the working class, be it by revolutionary or parliamentary means.[110]

For nearly a decade after its repression, the Commune continued to reverberate throughout the French political landscape. The government kept watch and accumulated dossiers on exiled Communards. Investigations continued into the activites of Parisians during the period between 18 March and 28 May 1871; while few were brought to trial, the Government and Paris police administration expended considerable resources researching individuals with similar names or physical descriptions to wanted Communards. After a Radical Party (in reality, the party of Gambetta and moderate republicans) victory in an 1873 by-election at Paris, conservative deputies warned of 'the legal revenge of the Commune.' In response, the monarchist majority in the National Assembly elected MacMahon as president of the Third Republic with a mandate to establish a new 'moral order.'[111] In the political climate produced by MacMahon's ascendance to the presidency, and following several pilgrimages by a large number of deputies to devotional sites, the National Assembly revived a project first floated by Darboy in 1870 to build a cathedral at Montmartre. Proposed in the immediate aftermath of France's loss as atonement for the moral weaknesses that caused France's defeat, its location at one of Paris's highest points was designed to make it visible throughout the capital. In 1873, however, the project took on increased immediacy for conservatives who argued that Paris's crimes during the Commune cried out for an expiatory cathedral.

On 24 July 1873, the National Assembly allocated public funds for the construction of the Cathedral of Sacre-Cœur at Montmartre. The locale not only maximized the Cathedral's visibility, but also represented a reappropriation of the site where the Commune had its symbolic origins on 18 March 1871 and, in contrast to the Commune's irreligion, the rededication of that site for ecclesiastical purposes.

Writers and journalists hostile to the Commune produced the first 'histories' of the event. Often premised on the faulty theories of criminologists and other social theorists, these accounts depicted the Commune as an abomination, the offspring of a mating between criminality, foreign influences, secularism, socialism, feminism, and challenges to authority. In other words, the Commune represented a compendium of all that threatened the stability of a parochial, patriarchal society forged in the image of bourgeois males. For conservatives it was a reaffirmation of their dedication to the values of the *ancien régime*; for moderates, it was a cautionary tale on the applicability, versus the ideal, of liberty, equality, and fraternity. With a heavy emphasis on melodramatic recreations of hostage executions, arson, and fabricated brutalities, these accounts either minimized, justified, or ignored the actions of the Versaillais; instead, the Communards, depicted as occupying a lower level on the evolutionary stage, appeared as incapable of rising above their station. Perhaps the most notable of these retellings is

Maxime Du Camp's *Les Convulsions de Paris*.[112] A close friend of Flaubert, du Camp's four volumes are little more than a hysterical screed against the Commune, whose members and supporters are described as uncultured alcoholics covetous of what others have obtained through their talents and industry. Though a stylistic disaster, *Les Convulsions* earned du Camp a spot in the Académie Française in 1880, and perhaps because of this, his work succeeded in establishing a definition of the Commune upon which others would build.

Until the republicans were able to seize control of the Third Republic in 1879, there was little chance for an amnesty of the Communards. Though such leading lights as Louis Blanc, Victor Hugo, Victor Schoelcher, Georges Clemenceau, François Raspail, Edouard Lockroy, and Auguste Scheurer-Kestner (later the principal parliamentary defender of Captain Alfred Dreyfus), among others, had proposed amnesty beginning in 1871, it was not until the legislative session of 1879–80 that the measure came to a vote. Central to the discussion in favor of the amnesty were the supporters of French Marxist Jules Guesde who argued that the Third Republic would never be stable as long as it repressed and marginalized opposition. By 1879, Auguste Blanqui, still in prison, had become 'the aging sage of the revolutionary tradition,' a symbol of republican unity who, had he been liberated in 1871, might have served as a mediating force.[113] In fact, voters in Bordeaux elected Blanqui to the National Assembly in 1879. On 11 July 1880, both houses of the legislature agreed to a full and complete amnesty of all Communards, including those who had been found guilty *in absentia*. With republicans for the first time in control of it, the Third Republic had finally reconciled with its past. Even still, as verified by documents at the Archives de la Prefecture de Police in Paris, after the amnesty Communards continued to be surveilled wherever they settled in France.

The Paris Commune stands as one of the seminal events in modern French history. For ten weeks in 1871, workers, artisans, students, and veterans of revolutions took control of the second largest city in Europe. Though the suddenness with which the Communards assumed power, and the conditions under which they exercised authority, precluded any consistency, the Paris Commune raised a number of compelling issues. First, it presented posterity with all sorts of interpretative nightmares. Was the Commune simply a nationalistic protest premised on a sense of betrayal by a government more determined to preserve the bourgeois order than to defend national honor and integrity? If viewed as such, the Commune represented a noble, though misguided, defense of repub-

lican ideals. However, through the combination of the Communards'
backgrounds and its actions, as well as their adversaries' characterizations
of it, the Commune represented something more ominous: a harbinger
of social revolution that raised the specter of irreconcilable social-class
interests and deep fissures that lay beneath a facade of republican unity.
Through their rhetoric, the Communards laid claim to a mission to complete the unfinished work of the French Revolution, thus presenting a
heterodoxical perspective on the bourgeoisie's historical patrimony.

The Commune was also novel for its response to, and the adhesion of,
heretofore marginalized segments of the population. The combination
of its members' youth and socialist convictions situated the Commune at
the crossroads of French socialism, quixotically revolutionary, yet at the
same time offering practical responses to specific problems. The
Commune reaffirmed the ideal first articulated during the French
Revolution that revolutions carry a regenerative imperative that mandates control over society's cultural past.

The Commune was also a slight departure from Jacobinism and
French socialism's misogynistic traditions. As the first revolution in
modern European history to give at least lip service to women's active
participation in the revolution, the Communards gave the impression of
supporting the idea that women must be constructive participants in a
society premised on liberty, equality, and fraternity. That said, we can
only speculate whether, given the opposition of some Communards
towards women's political activism, the reality would have matched the
rhetoric; but the ideal represented by the Commune did attract the
adhesion of numerous women whose participation was predicated on
more than just serving as appendages to their male partners. Beyond
this, the Commune's adversaries drew upon stereotypes in apportioning
much of the blame for what it characterized as the Commune's excesses
on women's participation in the public space.

The amnesty afforded Communards represented something of a *rapprochement* between the Third Republic and the Commune. Moderate
republicans (and even many socialists) were not entirely forgiving of the
Commune. As French pedagogists in the last decades of the nineteenth
century endeavored to develop the citizenry's allegiance to a republic
beleaguered by a close call with a monarchial restoration, Boulangism,
and the Dreyfus Affair, they defined the Commune as an aberration, a
contradistinction with the republican values represented by the Third
Republic. In the decades after its occurrence, the Commune continued
to produce revulsion in various parts of the globe, and working-class

uprisings and strikes were often viewed through the prism of the Commune. Though battles over the Commune might have faded over time, the ideals, memory, and martyrdom of the Commune continued to beckon socialists, communists, and political activists in France and abroad. The Commune has been the subject of a few polemical films, commemorative postage stamps, and comic books, in addition, of course, to serious scholarly study.

It is to the foregoing issues – the interpretation of the Commune, women's participation, and its mix of culture and revolution – that we now turn in the next three chapters.

Chapter 4: A Socialist Revolution?

While interpretations of the Commune have not been as contentious as those surrounding the French Revolution, it has been the subject of interpretive debates. In the absence of a precisely identifiable philosophy to guide and unite its members, and not existing long enough to define itself, the Commune left behind a rather ambiguous and malleable record. *Post-hoc* clarifications by exiled Communards and their adversaries left a distorted record that both facilitated the application of historical models to the Commune's interpretation while obfuscating the reality of its ten-week existence.

Reconstructing the past as its contemporaries knew it at the time it occurred is always fraught with pitfalls. Resolving the Commune's seemingly oppositional ideologies and bringing order to its influences has presented historians with particular difficulties. While socialist republicans laid its foundations, the Commune was not preordained, but resulted from the confluence of several independent factors. As such, circumstances forced the Communards into casting off their ideological moorings as they improvised Paris's governance and grappled with the residual problems from the war; this, however, does not imply a heuristic approach to governance. Invariably different approaches emerged, but the tendency of some historians to characterize the Commune as riven with philosophical differences has given too much credence to historical red herrings that were of no significance to the Communards or its supporters.[1] Scholarly attempts at redefining collective identities, highlighting Communard moderation and, in some instances, according special attention to the contentious debates over the formation of the Committee of Public Safety have occluded a clear view of the remarkable degree of unity on the Commune around revolutionary republican socialism articulated in the final years of the Second Empire.

The Commune's Contested Historiography

Socialism, nationalism, republicanism

On 30 May 1871, two days after the end of *la semaine sanglante* ('the Bloody Week' which culminated in the repression of the Commune), Karl Marx read his report on the Commune before the General Council of the International Association of Workingmen. Printed in a pamphlet entitled 'The Civil War in France,' Marx situated the Commune within a Manichean world of class conflict in which the bourgeois state endeavored to perpetuate itself after the fall of Napoléon III's empire, first, through the Government of National Defense, and then, the Government at Versailles. In opposition stood Paris, the historic ground zero of revolutionary change and the fount from whose source would spring a new social and political order. For Marx, class conflict in France culminated in the production of the Commune, 'the produce of the struggle of the producing against the appropriating class.'[2] As Marx viewed the Commune's progression and repression from his London home, the Commune's anticipation of a socialist order was not so much evidenced by its legislative accomplishments (though he did enumerate several of these), than by its symbolism as a harbinger of proletariat political activism and democratic things to come.[3] Furthermore, insofar as Marx accented the belligerence and violent hostility of the bourgeois government towards Paris, his account says more about bourgeois defensiveness than working-class consciousness.

Through his participation in the International Association of Workingmen, founded seven years prior to the advent of the Commune and dedicated to the construction of a transnational working-class response to questions posed by industrialization, Marx had become acquainted with several future Communards. Given his expectation that the historical dialectic, by which history moves through successive stages of class conflict to its culmination in a society devoid of class, was on the verge of entering the decisive conflict between the proletariat and the bourgeoisie, it is hardly surprising that Marx viewed the Commune as the actualization of modern society's fissure along a class divide.

Notwithstanding that Marx later modified his assessment of the Commune's socialism, both the Commune's subsequent defenders and detractors viewed it through a prism tinted by proletarian class consciousness.[4] A rash of histories of the Commune produced by participants in, and witnesses to, the events further situated the Commune within the matrix of class conflict. Highly partisan, personal, and often hastily produced, these accounts of the Commune are somewhat suspect as accurate reflections of events; but they do provide a portal into contemporary ideological perspectives on the Commune. For example, within six months of the Commune's repression, Benoît Malon, a member of the Commune, characterized it as the 'third defeat of the French proletariat,' positioning it alongside the Lyonnais *canuts* (silk workers) revolt in 1831 and the June 1848 uprising of Parisian workers in a seamless continuum of revolutions whose motivations and violent repression underscored the irreconcilibilty of class interests.[5] Prosper Lissagaray produced perhaps the best known account of the Commune by one of its participants.[6] Originally written in 1876 while Lissagaray was in exile in Belgium, it has been nearly continuously available in an English edition since Karl Marx's daughter, Eleanor, translated it ten years later. Lissagaray's account, while frequently erroneous, is an extremely well-detailed, dramatic narrative of events in which the culminating message of the Commune is the irreconcilability of class interests.

In the twentieth century, evaluations of the Commune continued to turn on its relationship to social-class dynamics and the lessons for revolutions it foretold. Few bothered to examine the historical record. Vladimir Lenin and Leon Trotsky, the architects of the Bolshevik Revolution of 1917, both expressed admiration for the Commune, but viewed its defeat as offering a cautionary tale on the fate that awaits revolutionaries who pursue a moderate course in the hope of building a revolutionary consensus across social classes. Despite this criticism of its practice, the Soviet state included the Commune in its revolutionary pantheon, thus solidifying an inextricable, though erroneous, association between the self-styled communist state and the Commune. Furthermore, in the wake of the Bolshevik revolution, some historians saw in the Commune 'the first concrete example of the workers' seizure of power,' and thus a harbinger of events that unfolded in 1917.[7]

The right-wing view of the Commune was no less prone to conceiving of it in terms of class conflict. Beginning with the publication of his four-volume screed against the Commune, Maxime du Camp established the tone for anti-Communard versions of events.[8] Influenced by France's defeat at the hands of Prussia and threatened by the prospect for social, political, and cultural upheaval represented by the Commune, du Camp's fears were anchored in pseudo-scientific theories of national and social degeneration. With social-class conflict more of a subtext, du Camp's portrayal of the Commune was of the proverbial inmates suddenly, and temporarily, taking control of the asylum. In du Camp's account, the Commune was orchestrated by an assortment of sociopaths – habitual criminals, alcoholics, the mentally deranged, the demimonde – whose temporary exercise of sovereignty over Paris culminated, predictability, in an orgy of disorder, characterized by death and destruction.

In 1930, Edward S. Mason, a political economist at Harvard, wrote of the Commune, 'its impetus and *raison d'être* are to be found in causes which lie outside the domain of socialism. The war with Germany, the events of the siege, disgust with a strongly centralized and incompetent government, were of more decisive significance.' In effect, while he acknowledged that there were socialists amongst both the elected Communards and its rank and file supporters, Mason challenged the conclusion that the revolution that produced the Commune was either proletarian or socialist. Focusing, instead, on a more temporally limited issue – the pervasive sense of betrayal at Paris – Mason distinguished the Commune's contemporary importance from the significance it achieved posteriorly, referring to it as a 'legend . . . of more importance in the molding of history than the historical reality itself.'[9]

Challenges to the socialist model of the Commune have continued with many historians viewing the Commune through the prism of republicanism, rather than class struggle. In 1971, Louis Greenberg advanced what he called, a liberal interpretation of the Commune, so named because it attributes predominantly political motivations to the communalist movement, namely the defense of political liberties and decentralization of political authority. For Greenberg, the greatest casualty of the Commune was 'the liberal dream of a self-governing France' that succumbed to the centralizing, dictatorial tendencies of a Jacobin majority.[10] To what extent can we bifurcate the Communards' advocacy of decentralization from their advocacy of socialism? Was the Commune simply a movement for municipal liberty? In viewing decentralization in purely political terms, Greenberg's approach to the Commune ignores Communard rhetoric that defined decentralized government as the purest, least diluted expression of democracy and the counterpoint to France's historically repressive centralized regimes.

Whereas the Commune's historiography was once largely a series of celebratory paeans to the origins of revolutionary proletarian consciousness, historians are now examining the Commune's relationship to republicanism, in general, and, in particular, its impact on the Third Republic, still the longest enduring of France's five republics. In most cases, these studies eschew the Marxist interpretation as too deterministic and reductivist; instead, they bind the Commune to Paris's aspirations for municipal liberties, its experiences during the Franco-Prussian War, and the development of an ideological rift between Paris and the nominally republican government and legislature of capitulators and monarchists. In a masterful survey of the Commune, William Serman's concluding words, describing the Communards' aspirations, encapsulate the republican interpretation of the Commune as having been driven by the tripartite aims of republicanism, patriotism, and social justice:

> [A]fter all what did [the communards] demand? The Republic and the victory over the invader, bread and a roof for all, justice and social solidarity, the recognition of their rights and their dignity, and, above all else, liberty.[11]

Though neither Serman nor Jacques Rougerie, the doyen of historians of the Commune, view the Commune as the first revolution of the proletariat, neither historian rejects the socialist motivations at the heart of the Commune.[12]

The position of republicans caught, in 1871, between the reactionary politics of Versailles and the Commune's association with socialism has been the focus of a few republican histories. The 'prudent revolutionaries' of the second *arrondissement* studied by Robert Tombs, inhabited a socially heterogeneous district whose east–west geographic axis corresponded to an artisanal-bourgeois class divide. As Tombs observed, 'In the second *arrondissement* what legitimacy the Commune possessed came not from revolutionary dynamism but from a common tradition of Republicanism . . . .'[13] Philip Nord's work on the 'party of conciliation,' many of whom (including Clemenceau) were sympathetic to the ideals of the Commune, though uneasy with its associations with revolution and the proletariat, addressed the Commune's integrality in the formation of 'the contours of future middle-class/working-class alliances,' the Radical Party, that galvanized in defense of the Third Republic, and enabled it to weather its many storms.[14]

Republican histories of the Commune differ over the impact of the Franco-Prussian War on, and the socialist motivations behind, the Commune. Bertrand Taithe's analysis of the Commune's practice of citizenship being bound to the particular experiences of the Franco-Prussian War has recently been disputed by Rougerie who noted the fallacy of considering the period between September 1870 and May 1871 as a bloc and interpreting it according to a single model of republican citizenship.[15]

Identity issues: Class, neighborhood, culture

In his pathbreaking study, *Procès des Communards*, Rougerie provided a composite portrait of the typical Communard as a male worker who, in his political activism and commitment to revolutionary social republicanism, was almost an unreconstructed copy of his eighteenth-century forebear, the *sans-culotte*. Both *sans-culotte* and Communard were identifiable by their habiliments – the *sans-culotte*'s trousers, and the Communard's National Guard uniform. Though their rhetoric was laced with violence towards their enemies, in the case of the Commune, the acts undertaken did not match the vehemance of the verbiage; both, though, liberally employed and believed in the rhetoric of revolution. While their political ideal grounded the republic in the revolutionary triptych (liberty, equality, fraternity), secularism, and manhood suffrage, the Communard and *sans-culotte* conceptualizations of virtue as being at the core of the republic also entailed a social agenda: price controls, increased taxes on the wealthy, rationing of essential food items, and redistribution of land. However, the Communards were not simply caught in a French Revolution time warp; the protypical Communard also demonstrated a familiarity with socialist rhetoric as he railed against class exploitation, bourgeois unproductivity, and class conflict.[16] As we will see, the typical Communard had imbibed the same general principles expressed by the elected Communards, and, without relinquishing his sovereignty, had confidence in his mandatory's fidelity to the realization of these ideals.

While the typical Communard was less than a correlate to the industrial proletariat at the vanguard of Marx's communist revolution, it was its prefiguration. According to Rougerie, 'there were still no unions, but only worker societies; no state-controlled collectivization, but only an experiment in generalized cooperation; and the working class which made the Commune is neither proletarian nor artisanal, neither old nor modern, it is intermediary.'[17] Standing at the cusp of the new industrial era, the Communard sense of identity was more a function of historical antecedents and contemporary circumstances than a future whose full implications were unclear. Their republican faith was founded, in equal measure, on revolution as the only means for establishing the republic, and social democracy, or socialism, as the ends with which it is indistinguishable.

Over the past decade, a sociologist, Roger Gould, and a cultural geographer, David Harvey, have breathed life into an interpretative debate over social-class identity and adherence to the Commune. At the center of the debate is the extent to which Haussmannization contributed to, or eradicated, working-class consciousness and cohesion. On one side, David Harvey's classical structuralist position holds that both a 'community of class' (social class interests) and 'class of community' (cohesion within a socio-geographic space) developed in the peripheral *arrondissements* in the wake of Haussmannization.[18] In other words, two Parises emerged out of Haussmann's work: one bourgeois, occupying the central *arrondissements*, reflected the opulence associated with the Second Empire and its encouragement of commercial and investment capital; the other, a less visible enclave of low-income housing and industrial production, where the working class had been relegated after being priced out of the post-Haussmann Parisian housing market.

The two Parises eyed each other with mutual suspicion and contempt, the bourgeoisie seeing the working class as irresponsible formenters of disorder, the working class viewing the bourgeoisie as selfish exploiters whose dehumanizing treatment of the working class was the source of the latter's problems.[19] In conclusion, Harvey argues that the economic, cultural, and geographic reconfiguration of Paris in the 1850s facilitated class cohesion. In turn, working-class unity in the more juridically relaxed, though highly charged, 1860s encouraged the working class, in conjunction with an assortment of political militants, to develop the political ideals expressed in the Commune.[20]

On the other side, the late Roger V. Gould's conclusions on working-class consciousness are a substantial revision of Harvey's thesis. According to Gould, whereas the structure of political discourse and political institutions in 1848 were conducive to the development of class-consciousness amongst Parisian workers, Haussmannization, if not actually destructive of class cohesion, was hardly preservative of it. In place of class identity, Gould argues, workers, in the decade preceding the Commune, gravitated around their respective crafts, rather than the larger solidarity provided by class identity.

Working under the general premise that class-consciousness was more of a construct than a reality, Gould claims that the most politically militant workers were employed in those trades in which social and community networks fostered and reinforced trade cohesion; by contrast, the least politically conscious workers were employed in trades where workers had more attenuated social relationships with each other and where worker control over the craft had diminished.[21]

In terms of the Commune, Gould argues that worker participation was less likely to be predicated on class, or trade, than on the geographic community in which a worker lived. In other words, workers who supported the Commune, according to Gould, did not do so as an expression of class-based grievances, but as an assertion of the communal independence of their district. According to Gould, scholars who view the Commune through the prism of social class conflict have largely been misled by the refractive lens of a solitary article that appeared on 21 March 1871 in the *Journal Officiel de la Commune.* That anonymously authored piece characterized the emancipation of labor and the proletariat as the Commune's objective. In contrast, Gould argues, the vast majority of justificatory communications issued by the Commune emphasized it as a struggle against institutions that transcended class – state and clerical oppression.[22]

Outside of the absence of direct references to class conflict in Commune communiqués, Gould discounts class as a motivating factor for workers who participated in the defense of the Commune, especially in the peripheral districts (e.g., Belleville, La Villette, Vaugirard, Grenelle, and Montmartre) from which the Commune drew its most dedicated support.[23] Instead, Gould postulates that the neighborhood community, a space where social bonds transcended class lines, provided the impetus to fight on behalf of the goal of municipal autonomy.

Gould's thesis and methods have generated numerous critiques. Harvey's 1985 essay has been republished as a series of chapters on a study of urban modernity.[24] Although Harvey's text is substantially unrevised, in a few newly added paragraphs he contested Gould's methodology and conclusions. Noting Gould's reliance on the incidence of bourgeois witnesses at working-class marriages as substantiation for the existence of cross-class solidarities, Harvey poses two counter-arguments. First, most working-class relationships were premised on the lines of concubinage, not marriage; those workers who sanctified their relationship were likely to be socially mobile or to aspire to be so. Consequently, this particular evidence is both quantitatively and qualitatively suspect. Second, Harvey asserts that distinctions

> between workers and small owners [the majority of those who served as witnesses] was . . . porous, and this was not the primary class divide – bankers and financiers, landlords, merchant capitalists, the industrialists, and the whole oppressive network of subcontractors constituted the main class enemy of workers, and I doubt very much if any of them ever turned up as witnesses in Gould's data.[25]

Rougerie has also entered into this debate. While acknowledging the importance of the questions he raised, Rougerie has recently challenged Gould's dismissal of class as simplistic and neglectful of the experiences of French workers between 1848 and 1871. For Rougerie, the stress Gould placed on community ignores previous studies that have established a multiplicity of forms – economic, political, ideological, and cultural – that worker solidarity assumed at the time.[26]

Class, culture and the Commune

Understanding the manner by which class and socialism functioned at the time of the Commune requires releasing class from its purely economic moorings. French cultural studies suggests an approach to the relationship between class and socialism in nineteenth-century France that is consistent with the experience of the Commune. In his study of the Parisian counter-culture of the nineteenth century, Jerrold Seigel explored the impact of urban bohemianism on the Commune.[27] Seigel's identification of the various, often complex, elements of bohemianism are beyond the scope of the present study; however, in the 1860s, Parisian bohemianism was identified with the ascetic lifestyle of young, educated bourgeoisie. United by their frustration with the restrictions of bourgeois society, bohemians divided over the meaning of bohemianism, some advocating strict morality, others celebrating a libertine lifestyle; some eschewing the pursuit of mainstream notoriety and the monetary rewards that attend it, others actively pursuing recognition, regardless of the price it entails. Although Seigel largely devoted his discussion to the bohemian credentials of Charles Longuet, Raoul Rigault, Gustave Courbet, and Jules Vallès, he also characterized their bohemianism as the pursuit of absolute freedom for the individual against institutional and cultural restraints. For Seigel, the ultimate dilemma for the bohemian was being 'torn between a sense of membership in the bourgeoisie and a contrary consciousness of exclusion and hostility that could not be firmly attached to any other class identity. In Bohemia, every social identification was undermined by a residue of refractory individualism.'[28]

To attribute (or at least to acknowledge) the confluence between Communard and bohemian aspirations leads to an erosion of the model of class inextricably wed to impregnable economic categories and historical materialism. An alternative construction of the relationship of social classes broadly construes itself as encompassing all societal elements detached from the cultural values constructed by the dominant class. In the case of Paris in 1871, urban bohemians, though bourgeois by origin, ontologically identified with the larger sense of alienation from bourgeois culture experienced by urban workers. Without necessarily sharing the same values, the two groups became revolutionary allies. The Commune suggests a different understanding of class struggle when posited as a challenge to French society's cultural praxis by workers and urban bohemians whose sensibilities positioned them on the outside of the dominant social order.

Kristin Ross has located the heart of the Commune in the oppositional cultures competing for control over a broadly defined public space of bourgeois cultural hegemony. In disputing that space, the Commune's challenge extended beyond the rigidity of an economic conflict; Ross's reference to the 'breakdown of the notion of "proper place"' during the Commune entails not only geo-political and social space (defined as the practices of everyday life), but also the less obvious cultural space.[29] Ross references the work of Paul Lafargue, a bohemian, married to one of Karl Marx's daughters (Longuet was married to another daughter). In 1871, Lafargue was an activist in Bordeaux on behalf of the Commune, and he later wrote that, at its most formidable, revolution in 1871 threatened to collapse 'the boundaries *between* labor and leisure, producer and consumer, worker and bourgeois, worker and intellectual.'[30] In short, understanding the Commune as a cultural revolution against bourgeois hegemony does not diminish the relationship between class and culture; rather, it situates it within the ontological experience of those alienated from a culture and society they perceived to be reflective of bourgeois values. In constructing a society based on a new set of cultural signifiers, the Commune not only posed a threat to bourgeois hegemony over culture, but also to the influence of its social, economic, and political dominance over everyday life.

Backgrounds and Ideologies of the Communards

Throughout the nineteenth century, republicans had never been able to coalesce into a monolithic movement, despite the challenges they faced from monarchists. Instead, factions as diverse as liberal constitutionalists and revolutionary socialists shared space within the genus 'republican,' the lowest common denominators being their commitment to a government chosen by the people and with no hereditary succession of power.

During the 1860s, all of the future members of the Commune positioned themselves as republicans, but through their advocacy of violence, their demands for a fundamental reordering of society, or a combination of the two, they added the adjective 'revolutionary' to that designation.

While republicans remained on the fringes of the Empire's political culture, all shades of republicans who had not been coopted by the Empire, from moderates to revolutionaries, remained united. In fact, as republicans declared the fall of the Empire at the Hôtel de Ville on 4 September, Jules Favre embraced future Communards Louise Michel, Théophile Ferré, and Raoul Rigault, referring to them as his 'dear children.'[31] Under such circumstances, when even moderate republicans lost the antipathy they harbored towards revolutionary republicans, the search for nuanced distinctions within the republican left obfuscates larger issues. Unity, however, does not presuppose absolute unanimity and once the euphoria surrounding the fall of the Empire faded, ideological fissures resurfaced between moderates and revolutionaries. Blanquists, internationalists, and neo-Jacobins remained united around both a revolutionary republican catechism forged and disseminated during the Second Empire and their critique of the moderate Government's conduct of the war, as they awaited the arrival of circumstances propitious for a revolution.

Those historians who attribute the Commune to circumstances largely related to the Franco-Prussian War are not incorrect; but to dismiss the commitment of elected Communards to socialism ignores the political and ideological culture of the late Second Empire. For example, Mason's characterization of Charles Delescluze as 'a Jacobin in the old tradition, passionately devoted to its abstract conception of political liberty and to revolution as the proper means of attaining it,'[32] failed to recognize that, in the late 1860s, neo-Jacobinism was largely just a form of historical identification, devoid of a distinct and identifiable ideology. If we examine Delescluze's opinions as expressed in his newspaper, Le Réveil, we find him applauding the International[33] and advancing a program that included administrative autonomy for communes and departments;[34] considering the Jacobin reputation for uncompromising centralization, and nationalism, bordering on chauvinism, these were decidedly un-Jacobin positions. Other contributors to Le Réveil promoted the virtues of socialism, some going so far as to call it the natural product of the principles of 1793.[35] Similarly, at Marseille, Gaston Crémieux's eclectic blending of Jacobin nationalism, socialism, and federalism reflected the hybridized, rather than oppositional, nature of these issues within revolutionary republican discourse. In the face of contemporary realities, neo-Jacobins adapted their historical preferences, rather than abandoning them altogether.

Though he does not completely discount the integrality to the Commune of the socialist political culture that developed during the final years of the Empire, Taithe has recently characterized the Commune's relationship to socialism as a *post-hoc* device by exiled Communards (like Malon) to give a larger meaning to their struggle.[36] This conclusion is justifiable, but only if our understanding of socialism is premised on a modern definition that connects it to industrial economic relationships and the irreconcilible class interests they produce. As previously noted, to socialists at the time of the Commune, the term 'bourgeois' was as likely to carry cultural and political implications as it was to connote an economic class. Within that context, socialism referenced a citizenry committed to social-class reconciliation around egalitarian principles.

Drawing on earlier works,[37] Martin Philip Johnson has identified 'association' as the lynchpin of the Communard revolutionary ideology. By association, Johnson referred to 'assemblies of interested individuals formed ... to regulate their interests,' rather than to Proudhonian-inspired workers mutual aid societies, as the term would have been understood in the nineteenth century; these assemblies (e.g., political clubs and vigilence committees) supplied the political culture for the Commune's revolutionary community.[38] In opposition to bourgeois individualism, the associations studied by Johnson advocated reorganizing society into collective bodies characterized by 'harmony, cooperation, and community.'[39] Most importantly, association was not privileged by any connection to a particular social class, but rather was 'a method of fraternal cooperation among republicans and revolutionaries of various hues and social positions.'[40] In short, it was the ultimate expression of utopian aspiration for a comprehensive revolutionary regeneration of society; in place of classic Marxian social-class tension, the Communards, according to Johnson, understood class in reference to a dialectic between oppressed and dominant, 'privileged and exploited or ... propertied and proletarian.'[41]

Given the vehemence of the rhetorical battle, the indisputable nature of the challenge posed by the Commune to the Versailles Government, and the exodus of a large chunk of moderate republican politicians from Paris, the men who were elected to, and who agreed to sit on, the

Commune understood the revolutionary nature of their enterprise; their fidelity to general principles was of much greater immediacy than any doctrinal battles. All had experience as journalists or club activists between 1868 and 1870, attending the same clubs and contributing to the same papers. Defining their struggle as a commitment to political, social, and economic democracy, they all professed 'profound solidarity with the armed Parisian "petit peuple" who constituted the social, electoral, and military base of the Commune.'[42]

The Communards

Occupationally, those elected to the Commune included manual workers (in workshops, not modern factories), independent artisans, small shopkeepers, students, journalists, artists, teachers, professors, lawyers, doctors, engineers, teachers, a veterinarian, an architect, and a pharmacist. Less than 20 percent were born in Paris or its suburbs, but the majority received their political educations as worker-activists or intellectuals in the capital's political clubs.[43] The biographical sketches of several prominent Communards, provided below, vivify the Commune as representative of the variegated nature of revolutionary republicanism.

At 24 years old, *Raoul Rigault* exemplified the Commune's youth (more than one-third of the elected Communards were 30 years old or less). A mathematics student from Paris and bohemian habitué of the city's Latin Quarter, Rigault became an ardent Blanquist and dedicated himself to forging a revolutionary alliance between students and workers (in anticipation of the efforts of student leaders in 1968). Sincere in his revolutionary socialist convictions, Rigault emulated his mentor's example, serving multiple stints in prison. Elected to the Commune from the 8th *arrondissement*, Rigault first held the position of the Commune's Prefect of Police before being named Commissioner of General Security, a post he held until 24 April. Posterity has reduced Rigault's role in the Commune to that of brutal executioner of hostages, yet he also saved the life of impressionist artist Auguste Renoir, wrongly suspected of being a spy for Versailles.[44]

Another fixture of Paris's student-oriented Latin Quarter was *Auguste Vermorel*, a journalist who arrived in Paris from the Rhône and started his first newspaper in 1861 at the age of 20. In and out of prison throughout the Empire for his stinging criticisms of the regime, Vermorel underwent a political odyssey that took him from liberal (before Napoléon III relaxed the laws) to Proudhonian to socialist republican. The latter incarnation dated from Vermorel's founding in 1867 of the newspaper, *Le Courrier Français* which, with a circulation of over 18,000, was one of the most influential socialist newspapers in the final years of the Empire. From 1865 to 1869, Vermorel edited the works of some of the leading lights of the French Revolution, from Mirabeau to Marat, citing them as pioneers on the revolutionary path to democracy. By contrast, in his analysis of 1848, Vermorel issued a cautionary tale to the contemporary republican movement: 'The men of 1848 have lost, treasoned, dishonored, smothered, disemboweled the republic . . . All their acts have been crimes against democracy and against liberty.'[45]

Vermorel epitomized the enigmatic and fluid nature of revolutionary republicanism, at once combining the class-based rhetoric of the Internationalists, the Blanquist devotion to revolution, and the veneration of Jacobin republicans. Libelously labeled a Bonapartist spy, Vermorel was unfairly maligned in 1869 by Delescluze in *Le Réveil*. The conflict was more personal than sectarian; on 25 May 1871, Vermorel and Delescluze, one-time adversaries gave up their lives while defending the Commune at the barricade at Château-d'Eau.

In contrast to the bourgeois backgrounds of Rigault and Vermorel, 29-year-old *Benoît Malon* was a largely self-educated son of day laborers. In 1863, Malon arrived on foot in Paris from the Loire Valley and became one of the first members of the International. During the Empire, Malon confined himself to the role of labor activist: organizing strikes, writing articles in defense of striking miners, and establishing (with Eugène Varlin) soup kitchens and other forms of assistance for the unemployed. As with Varlin and many of the younger internationalists (he was 30 years old in 1871), Malon represented a more militant, less conciliatory wing of the International. Before being elected to the Commune, Malon was elected to the National Assembly in February 1871, but resigned after the vote by the Assembly ended the war.

Félix Pyat, the son of a lawyer from the Cher, abandoned a legal career in favor of journalism and playwriting under the July Monarchy, mediums which allowed him to convey his socialist convictions. Elected to the Constituent Assembly in 1848, Pyat sat with the *démoc-socs*, but was forced into exile after his involvement in the 1849 demonstration against French assistance to Pius IX. From exile, Pyat relentlessly attacked the Empire, usually stretching the truth, his journalism having 'denigrated into irresponsible revolutionary rhetoric.' As was the case with most revolutionary republicans in the mid-1860s, Pyat was a communist when he returned to France, though few of his contemporaries, especially Marx, trusted his motivations, believing them to be self-serving and Pyat to be Janus-faced.[46] Largely on the basis of his reputation and oratorical skills, Pyat was one of the socialists elected to the Assembly from Paris in February, but like Malon, resigned his seat before being elected to the Commune.[47]

Twenty-seven-year old *Léo Fränkel* was the only foreign-born member on the Commune, the son of a Hungarian doctor in a Budapest suburb. Trained as a goldsmith, Fränkel settled in France in 1867 and took an active part in the International as a disciple of Karl Marx. As a delegate on the Commune's Labor Commission, Fränkel authored much of the progressive workplace regulatory legislation produced by the Commune.

Born in 1795, *Charles Beslay* was the only Communard born before Napoléon I's *coup d'état*. The son of a politician, he followed in his father's path and was elected to the first legislature under the July Monarchy. When he was not reelected, Beslay started a factory and unsuccessfully endeavored to initiate a Proudhonian-inspired *rapprochement* between capital and labor. Beslay's adoption of another Proudhonian idea – a bank of credit and savings for workers – led to his financial ruin. Within the International Beslay remained part of its old guard, maintaining his commitment to Proudhonian mutualism and antistatism. In the process, he languished on the margins of a socialist movement that took on more political, militant, and revolutionary hues. True to his conservative posture, Beslay, as the Commune's delegate to the Bank of France, chose to negotiate with the Bank's governor, rather than to nationalize the bank.

Edouard Vaillant, Gustave Lefrançais, and *Charles Longuet* were amongst the intellectuals to adhere to the Commune. Vaillant was the holder of doctorates in medicine and sciences before going to Germany between 1866 and 1870 to study philosophy. A native of the Cher, Vaillant initially delved into republican politics while still a student in Paris; in Germany, however, he joined the Marxist-influenced German section to the International. Upon his return to Paris, Vaillant threw himself into revolutionary politics, participating, along with Lefrançais, Pyat, Blanqui, Delescluze, Beslay, and a number of other future Communards in the ill-fated uprising of 31 October 1870. On the Commune, Vaillant was one of the most militantly revolutionary members and, befitting his background, was most influential in areas affecting education, museums, and theatres. Though associated with Blanquism, Vaillant, in fact, did not associate with the Blanquists until after the Commune's repression.

An outstanding student at the Teachers' College at Versailles, Angersborn Lefrançais was undone by his commitment to revolutionary politics. Mercilessly persecuted during the Second Republic for his efforts to combine socialism and pedagogy (even before Napoléon III's *coup d'état*, Lefrançais was forbidden from teaching), Lefrançais's conception of the republic inextricably linked it to socialism. Lefrançais was a popular club orator during the late 1860s whose commitments to both communism and individual liberty signaled the doctrinal variations of the period.

Longuet, from Normandy, was another brilliant student (while in exile after the Commune he was appointed a professor at King's College, Oxford) whose initiation into politics came, first, as a journalist opposed to the Empire. Forced into exile in the mid-1860s, Longuet joined the Belgian contingent to the International and became a close associate of Marx, eventually marrying one of his daughters in 1872. Unlike Vermorel who adopted a chauvinistic attitude as France and Prussia prepared to go to war in summer 1870, Longuet urged workers to remain united in opposition to war, articulating Marx's position on the subject. As Marx's principal supporter in France, Longuet often took positions contrary to those advanced by French internationalists, especially in his opposition to mutualism. In spite of some doctrinal differences, worker associations stood behind his unsuccessful candidacy in the February 1871 elections to the Assembly.

Eugène Pottier was a fabric designer who began composing political songs at age 14 in 1830 (the month after the Commune's repression, Pottier wrote the lyrics to socialism's anthem, the 'Internationale'). Pottier participated in both the February and June 1848 uprisings, and after the 1864 law on associations, organized a fabric designers' union. Though active in working-class causes, Pottier did not adhere to the International until 1870, and despite having signed the internationalists' July 1870 manifesto calling on German workers to refuse to go to war, Pottier joined the National Guard, ultimately being elected to the Central Committee.

The stories of these ten individuals, taken in conjunction with those of other Communards introduced in the previous two chapters of this study, reveal a fluid political milieu in which one's identity as a worker, a student, or an intellectual did not foretell doctrinal differences. They all participated in a political culture accurately defined as revolutionary, republican, and socialist, but lacking clear and precise theoretical underpinnings. Therefore, nominal divisions amongst the Commune's various sects, occasioned by the creation of the Committee of Public Safety (discussed later) during a moment fraught with grave uncertain-

ties, only posteriorily came to signify the *ab initio* existence of fundamental doctrinal differences. Both before and after the Bloody Week,
Communards expressed philosophical differences in only the most
general terms; the true battle within the revolutionary left would not
occur until Jules Guesde's embrace of Marxism in the 1880s.

The Commune in Action

In discounting the Commune's commitment to socialism, historians
invariably point to the paucity of socialist measures produced by the
Commune and its legislative moderation. Perhaps more than any revolution in French history, the Commune posed the problem of the dissonance between the revolutionary ambitions of its supporters and the
realities of governance. The challenges of administering Paris, fighting a
civil war, and not alienating all but its most committed supporters complicated the Commune's prospects for fulfilling the revolutionary
agenda at its core. Without losing sight of its long-term goals, the
Commune had to assure the functioning of public services. As the
Communards discovered, compromise, improvisation, and spontaneity
became the handmaidens of the exercise of revolutionary power.[48]
However, an examination of the Commune's legislative record reveals its
efforts at balancing municipal governance with larger revolutionary aspirations. In one crucial area, though, the Communards' trepidation may
have limited their ability to realize their goals.

Regeneration

In establishing the modern parameters of revolution, the French
Revolution defined it in terms of destructive and reconstructive
processes. During the Revolution, polemicists considered the prospects
for completely remaking social relationships, cultural references, and
political structures in the wake of the destruction wrought by revolution.
In short, embedded within revolutionary destruction was a regenerative
process that would facilitate the phoenix-like advent of a new society. On
one level, revolutionaries since the French Revolution spoke or wrote
abstractly, and ambiguously, about societal regeneration. On another
level, to provide regeneration with a tangible and identifiable form, revolutionaries had to devise policies that would facilitate their objective of
restructuring humankind. Two solutions proferred by the Communards
– restructuring political authority and secularizing society – were aimed

at altering the relationship between the citizenry and its institutions and inculcating a radically different set of values from those prevailing in society.

The Communards tethered societal regeneration to a refashioning of France's geopolitical structure along associationist principles described by Johnson. Replacing the heavily centralized French state with a decentralized federation of communes did not originate with the Paris Commune. During the final, liberal years of the Empire, discussions of municipal liberties and decentralization flowed out of political clubs and off the republican presses. Republicans, however, did not have an exclusive hold over the discourse on decentralization. During the 1860s, nearly all shades of opinion, including a prominent faction of Bonapartists, were advocating governmental devolution, but faced the dilemma of whether 'decentralization was an end in itself or a means to a further set of objectives.'[49] Being the shared expression of opposing political groups did not render decentralization a neutral objective; rather, conservatives, liberals, and socialists all pitched it as the necessary precondition for the furtherance of their goals.

Although decentralization was, in the first instance, a provincial reaction to Paris's historically dominant political role, Parisians were no less strident in their support for decentralized government, likewise demanding municipal autonomy within a republic of federated communes. Eager to dispel suppositions that they acted from cynical motivations, Parisian federalists were quick to acknowledge that, though Paris would be the most populous of the French communes, the capital had no pretensions of exercising a dictatorship or being anything more than a co-equal voice in the republic.

On 29 March, the newly elected members of the municipal assembly voted by acclamation to name their government 'the Commune,' a designation highly charged with revolutionary significance in 1871. In its 'Déclaration au Peuple Français,' the Commune endeavored to assuage concerns, confirming that its goals did not extend beyond municipal autonomy within a decentralized, though, nonetheless unified, republic.[50] Whether, in fact, the 'Déclaration' was a sincere statement of the Communards' position on decentralized government or merely an attempt at garnering provincial support cannot, however, be gleaned from this document.

Other statements, though, are perhaps more revealing of Communard intent. Characterizing decentralization as the antidote to France's history of plutocratic, authoritarian regimes, Communards of all stripes

– internationalists, Blanquists, neo-Jacobins – promoted it as the natural complement to the realization of a social republic. In April 1871, Pierre Vésinier, a former secretary to Eugène Sue who went on to become an internationalist, a member of the Commune, and editor of the newspaper, *Paris Libre*, defined the communal movement in the context of more expansive social and cultural aspirations:

> The communes of France in general, and those of Paris, in particular, must be revolutionary democratic and social federations, military and civil associations, organized by the entire people against all the privileges and monopolies; against the Church, the monarchy, the Empire; against industrial, landed, clerical, and military feudalism; against this brutal royal and imperial oligarchy which, after replacing the noblility, clergy, and the old feudal society, has, for three-quarters of a century, diverged from the revolution of 1789–1792. The Commune must replace the old world and become the base for a new world.[51]

For the Communards, authoritarianism, facilitated by centralization, was the principal impediment to the construction of a democratic and social republic. The devolution of power to the local level would liberate the sovereign people to build a society grounded on egalitarian principles and free of exploitation. In the final analysis, as conceived by the Communards, decentralized government was a political means for reaching social, economic, and cultural goals.

On another level, regeneration also entailed liberating society from both institutional and cultural reference points that inhibited the realization of sovereignty. The Communards focused on eradicating the institutions that they perceived as perpetuating society's servile ignorance. In 1869, Lefrançais and another future Communard, Gabriel Ranvier, argued that the nefarious influences of Catholicism and capitalism were destroying the family. On one level, they argued, marriage was still conditioned by material, rather than affectionate, considerations, specifically consolidation and transmission of property holdings. On another level, the Church remained influential in the functioning of the family through the agency of women, kept in ignorance by the Church which stridently resisted their formal education.[52]

With its focus squarely on the Church, the Commune resumed the dechristianization project commenced by its 1793 antecedent. One of the more confusing aspects of the Commune was the extent to which its actions were reflective of atheism – the complete denial of spiritual beliefs – or anticlericalism – the attenuation of any role by the church in the functioning of the community. Atheism was a central component of 1860s Blanquist philosophy. According to Blanquist Gustave Tridon, religious obscurantism, a relic of the Middle Ages, had retarded progress and maintained the people in a subservient state; during the Revolution, the Hébertists reawakened the people's atheistic sensibilities, empowering them to cast off the rituals and beliefs upon which oppression was justified and reified.[53] During the Commune, Rigault, in his capacity as the Commune's Delegate for General Security, placed the spotlight on the clergy as he waged war against subversive influences. For Rigault, monasteries, convents, and churches were staging grounds for counter-revolutionary activities, and spread fanaticism, ignorance, and debauchery.[54]

The Commune is indissolubly associated with some of the worst excesses against organized religion. The killing of religious hostages – Darboy and Deguerry, vicar of the Madeleine, on 24 May, and 11 priests on Rue Haxo on 26 May – as well as the arrest of more than 200 priests, led the Commune's detractors to malign it with accusations of secular fanaticism and intolerance. As has been pointed out earlier, those acts were instigated by individuals acting under color of authority, but not with the sanction of the Commune. In addition, the executions took place against a backcloth of despair, turmoil, and chaos, and only after Thiers, perhaps acting out of ulterior motivations, had steadfastly refused to negotiate Darboy's release.

In reality, when, as one of its first acts, on 2 April, the Commune decreed the separation of church and state, suppression of public funding for religion, and nationalization of clerical lands, it was merely providing the template for the secular state established in 1905. That the Third Republic appropriated some of the Commune's agenda should not diminsh its revolutionary nature more than three decades earlier.

The Communards entrustment of the laicization of public life to individual administrators resulted in little consistency as local conditions often determined the efficacity of attempts at secularization. Consequently, when a shortage of hospital personnel foreclosed the Communards from replacing nuns at hospitals, they, instead, instituted such symbolic gestures as having patients refer to the nuns as 'citoyennes' and renaming hospitals after revolutionary martyrs.[55]

Half of Paris's 67 churches were untouched during the Commune; of the 34 that were affected, several received a revolutionary rehabilitation – taken over by political clubs or turned over for military purposes, used as schools for girls, or rented back to their congregations. Churches were particularly attractive meeting places for clubbists; as spacious, centrally located, and symbolically charged structures, they signified the Commune's reconquest and regeneration of public space.[56] Although 23 were completely closed, only two – the expiatory chapel constructed during the Restoration as atonement for Louis XVI's execution and the Bréa chapel – were ordered to be demolished, though neither order was carried out. Damage to, and theft from, the churches came at the behest of overly zealous individuals or groups, fueled by decades of rhetorical violence and mutual antipathy of the Church and the Republic towards each other.

Much has been written about the ridicule, verbal violence, and profanities meted out to the Church, its representatives, and parishoners during the Commune;[57] outside of putting into motion the secularization of Paris, the Commune did not encourage abuse. Rather, the less salubrious instances of anticlericalism appear to have been spontaneous reactions by segments of the population to a changed political climate that no longer protected the Church.

Although the Church was the implacable enemy of the French Revolution, the rage of the average supporter of the Commune towards the Church was of more recent vintage. In 1862, the International Association of Free Thinkers, an anticlerical organization, was formed at Paris. Through the adhesion of internationalists such as Varlin, Malon, and André Murat (founder of the International in France, and later in charge of coinage during the Commune), anticlericalism extended its audience beyond bourgeois republicans. In fact, through the Free Thinkers, opponents of the Empire advanced the idea that a symbiotic relationship existed between authoritarian regimes and the Catholic Church. By the fall of the Empire, Blanquists and internationalists (including Varlin and Malon) were active Free Thinkers, viewing the Church as the handmaiden of despotism and oppression.[58]

Since the French Revolution, republicans promoted public education as the antidote to clericalism and the vehicle for society's regeneration. According to Blanqui, 'Education is both bread and liberty.'[59] Previous laws on public education simply confirmed the clergy's virtual monopoly over education while the reforms introduced by Napoléon III's Minister of Education, Victor Duruy, to secularize education and introduce critical thinking into the curriculum, were frustrated by the limits of Bonapartist liberalism. Both the republican movement and the International picked up where Duruy's reforms left off and in the

Belleville Program of 1869, Léon Gambetta declared that the creation of a secular and anti-authoritarian republic mandates an education system that is secular, free, and compulsory.[60]

The Commune concentrated its efforts on primary education, voting, on 9 April, for the removal of all clerical influences. As with its policy on churches, responsibility fell on the Communards to secularize the schools in their respective *arrondissements*. Faced with resistance in some *arrondissements*, and deprived of time and resources to effectuate the pedagogical agenda, the Communards, instead, were largely confined to issuing general philosophical statements. Thus, we have, for example, a statement by the fourth *arrondissment*'s delegation to the Commune in which it affirmed the sanctity of education and grounded it in the accumulation of scientific and philosophical principles. The delegation further announced that, in the interests of 'freedom of thought and religion, as affirmed by the French Revolution,' no religious authorities would be allowed to teach and no religious instruction would be tolerated in the *arrondissement*'s public schools. The declaration concluded with a mission statement on education that evidenced the influence of yet another nineteenth-century philosophical movement, utopian socialism, on the Commune: 'To teach the child to love and respect his peers; to inspire the love of justice; to teach him to be cognizant of society's interests; such are the moral principles on which will rest, from now on, the communal education.'

In spite of hardships, the Commune's Committee on Education worked prodigiously once Edouard Vaillant assumed control of it on 20 April. Under Vaillant's guidance, the Commune established two same-sex schools; while the one for girls opened on 12 May, the opening of the boys' school on 23 May was preempted by the entry into Paris of the Versaillais. The schools were to operate under a philosophy of 'integral education,' whereby schools dedicated themselves to the intellectual and professional development of their students. The ultimate goal was to establish a future citizenry that was both economically and politically productive and independent.[61]

By exposing students to the arts, sciences, and letters as a means for avoiding their regimentation into predesignated trades, the Communards were, again, signifying both their commitment to individual sovereignty and the influence of utopian socialist ideas on their reorganization of society. During the first third of the nineteenth century, the utopian philosopher Charles Fourier's prescription for a harmonious society entailed affording individuals the freedom to choose their occupational future in the confluence of their aptitude and interests. Similarly, the Communards conceived of freedom over one's destiny, be it in the micro world of the individual or in the macro world of the collective body politic, as a liberating principle essential to society's achievement of a harmonious equilibrium.

Maintaining public services

Maintaining public services during the Commune posed particular challenges as the Parisian economy had yet to rebound from the residual effects of the siege. Many Parisians were dependent on relief while the exodus of many public functionaries depleted the infrastructure. It is nearly impossible to determine the extent to which Communal policy on, for example, subsistence and rents, reflected a philosophical commitment to permanent social welfare or was simply a response to the exigencies of a war that had ended barely three months before the Commune's first round of elections. As noted earlier, amongst the first measures passed by the Commune were those which directly countermanded laws passed by the National Assembly.

Regardless of its commitment to revolution, the Commune also had to administer the capital and, amid difficult circumstances, maintain the quality of its inhabitants' lives. In spite of its financial shortcomings, the desertion of many functionaries, and a blockade of Paris by the Versaillaise, for the most part, there was little interruption in the functioning of public services during the Commune. Through improvisation, postal service out of Paris was largely successful; however, correspondence destined for Paris accumulated, undelivered, in a room at Versailles.[62] A Subsistence Commission maintained food stocks in the capital in spite of a blockade against Paris instituted by Thiers on 25 April. The Subsistence Commission operated a dual economy in foodstuffs: the private market continued to function alongside municipal butcher shops and restaurants that sold food at a significantly reduced price.[63] In addition, the municipality freely provided food to the National Guard and to indigents.[64] Judging by the notices inserted in the *Journal Officièl de la Commune*, the quality of life at Paris during the Commune was not adversely affected. Public parks, closed during the Franco-Prussian War for purposes of military security, reopened, while street lighting, fire protection services, and sewage disposal were all maintained.[65]

Believing that the self-regulatory autonomy of the medical profession would be better respected by the regime at Versailles, many doctors either left Paris or heeded the advice from Versailles to evade their duties. As it turned out, in spite of threatened reforms, the Commune was cognizant of its own limitations regarding health care and largely eschewed intervention in its provision. The Commune entrusted the task of organizing medical services to septuagenarian Camille Treillard. Treillard's brief tenure is notable both for his exercise of realpolitik and his scrupulous honesty and attention to duty. Though he endeavored to secularize hospitals and ambulance services, in his commitment to health care administration Treillard was not a rigid revolutionary ideologue bent on political purges of the medical profession. For Treillard, as long as medical personnel were not actively engaging in activities detrimental to the Commune, their services could not be rejected.[66] Given the growing demands for, and attrition of, medical personnel, this was a necessary strategy. That said, in spite of considerable obstacles, hospitals continued to function, and while some health care providers might have shirked their professional responsibilities or otherwise undermined the Commune (which included, among other activities, encouraging malingering and concealing logistical information), ordinary Parisians, even some who were not sympathetic to the Commune, cared for the wounded. Typical of the latter was Geneviève Bréton, a diarist, who, on 24 April, rhetorically asked, 'I cared for a Prussian, an enemy; should I not do the same for a *fédéré*, a brother, a Frenchman?' The following day, Bréton recorded that she had volunteered for the International Ambulance Unit.[67] On the other hand, the decision of Victor Desplats (professor of medicine and resolute foe of the Commune) to serve on an ambulance team appears to have been motivated strictly out of self-preservation.[68]

The Commune applied its philosophical commitment to demilitarization, popular sovereignty, and decentralization to the reorganization of the police and fire departments. Whereas some ardent Proudhonists, ever hostile to the state, preferred to see the elimination of the police force altogether, the majority of Communards viewed the police as agents in the creation of a new regime. Though revolutionaries had no theory on policing, ten years after the Commune, Alfred Breuillé, a Blanquist, who served as an adjoint to Prefect of Police, summed up the attitude that prevailed on the Commune: 'Policing is an aspect of the social question ... The Revolution alone will be able to resolve this problem in wiping out the enemies of the people.'[69] In practice this meant that the political function served by the police under the Commune was not dissimilar from the highly politicized operations of the police forces of the various regimes since the Revolution; what constituted public order, predictably, was a function of differing ideological conceptions. In contrast to prior regimes, for the Communards, order was not synonymous with the sanctification of property interests.

As with many of the Commune's plans, the combination of the exigencies of the defense of Paris, the hasty recruitment of a police force from the ranks of artisans, laborers, and intellectuals, and ill-conceived ideas presented particular challenges for effective policing. Indeed, the Commune's policing efforts provided both its supporters and detractors with plenty of grist for their critical mills. For its detractors, the Commune was a period of unrestrained criminality, where the police expended more energy terrorizing political and cultural opponents than in bringing order and security to the streets of Paris. On the other hand, its defenders, like Lissagaray, faulted the Commune for not acting with enough fortitude in suppressing the activities of its opponents.

The truth lies somewhere between these two interpretations. On the one hand, policing efficiency was bound to be hampered by hastily conceived, ill-defined, overlapping jurisdictions. Although the ex-Prefecture of Police (as Rigault rechristened it) technically maintained control over policing, the Commissioner of General Security largely undermined its authority. In the two months of its duration, the police force did arrest an assortment of common criminals – from murderers and thieves to drunks, vagabonds, and prostitutes – in addition to executing the decisions rendered by the Commune relative to requisitions and tenant rights.[70]

On the other hand, the Versaillais attributed blame for the excesses committed amidst the Bloody Week – in particular, the execution of hostages, including Georges Darboy, archbishop of Paris – on the Commune's policing apparatus. Just as the voracity with which executions were carried out during the French Revolution's 'Reign of Terror' was largely due to the actions of individuals, so too responsibility for Darboy's execution was largely the responsibility of Théophile Ferré and Gustave Genton of the Commune's Commission of General Security. Occurring during the final days of the Commune, and in response to reports of the indiscriminate murder of prisoners by the Versaillais, Darboy's execution is best understood as either an act of desperation, an act of revenge, or, perhaps, as an inseparable feature of revolution, but not a calculated, officially designed policy.

The Bank of France: A missed opportunity?

Whether the Communards limited their aspirations to municipal rights or had more expansive national goals, the fact is that they took over a city with a severely compromised infrastructure. An already difficult situation was hampered further by the need to devote resources and energy to the war against Versailles.

Although it had near unfettered access to the Bank of France, for the Commune's delegate to the Bank, Beslay, pragmatism dictated a policy of accommodation, rather than confrontation. Persuaded by the patriotic appeals of the Bank's governor, Beslay argued that if it colluded in pillaging the Bank's reserves, the Commune risked losing both support, confidence, and, come what may, France's future financial credibility. Most immediately, Beslay reasoned, should this occur, the Commune would be traveling down the same path previously trodden by the French Revolution in its issuance of *assignats* and risked evoking the enmity of its constituents as their purchasing power declined.[71] While the Bank verbally acceded to the loan requests made by Francis Jourde, the Commune's Finance delegate, the sums actually dispersed rarely matched the requests, and were usually paid after a delay. In addition, nearly half of what the Bank disbursed to the Commune originated from the City of Paris's own account.

Jourde was no less cautious than Beslay.[72] While he remained more committed than Beslay to a socialist agenda in the long term, and the satisfaction of the Commune's commitments to those who suffered or sacrificed on behalf of Paris, he was resolutely opposed to revolutionary means for filling the Commune's coffers through forced appropriations. Instead, the Commune's financial state depended upon collection of existent regressive taxes (e.g., taxes on consumer goods, city tolls) and what disbursements it received from the Bank. By consequence, the Commune, a revolutionary government in one of Europe's wealthiest cities, deprived itself of the means for realizing its objectives.[73]

Lefrançais noted that one of the chief shortcomings of the Commune was its failure to understand that it could not be, at once, legal and revolutionary, but that it had to choose between the two.[74] Later, Lefrançais called the failure to take control of the Bank 'the irreparable mistake' of the Commune.[75] Not only would possession of the Bank's resources have solved the Commune's financial woes, but also would have provided the Commune with a most formidable hostage. Instead, however, the cautious approaches adopted by Beslay and Jourde provided the Commune with no tangible benefit; in the aftermath of its destruction, the Commune was still maligned as an orgy of lawlessness, pillage, and destruction. Second guesses aside, we should not read a lack of socialist convictions into a decision motivated by pragmatism.

The legislative record of the Commune

Much of the Commune's rhetoric had the twin aims of confirming its fidelity to the French republican tradition and contrasting this with the government and National Assembly's apparent antipathies towards the republican catechism. It is undeniable that these were seductive arguments in urban France, especially Paris, the foyer of republicanism, where republican sympathies were at their strongest. If the results of the February elections are any indication, the majority of the nation had not embraced the Parisian brand of revolutionary republicanism. That said, the large vote for conservatives might have been more a rejection, by the war-weary nation, of republican bellicosity towards the surrender than hostility to the core republican ideals.

When it decreed that public employees ignore orders or directives emanating from Versailles, the Commune established itself as the exclusive authority over Paris and raised hopeful expectations in some quarters, and fears in others, over how it perceived the breadth of its mandate.[76] A review of the Commune's legislative record reveals that, given the revolutionary convictions of most of its members, and the opportunity that presented itself, it acted with astonishing moderation, if not reticence. Most of its decrees were little more than faithful echoes of the standard nineteenth-century republican orthodoxy regarding separation of church and state and protection of civil liberties, others were sometimes tepid responses to the realities of a struggling city. For example, concerns over indebtedness prompted the Commune to issue a decree reaffirming debtors' responsibility for their debts, but extending the payment period to three years. The measure was a response to both the realities of a sluggish economy while, at the same time, a reassuring signal to creditors that the Communards were not simply determined to extinguish all debts.

However, considering the brevity of its existence, the Commune was also remarkable for the prodigiousness of its output and the zeal, if not naivety, with which it seized a very small window of opportunity. Though it is sometimes faulted for being bogged down in didactic debate, the Commune's legislative and administrative accomplishments in ten weeks exceeded, or at the very least equaled, those produced by the Third Republic in its first 30 years.[77] Its ability to implement those measures, on the other hand, was a different matter altogether.

In his history of the Commune, Arthur Arnould, who represented the fourth *arrondissement*, categorized the body's decrees as responses to either immediate needs (i.e., the residual circumstances of the siege) or exigent circumstances (i.e., the war against Versailles), or as having been based upon principles and designed to have a more enduring lifespan.[78] It was these latter acts that gave rise to Goncourt's fears of the Communards' commitment to both social reorganization and its transcendence of a purely municipal mandate.

Many of the Commune's decrees demonstrated fidelity to the larger principles articulated by revolutionary republicans during the final years of the Empire. At its first official meeting, the Commune abolished military conscription, and replaced the permanent army with the National Guard. Though the National Guard originated as a bourgeois militia, by 1871 it was widely understood to be a democratic body of citizen soldiers, premised on principles very different from the army's authoritarian and militaristic traditions. Other decrees straddled the line between social revolution and responses to ephemeral conditions. The Commune prolonged the moratorium on rents declared during the siege, but did not establish a rent control policy. Homelessness caused by the bombardment of Paris, first by the Prussians, then by the Versaillais, was an immediate and pressing problem. Putting a twist on the precedent established by the French Revolution in confiscating the lands of émigrés, the Commune requisitioned apartments abandoned after 18 March and, rather than selling them at auction, distributed them to the homeless. Even though many of the Communards had professed support for communism during the public meetings at the end of the Second Empire, at no time, once in power, did they enact laws restrictive of property rights. Rather, the measure on apartments was both a response to a pressing problem and a punitive measure against those who, through their actions, were irreconcilible to the revolution.

In other areas, the Commune endeavored to alter social relations. Although Arnould classified the decree prohibiting the sale of objects deposited at the three Parisian pawnshops, the *monts-de-piété*, as a response to immediate concerns, the Commune's long-term plans relative to the *monts-de-piété* were more ideologically based. Originally created in the fifteenth century to combat usury, the Mont-de-Piété was privately operated, but government-licensed and protected. Its clients were, preponderantly, unskilled workers and artisans; during periods when the economy was depressed (such as the siege), business was brisk. When the economy did not recover after the armistice, many workers were caught in the double bind of having pawned the tools of their trade; with no tools in a sluggish economy, workers were unable to produce the goods that would allow them to reclaim their tools.

On 1 May, Fränkel, the head of the Commission on Labor and Exchange reported on a plan to liquidate the *monts-de-piété*. Characterizing the *monts-de-piété* as symbolizing the rule of exploitation, lacking in moral principles, and serving no useful economic purpose, Fränkel's plan further asserted that the conditions which allowed for the existence of the *monts-de-piété* would no longer exist once 'a social organization [is created] which gives workers some genuine assistance and support in the event of unemployment or debilitation.'[79] More immediately, the Commune made plans to release without charge to their owners all objects worth 20 francs or less; however, the entry of the Versaillais into Paris caused the abandonment of this plan.[80]

At its third meeting, on 31 March, the Commune set the reimbursement for those elected to the Commune at 15 francs per day and, on the following day, set the maximum salary of municipal functionaries at 6000 francs per year.[81] To put this in context, in 1871 the average male Parisian worker earned five francs per day; National Guardsmen received 1.50 francs per day, but senior officers were paid around the same salary as elected Communards.[82] On the other hand, Arnould wrote that '[f]or fifteen francs per day, [the Communards] each filled three or four functions which, under whatever monarchy, as under MacMahon's republic, are evaluated at 30,000 to 100,000 francs per job.'[83]

One of the more revolutionary measures adopted by the Commune relative to wages was in the area of teachers' remuneration. In addition to raising teachers' salaries to 2000 francs per year and teacher-aides to 1500 francs per year, the Education Commission also decreed that there should be no differential in the remuneration of male and female teachers. In recognizing that all teachers, regardless of gender, performed the same functions, this measure represented the first application of the principle of equal pay for equal work. Again, its publication, on 21 May, coincided with the entry of the Versaillais troops into Paris.

Drawing on nineteenth-century French socialism's penchant for worker cooperatives, the Commune premised its plans for the alleviation of unemployment on the establishment of readily available credit and the encouragment of worker-producer associations. A succession of measures decreed on 15–16 April called for the confiscation of property belonging to Napoléon III, the Versaillais, and émigrés from Paris, and requisitions of abandoned factories and workshops. On 4 May, the Commune decreed the final piece of this social reorganization puzzle – conveyance of requisitioned property to worker cooperatives to be funded through the creation of publicly administered lines of credit.

Not only did the Commune lack the resources to see this plan through to its finality, but within four days, the army overran the Communard defenses at Issy, signaling its imminent entry into Paris and a reorientation of governmental priorities.

Executive authority and the Committee of Public Safety

The Commune's establishment of an Executive Commission appeared to represent a violation of its stated commitment to undiluted democracy; in keeping with its stated aversion to centralized authority, though, the Commune limited the Commission's jurisdiction to the implementation of decrees produced by the other nine commissions.[84] However, by 21 April, a majority of Communards began to sense that their ability to defend Paris was being undermined by too much departmental autonomy and the absence of executive leadership. The Communards initially reorganized the commissions, most notably reconstituting the Executive Commission as a centrally structured ministerial cabinet staffed by those appointed to head the other nine commissions. However, within two weeks of this change, on 1 May, a majority on the Commune voted to vest complete authority in a five-member Committee of Public Safety. Proposed by Jules Miot, a 61-year-old veteran of revolutionary republican movements who had spent a good portion of the Second Empire in prison or in exile,[85] the Committee of Public Safety was the Commune's most direct, and some might argue most pathetic, imitation of the French Revolution. Prompted by the inefficient functioning of basic services and, more directly, an increasingly grim military situation, the majority on the Commune who supported Miot's proposal characterized the Committee of Public Safety as the 'magic bullet' of French republicanism; a painful, albeit temporary, suspension of revolutionary ideals in the midst of a crisis. Given the 1793 Committee of Public Safety's inextricable connection with the 'Reign of Terror,' and dictatorship, however, the choice of this title was bound to engender fear, revulsion, resolve, and hope in equal measure.

Beyond this, the proposal nullified prior efforts at forging unity in the Commune, while signaling the Commune's majority as being locked in the time warp of the Revolution. The debate over Miot's proposal lasted for four days, yet another enduring symbol of the endless debates that seemed to characterize, and one could argue, compromise the Commune's work. A review of the rhetoric during the debate, though, underscores the extent to which this issue encapsulated so much of the essence of the Communards' sense of identity.

Opponents of the proposal ultimately objected to it as a usurpation of the people's sovereignty (and thus closer to royal absolutism than republicanism).[86] However, during the debates, others took issue with its historical connotations. Vermorel, representing the eighteenth *arrondissement*, noted the need for a fortified executive branch, but objected to calling it a Committee of Public Safety. Vermorel would form part of the minority which, on the day of the vote, issued a collective statement that characterized the Committee of Public Safety as a dictatorship contrary to the representative mission of the Commune and, as such, 'a veritable usurpation of the people's sovereignty.'[87] In addition to highlighting the Commune's slippery slide along the path of revolutionary dictatorship, various opponents of the measure also noted how the name would generate a sense of alarm and panic. Gustave Courbet, perhaps the most renowned artist of the social realist school of the mid-nineteenth century, and a representative of the sixth *arrondissement*, stated the problem in the following terms:

> I desire that all titles or words belonging to the Revolution of 89 and 93 remain confined to that epoque. Today they no longer have the same significance and can no longer be applied or received with the same justification.
>
> The titles: *Public Safety, Montagnards, Girondins, Jacobins,* etc., etc., should no longer be employed in the socialist republican movement.
>
> We represent the time that has passed from 93 to 71, with all the genius that must characterize us and elevate our proper temperament.
>
> This appears so much more pressing than appearing to be a bunch of plagiarists who, to our detriment, reestablish a terror that is not of our period. Employ terms that will suggest that this is our revolution.[88]

For every Courbet, though, there were others in the majority who took comfort in the historical affinity. Pottier objected to the name, but believed the gravity of circumstances overrode nominal objections. Pyat expressed his support by noting that the first incarnations of the French Republic and the Paris Commune were of the same era as the Committee of Public Safety. Similarly, Rigault stated his hope that the 1871 Committee would emulate the energetic verve of its nominal predecessor.[89]

However, from a practical standpoint, the Committee of Public Safety's jurisdiction was ill defined. The antagonism expressed towards the Committee of Public Safety's creation was largely a function of what it symbolized, rather than a comment on either the manner by which it exercised authority or the conditions that led the Commune to invest it with absolute authority. In fact, the conduct of the defense of Paris remained within the Central Committee of the National Guard's jurisdiction; nevertheless, blame for breaches in Paris's defense during May settled on the Committee of Public Safety.[90] Inextricably connected to the failed defense of Paris, the Committee of Public Safety has symbolized both the Commune's inability to accomplish more than mere symbolic acts and its dubious distinction of fomenting internal conflicts over the revolutionary legacy to which it adhered.

The Communard split over the Committee of Public Safety has also been cited as evidence of sectarian divisions in the Commune with internationalists, sometimes confused with Proudhonians, opposing the Committee's creation out of a commitment to anti-authoritarianism. However, nearly every Communard had some association with the International (including many who favored the founding of the Committee), and Proudhon's legacy exercised a negligible influence on the Commune.

To understand the vote as evidence of divisions on the left is to attribute a false synchronicity between political designations (e.g., neo-Jacobin, internationalist, and Blanquist) that did not exist in 1871 and actions undertaken during exigent circumstances. In fact, nine of the 23 votes against the Committee of Public Safety, were cast by Communards who, according to Serman, had no prior affiliation with the International (Andrieu, Victor Clément, Courbet, Jourde, Ostyn, Rastoul, Tridon, Vallès, and Vermorel). Furthermore, as we have previously seen, Tridon was an active Blanquist, Vermorel had lauded the Jacobins, and Longuet (also a *minoritaire*) was as close to being a French Marxist as one could be in 1871. By contrast, 19 of those voting in favor of the measure were members of the International.[91]

In the decades after the amnesty, the Commune continued to reverberate on the French political landscape. The French state exerted some effort at marginalizing the Commune as, at best, an aberration, occasioned by a disastrous war. As much as the French Revolution, the Commune was resplendent in the deep fissures occasioned by class conflict, ideological divides, cultural chasms, and competing historical memories that lay beneath the surface of republican unity. However, unlike the French Revolution, the Commune left behind no tangible legacy, other than a cautionary tale of the futility of revolution. The repression of the Commune and the Third Republic's subsequent embracing of the

French Revolution's historical patrimony closed the curtain on a revolutionary tradition forged out of the uncertain conclusion to the French Revolution. In the aftermath of the Commune's repression, the republican left was moribund for the better part of a decade. However, it did recover – in the form of the Socialist Party at the end of the nineteenth century. Although the Third Republic had weathered a series of formidable challenges from the right – the threat of a monarchial restoration, the allure of Boulangism, and the divisions of the Dreyfus Affair – the Commune symbolically reemerged, displacing the Revolution as the reference for the class-based political culture of the Third Republic.

Chapter 5: Women and the Commune

Upon their return to Paris from Versailles during the first week of October 1789, the women of Paris unexpectedly altered the course of the French Revolution by shifting the locus of governmental authority to the volatile political climate at Paris. In spite of having played the crucial role in one of the seminal events in the French Revolution, on balance, women's position in French society remained unchanged. Laws that potentially helped women (e.g., providing for divorce) were nullified by republican constructs of gender that relegated women to the private space; in other words, while women could extricate themselves from bad marriages, they had few opportunities for an independent existence. Matters rapidly went from bad to worse when the Napoléonic Code (a.k.a., the Civil Code) of 1804 defined and codified their subordinate status, eliminating some of the few gains made by women during the Revolution.

That the French Revolution's regenerative mission fell short when it came to gender should not have surprised anyone. Jacobins, liberals, and Bonapartists alike, all relied on old distinctions between male reason and female emotion to exclude women's voices from the public space and grounded misogynistic constructs of gender that dated back to antiquity in the philosophical currents of eighteenth-century reason. Steeped in Rousseauean ideas in which the public and private spheres were separate and gendered, polemicists argued that the decadence, corruption, and frivolity of the *ancien régime* was due to women who, in exercising political and cultural influence, transgressed their maternal function.

During the 1830s utopian socialism appeared to offer women some hope. In their pursuit of a society premised on social harmony, utopians preconditioned the attainment of this goal on, amongst other things, women's emancipation. Ultimately, female adherents to Saint-Simonianism,

143

frustrated by the dissonance between the discourse of the male leaders and women's positions within the movement, formed the first autonomous feminist movement in French history. Through their experiences with the contradictions between Saint-Simonian discourse and rhetoric, French feminists understood that women's oppression transcended social-class hierarchies; in other words, within their respective social orbits, working-class women and bourgeois women were subordinate to, and dominated by, males. French feminists in the nineteenth century, though, did not challenge the essentialist constructs of gender that, ironically, also rationalized women's subordination. In fact, feminists in the first half of the nineteenth century embraced gender distinctions as complementary and motherhood as justifying women's full participation in the public life of the nation.[1]

The 1848 revolution engendered an upsurge in feminist political activity, but few tangible results. However, as revolutionary optimsim turned to disappointment after the April 1948 election, feminists suffered a corresponding loss of potential fortunes. Although women did not play a particularly distinctive role in the workers' revolt of June 1848, feminism became an additional casualty of the repression as it was linked, along with socialism, with progenitors of social disorder and revolution.[2]

Reflecting the commanding influence of Proudhon, post-1848 French socialism was particularly virulent in its opposition to feminism. Proudhon characterized the family as forming the center of his social structure, a fount of moral authority, justice, and sociability. In contrast to the utopian socialists of the 1830s who emphasized the sexual satisfaction of men and women as integral to social harmony, Proudhon viewed sex as a distraction, and limited its social utility to reproduction.[3] The husband's position as head of household is justified, according to Proudhon, by the innate intellectual, physical, and moral superiority of men, which Proudhon purported to establish through a bizarre mathematical equation.[4] Throughout the 1850s and 1860s, feminism remained a largely middle-class movement. Although feminists argued in favor of marital reform, divorce, women's education, and women's rights to employment, their messages did not resonate with working-class women, most of whom 'either remained mute over their secondary position in the labour market or took greater comfort in idyllic familiarity with the dominant bourgeois ideal of domesticity.'[5]

In the political clubs of 1868–70, out of which the Commune emerged, 'the female question was at the heart of the political meetings.'[6] A new feminist organization, the Association for the Rights of

Women, was formed by, and included, both liberals, including M. and Mme. Jules Simon, and socialists, such as Louise Michel, André Léo, and Paule Minck, but no female workers. Female workers, such as Nathalie Lemel, a bookbinder active in the International, limited their participation to working-class organizations. Along with Eugène Varlin, Lemel established a cooperative restaurant, the *Marmite*, and actively worked on behalf of workers' rights without restricting herself to gender issues. Although female workers were conscious of the hardships endured by working-class women, they tended to frame their discussion of the issue more in terms of class oppression than gender inequality.

While liberal feminists advocated redressing gender inequality through legislation, those working-class leaders who were sensitive to gender exploitation, like Varlin, characterized the symptoms of gender inequality – prostitution, dependence on charity, bad marriages – as indictments of capitalist rapaciousness.[7] As has been noted earlier, Varlin represented a young generation of working-class advocates who departed not only from Proudhonian mutualism, but Proudhonian misogyny, as well. In 1867, Varlin rejected the stance against working women of the French delegation to the International: 'Whether the work is done by a man or whether by a woman, it's the same product, therefore it should be the same wage. If this happens, women will no longer lower men's wages, and women will be liberated by their work.'[8]

During the siege of Paris, women were particularly hard hit as inclement weather and food shortages hampered fulfillment of their socially appointed role. Women also suffered emotionally and economically as their husbands died in combat or their children perished from exposure or malnutrition. In response, future Communard Jules Allix, a veteran of the republican movement who went into exile after Napoléon III's *coup d'état*, founded the Committee of Women, a committee dedicated to 'work, education, social welfare, and rights for women.'[9]

Women endeavored to participate in the defense of Paris. Félix Belly entered the annals of the period for having suggested, during the siege, that an all-female battalion, to be known as the Amazons of the Seine, be formed. Belly premised his idea on essentialist notions: women are moral, have a penchant for uniforms, and have a knack for ambush. According to Belly, 1500 women signed up for the Amazons, only to be rebuffed by General Trochu, the president of the Government of National Defense. Apparently, to Trochu, patriotism was biological and implicit in Trochu's rejection of the Amazons was the perpetuation of the idea that women are not worthy citizens of the republic (ironically, by one who was never known as a republican, himself!) Consequently, in their determination to contribute to the defense of *patrie*, Parisian women formed various neighborhood committees to succor the sick and wounded. At Montmartre, Louise Michel organized a women's complement to the all-male Eighteenth *Arrondissement* Vigilance Committee, all the while declaiming that, at Montmartre, the siege had rendered traditionally designated gender roles irrelevant.[10]

Through the combination of 'shared hardship' and their experiences in quasi-official roles, Parisian women under the siege served political apprenticeships and developed bonds of sisterhood that, under the Commune, translated into new perspectives on female participation in the public sphere.[11] We now turn to an overview of women in the Commune, looking briefly at three of the more prominent women, Communal legislation on women, women's roles during the Commune and the manner by which gender constructs functioned in the analysis of the Commune by its adversaries.

Three Communardes

Thousands of anonymous women participated in some capacity in the public life or defense of the Commune. Of the 1051 women arrested in the aftermath of the Commune's repression (not including, of course, those who were summarily executed), well over 90 percent were working class; nearly 25 percent were either suspected or convicted prostitutes. Outside of their place and date of birth, most of their backgrounds have been lost to history and all that remains were the accounts of the offenses for which they were convicted – most were accused of incendiarism, a topic we will revisit, but those charged also included a nun who had given a sip of water to some *fédérés*.[12] Only 158 women, though, were convicted.

Amongst those pursued and convicted (often *in absentia*) were women who had played prominent roles in the republican clubs and press at the end of the Second Empire. Perhaps the most celebrated non-elected member of the Commune, male or female, was *Louise Michel*. The product of a union between a servant and a member of the family who employed her, Michel's paternal family provided her with a solid bourgeois upbringing. Michel earned her teaching certificate and, in 1852, opened a private school in her native departement of the Haute-Marne; though she claimed to have done so after refusing to swear an oath to

Napoléon III, one of her biographers doubts whether she had, at that point, developed a deep-seated commitment to republicanism.[13] In any event, after relocating to Paris a few years later, Michel threw herself into oppositional politics. She exposed herself to an eclectic mix of ideologies, including bourgeois feminism, moderate republicanism (even taking a course offered by Jules Favre!), Blanquism, and Internationalism.[14] Michel also earned a reputation for her sensitivity towards the plight of the poor, a concern that ultimately situated her in the camp of revolutionary socialists. Yet Michel was also a forthright critic of the misogynistic tendencies within socialism.

As previously mentioned, during the winter of 1870 Michel was an activist at Montmartre, participating on both the men's and women's Eighteenth *Arrondissement* Vigilance Committees and the political clubs that met in the district. It was hardly a coincidence that the Commune would have its symbolic origins with the defense of the cannons at Montmartre on 18 March; during the siege, the revolutionary idiom that flowed so freely during the Commune became the standard discourse at the clubs and committees of the eighteenth *arrondissement*. As an integral participant within this vibrant political milieu, Michel's revolutionary republican evolution was completed and she participated as an armed combatant on both 22 January and 18 March 1871.

Michel maintained a ubiquitous presence during the Commune, even if she was restricted from pursuing a seat on the Commune. Clad in a National Guard uniform and a member of the Montmartre 61st battalion, Michel claimed, not with total plausibility, that, from 3 April until her arrest on 24 May, she only abandoned her combat position two times, each for only a few hours. That said, Michel and other female combatants fought a two-front war: against the Versaillais and against the entrenched misogyny of their fellow male combatants. Romantically attached to Théophile Ferré (and, purportedly during the siege, to Victor Hugo), Michel combatted Ferré's chauvinism with audaciously revolutionary suggestions, including a plan to assassinate Thiers at Versailles; Ferré rejected the plan as both impractical and a potential public relations disaster.[15] Determined to serve the Commune, but hamstrung by the persistence of conventional misogyny amongst the majority of Communards, Michel not only fulfilled the acceptable role of *ambulancière* (ambulance nurse), but also demonstrated her revolutionary verve as a soldier, who likely killed some Versailles soldiers.[16] The many facets and complexities of Michel's character were revealed during the Bloody Week when she not only fought on the barricades but also laid flowers on the grave of Henri Murger, the patron saint of nine-teenth-century French bohemianism, whose writings addressed the stul-tifying effect of materialism on artistic creativity.[17]

Michel turned herself in to the authorities after finding out that her mother had been arrested, and would be executed in her place. At the time of her arrest, she had a notorious reputation amongst the Versaillais; her notoriety would become more widespread after her trial. Until the Third Council of War sentenced Ferré to death, Michel dimin-ished her role in the Commune, denying she had been anything more than a battlefield nurse and entertaining a romanticized idea of being transported with Ferré to the French penal colony at New Caledonia. After Ferré's execution on 28 November, Michel became far more stri-dent in admitting to her participation in a greater range of activities during the Commune (if anything, she exaggerated her exploits). Though shocking, her admissions were both an affirmation of her con-victions and an example of the lengths she had to go, as a woman, to establish herself as a revolutionary.

Still, it is difficult to determine whether Michel was motivated by a determination to join Ferré in death, to exculpate others (by assuming responsibility for the crimes of which they were charged), or to serve as a martyr for the Commune (she persistently invoked her dedication to the social revolution represented by the Commune and swore that the dead would one day be avenged); regardless, the prosecution also went to great lengths to inculpate Michel in every act from the executions of Lecomte and Thomas to the fires of the Bloody Week (even citing, as evidence, the songs from the French Revolution, including *La Marseillaise*, that Michel taught the students in her school). In the end, despite Michel's stoicism and demand that her judges demonstrate courage by ordering her execution, the Fourth Council of War con-demned Michel to banishment on New Caledonia. As previously noted, there she endeavored, in spite of her Western cultural baggage, to dis-seminate indigenous Kanak culture.[18] Returning to France with the 1880 amnesty, Michel became an icon to the republican left. She main-tained her faith in the social revolution and was outspoken in her con-demnation of imperialism abroad and capitalism at home. At times, Michel vacillated between passive resistance and violent confrontation. By the 1890s she had fully embraced anarchism and became a patron saint to a younger generation of revolutionaries, including the American Emma Goldman (with whom Michel shared the stage at a London rally in 1895), until her death in 1904.

Léodile Champseix (known as *André Léo*), was the daughter of a military officer, educated, and a reasonably successful author in the 1860s of fictional works where the plots served as indictments against the institution and indissolubility of marriage. By 1866 she was one of the animating forces behind the Society for the Rights of Women. In her 1869 work, *La femmes et les mœurs*, Léo decried the argument that affording women political rights would distract them from their maternal duties. In addressing marital oppression, Léo raised the spectre that marriage was a microcosm of society; just as the latter was structured on superior–subordinate relationships, so too, was equality denied in marriage. Along with Michel, Léo was a member of the Eighteenth *Arrondissement* Women's Vigilance Committee during the siege.

During the Commune, Léo was a member of the commission charged with organizing and overseeing girls' schools, but her greatest skill was as a journalist for the newspaper, *La Sociale*, which she founded with *Anna Jaclard*, the daughter of Russian aristocrats, a member of the Russian section to the International, and, like Léo, a member of the Eighteenth *Arrondissement* Vigilance Committee and commission on girls education. In the pages of *La Sociale*, Léo committed herself to the Commune, but did not shrink from criticizing the dissonance between its ideals and its pointed neglect of women. If there was a unifying theme to Léo's journalism, it was the idea that revolution required the solidarity of society's dispossessed – workers, peasants, women – in a regenerative mission based on equality and fraternity. In an article that appeared on 3 May, Léo appealed to the peasantry to rise in defense of Paris, reminding them that they shared a community of interests with the urban working class as victims of the rich and powerful. Three days later Léo reported insults meted out to nine female ambulance and canteen workers by National Guard officers and a physician, as opposed to the respectful treatment they received from working-class soldiers. This anecdote revisited the theme of women's participation, an issue that Léo considered to be a litmus test of one's true revolutionary convictions. In other words, Léo contrasted bourgeois officers, professionals, and journalists, whose commitment to revolution ended with their own empowerment, with the working class who were intrinsically committed to a comprehensive social revolution that also encompassed gender roles. Léo fled France during the Bloody Week and took refuge in Switzerland with her common-law husband, Benoît Malon.

The illegitimate daughter of a large landholding Russian officer,

Elisabeth Dmitrieff, became an adherent to socialism while a student at Saint Petersburg. Dmitrieff entered into a fictitious marriage at age 17 in order to travel abroad. Arriving in Geneva in 1870, Dmitrieff joined the Russian section of the International where she established herself as a professional confidante, though not necessarily an ideological soul mate, of Karl Marx. Dmitrieff arrived in Paris as the General Council of the International's special delegate.

In early April, Dmitrieff, along with *Nathalie Lemel,* organized the *Union des Femmes Pour la Défense de Paris et les Soins aux Blessés* (Women's Union for the Defense of Paris and Care for the Wounded). The Union's principal objective was to organize the defenses in each of Paris's 20 *arrondissements* and care for the wounded. Increasingly, the Union devoted itself to organizing work for Parisian women, many of whom, in the absence of male support, were desperate for work. The Union was able to secure work for women related to Paris's defense: sewing sandbags for barricades and manufacturing cartridges and other military equipment.[19] Although it appeared as though the Union directed itself simply at ephemeral conditions occasioned by the war, under Dmitrieff's inspiration, it might have been the vehicle by which the Commune would alter social and gender relations by ensuring women's rights to work.

Accounts of Dmitrieff's activities during the Bloody Week are a little sketchy. In a report filed by a Russian diplomat, Dmitrieff allegedly was last seen in Paris behind a barricade, encouraging the *fédérés,* distributing ammunition, firing at the Versaillais, before being wounded. The diplomat's report ended on a note of alarm regarding the prospects that Dmitrieff would resurface in Russia to foment dissent.[20] In fact, after escaping to Switzerland, Dmitrieff did return to Russia, but did not engage in revolutionary activities.[21]

Women and Legislation

In the years leading up to the Commune, feminists addressed issues ranging from marital equality to suffrage to employment rights to access to education. As we have seen, many of the feminists of those years actively supported the Commune, but their support for the Commune was not conditional upon the latter's satisfaction of the feminist agenda. Although Louise Michel subordinated women's equality to the Commune's survival, André Léo was not as compliant, regularly pointing out instances under the Commune where, as regards women, the more things changed, the more they remained the same.

While certain members of the Commune – most notably Eugène Varlin – had a commitment to female emancipation, there is little evidence that many of his colleagues harbored similar sentiments. Ameliorating women's social condition was not high on the Communard agenda, except to the extent that it was enveloped in issues that were of overarching importance, such as separation of church and state.

Pedagogical reform was crucial to Communard plans for developing an informed and productive republican citizenry; to this end, the Communard policy relative to public schools situated girls' education on an equal basis as that provided boys. While the plan's impetus lay in the larger objective of regeneration, it was also a tacit step towards equality and an effort at weaning French women off their traditional allegiance to the Church. Furthermore, regardless of the motivation for the measure, it must be considered in the context of nineteenth-century French society. Though a string of reforms and treatises testify to the treatment of education with increasing seriousness, girls' education continued to be entrusted to nuns (who were largely uneducated).[22] The import of this was that girls needed little more than moral and devotional training, as their lives would be limited to the household.

In its first few weeks the Commune adopted a series of measures for the benefit of its defenders' families. On 10 April the Commune voted a 600-franc pension to the partners, whether concubines or wives, and 365 francs per annum pension to the children, whether recognized or not, of soldiers killed defending Paris against Versailles. As Arthur Arnould, a member of the Commune from the fourth *arrondissement,* wrote in his memoirs, this act was significant because it acknowledged relationships heretofore rejected by the French state: common law spouses and children born out of wedlock. By this measure, the Commune 'raised the woman to the rank of the man, in placing her, in the eyes of the law and morality, on an absolutely equal civil footing with man . . ..'[23]

The most decisive measures taken by the Commune relative to women's independence was in the area of work. The combination of war against Prussia, the siege, and the war against Versailles, had wreaked havoc on the Parisian economy while often depriving women of the financial support of a male family member. Historically, women's pay was significantly lower than that paid to men. Although women's positions in the industrializing economy of the nineteenth century was arguably more prominent, their remuneration remained one-half to two-thirds of a man's wages. Various justifications were advanced for women's low pay, from tradition to claims that women, whose socially-appointed role was in the household, had no expectation of earning a 'living wage'; by consequence, when women worked, the argument followed, it was merely to supplement their husband's pay. However, women often depended on their wages and, for many working-class women, prostitution became the 'fifth-quarter' of their working day.

Whether as a response to the sluggish economy or, as Edith Thomas suggested, an attempt to undermine the Commune, manufacturers who remained at Paris after 18 March reduced women's wages by nearly one-third.[24] Beginning on 3 May, the Women's Union petitioned the Commune to establish workshops for women. Dmitrieff, for one, understood that women's support for the Commune was conditional upon the Commune securing their material well being.[25] Influenced by the Women's Union's request, Leo Fränkel and Benoît Malon, on behalf of the Labor and Exchange Commission, drew up a plan for the organization of cooperative workshops run by a committee of women with funds initially provided by the Commune. Denying that the establishment of female cooperatives was a charitable expedient, Fränkel and Malon's plan characterized it as a socially regenerative measure whose life would extend beyond the crisis that prompted it.

The first and only all-female cooperative ventures were limited to the production of sandbags to be used on barricades. Women would fill and sew the bags at home, bring them to a central distribution center, where the Commune would purchase them, thus avoiding intermediaries. The plan responded to concerns over women's impoverishment and the prevailing view that women should remain in the household by establishing production within the home. In other words, this measure was clearly designed to grapple with exigent circumstances without challenging gender boundaries.

The Labor and Exchange Commission had more extensive plans for the women's cooperatives. As outlined by the Women's Union's Dmitrieff, cooperatives would pay their workers a living wage – 6 francs for the manufacture of National Guard jackets and trousers – as opposed to the piece-rates of 3.75 and 2.50 francs paid by private industry for the manufacture of the same items, respectively; Fränkel agreed that, for the Commune to be consistent with its principles, it would purchase exclusively from the cooperatives.[26] On 15 May, Fränkel called for the Union to enlist women in the cooperatives; in response, more than 300 women registered in the tenth and eleventh *arrondissements*. However, less than one week later, the Versaillais were inside Paris.

The Communards' commitment to larger revolutionary principles, in the economy and in labor relations, inspired women to develop plans to overcome obstacles to their participation in the economy. On 15 and 17 May, Marie Verdure, daughter of Augustin Verdure, a member of the Commune from the eleventh *arrondissement*, along with Félix and Élie Ducoudray, presented a plan for the creation of crèches in the 'districts inhabited by workers, near factories.' Inspired by the recognition that working-class women were driven to seek employment outside the home by economic realities, rather than the desire for independence, the plan was intended to be a stopgap measure until the day that mothers would be granted maternity leave 'by means of the social reforms' its sponsors were expecting to propose.[27] In the meantime, though, crèches, staffed with wet nurses, would relieve working mothers of having to decide between their maternal obligations and their economic requirements. As conceived, nurseries were more than simply drop-off centers for the off-spring of working-class women. In fact, according to the plan, they would be veritable laboratories of utopian socialization employing young, cheerful women, clad in brightly colored outfits, whose positive attitude would be maintained by daily rotation amongst the various positions at the nursery.[28] Creating a pleasant, secular first-learning environment for pre-school aged children was consistent with the Communard objective of grounding society on cooperative, rather than authoritarian, ideals.

The Commune was at its most regressive and conventional when it addressed prostitution. Throughout the nineteenth century, politicians and medical authorities grappled with prostitution as both a physical and moral peril. Prostitutes were not only potential conduits of syphilis and symptoms of degeneracy; they also represented an insidious threat to gender and social hierarchies. On one level, in exploiting their customers' libidinous desires, prostitutes achieved a level of empowerment that conventional standards deemed inappropriate for women. On another level, they represented 'a gangrene rising from the lower depths of society and invading the entire social body during the Second Empire.'[29] During the Franco-Prussian War, the prostitute, and the contagion she threatened to unleash, became the poster child for national degeneration, in general, and the vulnerability, lassitude and impotency of the military, in particular.

The Commune never arrived at a comprehensive policy regarding the regulation or deregulation of prostitution.[30] Instead, the ex-Préfecture de Police attempted to register all prostitutes; in registering, but in failing to perform physical examinations on the prostitutes, the authorities may have been more concerned with demonstrating the Commune's adherence to conventional morality and public order than eradicating the spread of disease. If so, it would confirm Taithe's conclusion that 'when the Commune had any will to legislate on sexual matters it proved authoritarian and prudish.'[31]

Male leaders of the Commune were more disinterested in, than hostile to, women's rights. The Commune produced no legislation that was directed specifically at the condition of women; the measures discussed above were either proposals by *ad hoc* committees of women or were orders promulgated by the Education and Labor and Exchange Commissions of the Commune. Nonetheless, feminists praised the Commune, as even its paltry reforms amounted to more than any previous government had provided women, while its encouragement of support amounted to more than either the French Revolution or the revolution of 1848 had accorded women.[32] If feminist support for the Commune transcended what the Commune actually produced, it was a function of expectations engendered by Communard rhetoric that appeared to herald a brighter future for all of society's dispossessed.

Women's Roles in the Commune

Thus far we have examined the activities of the most politically active women who, through their actions, endeavored to influence policy. The Commune also witnessed the participation of thousands of Parisian women, drawn to it either from ideological, historical, or familial reasons. Women, of course, played the instrumental role on 18 March, beseeching the soldiers sent by the government not to remove the cannons at Montmartre. Eighteenth March was the Commune's equivalent of 5–6 October 1789 when thousands of women from Paris marched to Versailles to appeal to Louis XVI to relieve the food shortage at the capital. In both instances, women played a pivotal role in an event that proved crucial to the unfolding revolution. But whereas female revolutionaries in 1789 and 1871 formulated similar conceptions of revolutionary citizenship based on a politics of violence, the Paris Commune, alone, provided women with opportunities for sustained participation in the revolutionary project.[33]

Within days of the opening of hostilities during the first week of April, delegations of women, recalling the memory of their foremothers in October 1789, prepared to march to Versailles to persuade the government to negoitate a peaceful end to the conflict. Their efforts ended in confusion, with National Guardsmen blocking most of the marches to Versailles out of concern for the womens' safety. On the other hand, as Martin Phillip Johnson points out, the event galvanized women's support for the Commune as they drew upon their collective memory of their forebears' participation in the French Revolution and October 1789.[34]

The Commune inverted the notion of citizenship, limiting it to those who affirmatively supported the Commune, but also expanding the range of potential claimants to citizenship. Anyone, male or female, whose actions manifested support for the communal revolution, qualified for the nominal designation of citizen, even though the enjoyment of political rights normally associated with citizenship were reserved for men. Whether serving in traditional roles as canteen workers, ambulance nurses, or as soldiers, women could actualize their claims to citizenship in a way never before allowed them. Whereas the French Revolution created legal obstacles against women manifesting their adhesion to the Revolution, and the Second Republic clamped down on women's political activities even before the June Days, the prevailing political culture encouraged women to demonstrate their devotion to the Commune on the battlefield. To this end, the founding of, and recruitment for, the all-female *Légion des Fédérées* in the twelfth *arrondissement* on 10 May suggests official sanction.[35] Most likely formed at the behest of the Women's Union, the Légion led demonstrations in support of the Commune, organized women to fight on the barricades, ferreted out draft dodgers, and policed the activities of potentially counter-revolutionary women.[36] However, the assumption of public roles by women was confirmation for the Commune's opponents of its transgression of all established boundaries.

Gender Constructs and the Commune

The Commune's inversion of citizenship, whereby male entitlement to the rights thereto was discarded in place of a sort of revolutionary meritocracy, led many women to aspire to *citoyenneté*.[37] On the other hand, the very suggestion that women could be afforded rights to citizenship (though short of being enfranchised), added another layer to the opprobrium heaped on the Commune by its detractors, already fearful of social disorder; perceptions and depictions of women participating in the public space lent a particularly shrill and insidious tone to their characterizations of the Commune. In fact, no revolution has been as gendered and as inextricably enveloped in misogynistic analyses as the Commune.

In *The Unruly Women of Paris*, Gay Gullickson reminds us that narratives of the Commune, written in the immediate aftermath of the event, 'were part of a nineteenth-century discourse about women's nature and appropriate female behavior.'[38] Scripture provided Western civilization with conceptions of gender that alternated between castigating woman as sinful and evil when in the public realm (e.g., Eve), and holding them up as paragons of virtue and purity when their activities were confined to maternal duties (e.g., Mary). The model became an unchallenged cultural trope. However, the realities of nineteenth-century economic, social, and cultural transformations challenged the neat and tidy bifurcation of the public and private along this gendered axis; cities and industries required female workers, but tempered this need by paying them sub-subsistence wages, in the process maintaining marriage as a social and economic necessity. Nonetheless, the more visible presence of women in the public space sent conservative discourse into overdrive, as it stressed the inconsistency between historical characterizations of women's essence and the attributes necessary for participation in the public life of the community; not that there were many demands that political rights be afforded women.

Dichotomously, the French republic was visually packaged in a female form. While this metaphor reflected the ideals of liberty, wisdom, and justice personified by the Roman goddess Minerva, it represented an idealized woman, too ethereal or fantastic to be considered real. The values were clearly extricable from the image, and conventional thinking maintained that women were intellectually and emotionally incapable of being constructive participants in the civic life of the community.

With women playing so visible a role in the Commune, both supporters and opponents of the Commune drew on stereoptypes, alternating between sympathy for, or condemnation of, women depending upon whether their place on the revolutionary stage was circumstantial or volitional. In the former category were women who became participants by virtue of circumstances, 'damsels in distress' – orphaned girls, widowed wives and mothers, innocent victims caught in the crossfire (at present indelicately referred to as 'collateral damage'). For example, as the Versaillais fired upon Paris's western districts, residents of Neuilly, a bourgeois suburb, became casualties of errant shellings. The war's senselessness could not have been more potently symbolized than by the specter of defenseless women and children being mowed down in an orgy of bombardments; that the victims were bourgeois and that the Communards, wrongly, were accused of being responsible for the carnage, only added to the revulsion.[39]

By contrast, women who voluntarily played a role in the Commune, whether as *cantinières* (battalion food and drink servers), *ambulancières* (battalion nurses), political activists, or combatants evoked little sympathy, even from most proponents of the Commune. Conservatives, in particular, fixated on the female activist as an agent in Western civilization's decline and the Commune's role in encouraging gender confusion. The message was a simple one: in blurring the carefully crafted lines that demarcated acceptable and natural gender behavior, no principles were sacrosanct to the Commune. In one widely disseminated illustration, a militant working-class woman, rifle on shoulder, leads her comrades into battle while her husband tenderly, though awkwardly, cares for the couple's baby. The illustration revisits 1848's fears over *vésuviennes*, the metaphoric name taken by feminists in the early days of the Second Republic, who, likewise, were often depicted as bearing the accoutrements and assuming the roles of masculinity.[40]

During autumn 1870 women became active in the civic life of the besieged capital. Whether queuing for hours for rations, serving as *ambulancières* or *cantonières*, or distributing alms as part of *arrondissement* Vigilance Committees, activist women were the foil to male lassitude as civic life and domestic duty became conflated. As tempting as it may be to interpret the significance of these public roles as a first step towards women's liberation from the foyer, it is equally important to remember that the siege presented Parisians with a peculiar and unprecedented set of circumstances; the exigencies of the moment were not conducive to the insistence that the genders confine themselves to the predesignated spheres. That said, in filling glorified nurturer/caregiver roles, the functions women performed deviated little from those they traditionally played.

Women's participation, and the forms it assumed, became something of a self-fulfilling prophecy for opponents of the Commune. Descriptions of women's activities highlighted how their emotional excesses gave rise to innumerable examples of ferocity, cruelty, and insanity. Shocking, though trivial, events loomed larger in the histories when the author identified the perpetrators as women.[41] On the other hand, as Paris smouldered (though not as fiercely as reported) during the Bloody Week, blame for the fires that engulfed the capital and destroyed some of its cultural patrimony settled on women, giving rise to the legend of the *pétroleuse.*

To be sure, women participated on the barricades, most doing so in conjunction with a spouse or lover or in defense of their neighborhood.[42] The image of women with rifles and bayonets attracted the attention, though not necessarily the respect, of pro- and anti-Commune commentators, alike. For the Communards, there was something poetically apt about women fighting to preserve the Commune during that desperate week; after all, the drama had originally opened with women defending the cannons at Montmartre on 18 March.

The commonly held belief that the Communards transformed Paris into a veritable inferno during the final full week of May 1871 was, like much of the reportage on the Commune, only partially true. In the first place, while several famous buildings were on fire, this was no general conflagration. Nonetheless, rumor became currency, and terrified observers should be forgiven if, in their panic, they mistook the few fires they observed with a fear that the entire capital was being razed to the ground. Once the smoke cleared, and the Versaillais were in control of Paris, exaggerated stories of fires deliberately set by the property-despising Communards continued to circulate. In the wake of the most indiscriminate bloodfest in French history, the fires served as a public relations coup for the Versailles government, desperately needing to divert attention away from the 20,000 to 30,000 corpses scattered across the capital and its neighboring suburbs. In other words, whatever acts of brutality were meted out by the 'forces of order' either paled in comparison to, or were necessary measures against, the savagery of the Communards.

However, the Communards did not instigate the arson. The first fires came courtesy of bombs lobbed by the Versaillais at *fédérés* encampments on the Champ-de-Mars and, presumably, misdirected ones that found the attic at the Ministry of Finance building. The Communards did follow suit, first starting fires to aid their retreat, then, on 23 May, torching a number of structures, including the Tuileries Palace. After the Commune concluded its final meeting on the following morning, Jean-Louis Pindy, a representative from the third *arrondissement,* ordered the Hôtel de Ville be set on fire; within a short while, the Palais de Justice and the Prefecture de Police were also in flames. By the end of the day, fires burned along the right bank of the Seine and on both sides of Place de la République, at the Porte Saint-Martin and in Belleville.

While the supporters of the Commune accepted responsibility for many of the fires, including those buildings they characterized as vestiges of France's tyrannical past, much of the incendiary damage resulted from the incessant and indiscriminate shelling by the Versaillais. It has also been suggested that Bonapartists, desirous of concealing embarrassing documents, might have been behind some of the fires.[43]

While it is understandable that the Versaillais would level blame for the fires on the defeated Communards, less clear is how suggestions of female involvement in the fires evolved into a national psychosis that endured throughout the summer. As fires were still burning, several newspapers, French, British, and American alike, raised the specter of female incendiaries. By 28 May, the last day of the Bloody Week, the press reported on teams of arsonists, comprised of women and children, being paid 10 francs for every fire started. A mass hysteria ensued and possibly hundreds of women were executed because they fit the designated profile of a *pétroleuse*: 'poor and ill-dressed, and ... carrying a basket, box, or milkbottle,' or, better still, smelling of kerosene.[44]

To be fair, Article 14 of the Women's Union's statutes mentioned that kerosene and weapons would be provided to women fighting on the barricades. Whatever the inculpatory nature of this document, none of the women investigated for arson were members of the Women's Union.[45] There were two sets of trials of *pétroleuses* involving only eight women. At the first trial of five women accused of arson, no witnesses testified to actually seeing any of them toting kerosene or lighting fires, though all five admitted to having been at the barricades, either as *cantinières* or *ambulancières*. The five were convicted and three were sentenced to death before the Commission of Pardons, underwhelmed by the lack of evidence, commuted their sentences to hard labor for life. The second batch of trials occurred in 1872. Of the three accused, witnesses testified that two had some connection to fires, in one case as one of the Tuileries' arsonists, in the other case, as having had prior knowledge that buildings were to be torched. All three were convicted.

In addition to being working class and, for the most part, outspoken supporters of the Commune, prosecutors noted that the eight had demonstrated contempt for society's moral codes. All had lovers, but two were married, separated from their husbands, and involved in relationships with *fédérés*, no less! The three who were sentenced to death also had criminal records for offenses ranging from buying military clothing to assault to theft.

Accused *pétroleuses* were not judged so much by the evidence of their culpability as arsonists, but for what they symbolized. In fact, the convictions were more an indictment of the Commune as the *bête noire* of bourgeois morality than an affirmation of the women's actual culpability. Stigmatized for endeavoring to destroy the family by recognizing 'free union marriages'[46] and deregulating prostitution,[47] the Commune's violence was readily understood as the consequence of giving women too much freedom. Referred to in the indictment as 'unworthy creatures who seem to have taken on the task of becoming an opprobrium to their sex, and of repudiating the great and magnificent role of woman in society,'[48] the accused women personified the deepest bourgeois fears of what the Commune represented. As Gullickson reminds us, male defenders of the Commune had simply made a poor choice; female defenders, on the other hand, had not only made a poor choice, but, more seriously, challenged the foundations of social stability by venturing out of the sanctity of domesticity and into the public space.[49] Ironically, at the same time, many men were sexually attracted to an image that was meant to inspire revulsion.[50]

In the aftermath of the Commune, both conservative commentators and bourgeois feminists noted that working women and prostitutes posed the biggest threats to the stability of the family. In the official postmortem of the Commune, commentators, like Hippolyte Taine, attributed much of the violence during the Bloody Week to the participation of women. Taine, arguably the most influential French historian of the second half of the nineteenth century, simply reified conventional ideas that women are closer to nature, and therefore more primitive, more instinctive, and less reflective, less civilized.[51] Though Taine's conclusion was more cultural than scientific, it not only justified the criminal accusations for which tangible evidence was lacking, but reconfirmed French fears that the path to social disorder was paved with female independence from the household and their presence in the public space.

Through visual imagery, caricaturists and artists of the period demarcated and defined the boundaries separating acceptable from forbidden female behavior. By their presence in the public space, women had obliterated that boundary; for the Commune's detractors, the devastated capital was both a symbolic and real testament to what ensues from womens' emergence out of the private sphere. As we turn to the Commune's relationship to the art world and its effort to shape history through the creation of indissociable bonds between political ideas and cultural practice, we will examine recent scholarship on the Commune's representation through visual media, including the ubiquitously exaggerated image of female Communards.

Chapter 6: Revolution, Culture, and the Commune

Art and Revolution

Coinciding with the 1747 resurrection of the Salon, La Font de Saint-Yenne, credited as the first modern art critic, inadvertently initiated a campaign that challenged the dominant artistic style of the first half of the eighteenth century, rococo. Suited to the frivolity and sensuality of Louis XV's France, rococo lost its viability amid demands that art serve a civic, as well as aesthetic, function. As the official art institution of the *ancien régime* and showcase of the French Academy, the Salon's intention was to expose the public to new currents in art; the movement of art to the public arena required art had to resonate with an increasingly politicized public. In the 1780s, Jacques-Louis David led a revival of neo-classical art, a style that better responded to the evolving dictates of the French Academy for 'didactic, elevated, and heroic' themes.[1] Although David was hardly a republican in the 1780s (even Robespierre had not yet embraced republicanism), his major works, including *Oath of the Horatii* (1785) and *The Lictors Returning to Brutus the Bodies of his Sons* (1789), conveyed the artistic language of the pre-Revolutionary radicals and its 'idiom of virtue.'[2]

During the Revolution, David was the leader of a cadre of artists whose work immortalized the Revolution, visually commemorating the revolutionary drama, allegorizing its ideals, raising its actors to mythological proportions, sanctifying martyrs to liberty, and parodying one's political opponents.[3] Interestingly, 'revolutionary art' comprised a surprisingly small percentage of the artistic output during the Revolution, and, in fact, the high point of didactic art were the years immediately preceding the Revolution.[4] However, the most memorable works from the 1790s captured the revolutionary moment and emotionally connected the viewing public to the events, personalities, and ideals portrayed, positioning the audience as both spectators and participants, while conveying the power and sublimity of the revolutionary project.

The Functioning of the Arts During the Commune

In his work on artists and the Commune, Gonzalo Sánchez observes that the French Revolution of 1789–94 provided a model for the revolutionary mobilization of artists under the Commune.[5] On one level, issues of artistic freedom were common to the years leading up to the French Revolution and the Paris Commune. In both instances, artists denounced the Salon, and the official, governmental patronage it received, as an impediment to artistic expression. In response to the *Salon des Refusés* (an alternative to the Salon organized, in 1863, by artists whose works were rejected by the Salon), and as part of its more general liberalization, the Empire instituted some peer-review reform. In the turbulent final years of the Empire, artists joined in the chorus of republican dissent; anxieties over their livelihoods and demands for artist self-administration of the Academy morphed into a more generalized critique of the imperial administration.

With the fall of the Empire, and the looming threat of a Prussian invasion of Paris, the Government of National Defense established the *Commission artistique pour la sauvegarde des musées nationaux* (Artists' Commission for the Protection of National Museums) under the auspices of Jules Simon's Ministry of Education. The Artists' Commission not only viewed its mission as safeguarding Parisian art treasures from the Prussian army, but also from the Napoléonic administrative staff left in place at, for example, the Louvre by Simon.

Led by Gustave Courbet, most of the artists selected to serve on the Artists' Commission had been ardent opponents of the Empire. Courbet was perhaps the most renowned artist of the social realist school of the 1850s and 1860s. Whether disparaging the rural bourgeoisie's ennui (e.g., *Burial at Ornans*[6]), subverting classical styles of art (e.g., *The Bathers*), or presenting a grim portrayal of peasant labor (e.g. *The Stonebreakers*), Courbet's work challenged artistic conventions and drew connections between art and social criticism. As a close friend of Proudhon (in fact, he painted Proudhon's portrait for the Salon), Courbet advocated the application of Proudhonian corporatism to artists (through self-regulation). While presiding over the Artists' Commission, Courbet juggled national cultural concerns with his professional dedication to artistic reform and political distrust of Bonapartism.

By the end of January 1871, the Artists' Commission ceased to exist. Its principal function – preserving the nation's artistic treasures – had been fulfilled and it was doubtful that they would be endangered after the declaration of the armistice. It was doubtful that, in the conservative atmosphere that prevailed between January and March, Courbet's professional and political objectives would be realized. The declaration of the Commune breathed new life into these goals.

On 6 April, Courbet issued a call to Paris's artists to follow the lead of the newly declared Commune and establish corporatist and cooperative autonomy over art.[7] The new commission – the *Fédération des Artistes* (Federation of Artists) – was actually an enhanced version of the Artists' Commission. Comprised of 47 representatives of the five fine arts disciplines[8] democratically elected by recognized or exhibited artists, the Federation was, according to its mission statement, determined to defend the principle of artistic self-governance. By self-governance, Courbet was referring to artist control over official exhibitions, peer-reviewed committees for grants, and instruction.

As Sánchez reminds us, 'The Fédération was an initiative *under* the Commune, not *of* the Commune.' Though the Commune gave its approval to the Federation's first meeting and elections, it withheld official recognition of it until 1 May. In fact, the Commune and the Federation had a somewhat uneasy coexistence that, in some respects, was aggravated by Courbet's position as an elected member of each body (after an unsuccessful candidacy in the first round of elections to the Commune, voters in the sixth *arrondissement* elected him in the by-election held on 16 April). As the Federation adjourned a motion by Courbet on 20 April that its members pledge their allegiance to the Commune, at least one member affirmed that delegates to the Federation were responsible to their artist-constituents and not to the Commune. Five days later, the Federation rejected Courbet's claim to serve as a mediator between the two bodies, insisting that he served on the Federation strictly as a representative of his fellow painters. Interestingly, though, when six members of the Federation attempted to resign from it, the Federation invoked the authority of the Commune in refusing to accept the resignations.[9]

In terms of the Federation's actual as opposed to idealized activities, it spent considerably less attention on the preservationist duties that the

Artists' Commission had taken so seriously. On the contrary, once the Commune recognized it, the Federation devoted much of its attention to reopening and restocking the Paris museums and replacing the Bonapartist curatorial staff at Paris museums. Although accused by opponents of the Commune of being agents of destruction, at the commencement of the Bloody Week, Federation artists turned their attention to preserving the artworks under their care from being destroyed.[10] Even before that, at a meeting on 12 May regarding the Commune's order to demolish Thiers's house, Courbet and several other Communard preservationists protected the artwork, literary sources, and historical artifacts in the private collection.[11]

Although not every artist shared his vision for the Federation, Courbet largely established the revolutionary agenda that distinguished the Federation from the Artists' Commission. As his initial statement on the Federation fêted Paris as the nurturer of artistic talent, Courbet echoed the revolutionary creed that privileged Paris for its political militancy. While Courbet's emphasis on corporatism and anti-statism represented an anachronistic fealty to Proudhonian ideas, his insistence on democracy was consistent with the spirit of anti-authoritarianism ushered in by the Commune. However, as regards anti-statism, it is difficult to determine whether the demand for attenuating the relationship between artist and state was borne out of concerns for pure artistic freedom or suspicions over conservative governments. Proudhon, himself, was a bundle of contradictions on this point; his advocacy of art as a moralizing force represented a denial of artistic freedom. Although the Commune did not reference Proudhon on this point, by placing the Federation under the jurisdiction of Vaillant's Committee on Public Instruction, it implicitly recognized art and art education as agents for social regeneration.

Whereas most members of the Federation were reintegrated back into the art world (Courbet, whose fate will be discussed below, is the most notable exception), state art policy was a mixture of retreat from reforms – even those initiated by the Second Empire – and gradual, though largely unacknowledged, acceptance of Federation ideals. On one level, the post-Commune art administration enhanced the role of the Academy as arbiter of Salon submissions, thus de-democratizing the selection process, and raising the specter of another *Salon des refusés* in 1872. On another level, as fine arts administration grew more conservative in 1874, it adopted a more libertarian stance; ironically, and without acknowledging it, the state had facilitated artistic self-regulation.[12]

Perhaps the most contentious artistic issue concerned the functioning of theatres. During the Second Empire, theatrical productions reflected the decadance of the era and rarely touched upon serious themes. During the Commune, authors, musical composers, playwrights, and lyricists endeavored to take control over their art by forming an Artistic Federation. Upon a petition by the Artistic Federation that it be granted the right to take over unoccupied theatres to stage productions for 'widows, injured, orphans, and dependents of the National Guard,' the Commune turned over operation of the theatres to the more than 600 theatrical artists who adhered to the Artistic Federation.

When the Commune considered the administration of theatres, a spirited debate ensued that pitted advocates of artistic social utility versus supporters of artistic freedom. On 19 May, Edouard Vaillant declared that, following the example set by the National Convention during the First Republic, theatres would be under the jurisdiction of the Commune's Education Committee. According to Vaillant, 'the theatres must be considered, above all, as a great instructional establishment; and in a republic, they must be only this.'[13] In response, Félix Pyat, a one-time playwright, challenged Vaillant's proposal to channel artistic production in the service of the state as anti-republican and tyrannical, characterizing state control over culture as identical to religious tyranny. Claiming that he had no intention to challenge artistic freedom, but was endeavoring to end the exploitation of theatrical artists, Vaillant's proposal called for the creation of an association of theatrical artists to be subsidized by the state.[14] In the end, the Commune adopted Vaillant's proposal, but two days later the entry of the Versaillais into Paris lay to rest any plans for artistic regulation of the theatrical output or collectivization of Paris theatres.

Culture, National Regeneration, and the Public Space

As the debate over theatres made manifest, the Communards believed in art's revolutionary role and understood the theatricality of revolutionary acts. On 6 April, a group calling itself 'the sub-committee of the eleventh *arrondissement*' ordered the seizure of a 'more mobile and quicker' guillotine found on the Rue de la Folie-Méricourt. Taken to the town hall of the *arrondissement,* the guillotine was burned in front of the statue of Voltaire, 'the apostle of humanity and precursor to the French Revolution.'[15] As an instrument first introduced during the French

Revolution, the guillotine would appear to be connected with the past to which the Communards identified; since the Revolution, the guillotine served as a symbol of barbarity and the ultimate authority of the state over the individual. Though the Commune had nothing to do with the the act, the guillotine's destruction, in front of a monument to Voltaire, was perhaps an expiatory act designed to make amends for the Revolution's deviation from its original enlightened ideals. If so, it was the first of several theatrical acts in which the public space was utilized to ritually exorcise France of unpleasantries that bedeviled its history.[16]

As controversial as any measure undertaken by the Commune was its decree on 16 May ordering the toppling of the Vendôme Column. Inaugurated in 1810 by Napoléon I to celebrate his empire, the column was forged from captured Austrian and Russian cannons and was topped by a bronze statue of Napoléon clothed in the vestments of Roman emperors. The column had, since the fall of Napoléon, suffered the slings and arrows of French regime changes. The Restoration removed Napoléon from the top of the column, replaced him with a large white flag, melted down the bronze, and recast it for the statue of Henri IV on Pont Neuf. During the July Monarchy, Louis-Philippe had another statue of the Emperor, clad in riding coat, the citizen-emperor, placed atop the column.[17] In 1864, Napoléon III had that one replaced with an enormous bronze statue of his uncle 'draped in the mantle of a Roman emperor, a globe resting in one hand from which soared a winged victory.'[18]

Having gone through various transmogrifications, the statue atop the column was hardly inviolable. Upon the fall of the Second Empire, a homage to the First Empire seemed to be a perversion of republicanism and even moderate republicans like Jules Simon suggested more suitable uses for the Column's bronze.[19] Courbet, in particular, launched a spirited campaign to destroy the entire column. Obviously, with the onset of the siege, dealing with the Column's offensiveness was a very low priority and it was not until the scission in March that the Column, again, became a pressing issue.

On 12 April, four days before Courbet's election to the Commune, the latter ordered the toppling of the Column, characterizing it as 'a monument to barbarity, a symbol of brute force and false glory, an affirmation of militarism, a negation of international law, a permanent insult by the conqueror over the vanquished, a perpetual assault to one of the great principles of the French republic, fraternity.'[20] Because the crowd that wanted to witness the Column's demolition was larger than Place

Vendôme could accommodate, the Commune distributed special admittance passes to those who had rendered service to the Commune. Under a beautiful Spring sky, the crowd listened as an orchestra turned out 'Le Chant du Depart,' an anthem from the French Revolution which extols the virtues of sacrifice on behalf of the republic; at the moment the Column fell, the orchestra played 'La Marseillaise' and observers scrambled for pieces of bronze or to have their photographs taken with the fallen symbol. In place of the Column, Courbet suggested a monument to commemorate the revolution of 18 March.[21]

9   The toppling of the Vendôme Column, five minutes before it fell
Source: © Photothèque des musées de la ville de Paris, France.

The Column had its defenders and probably picked up more amongst the moderates and conservatives at Versailles, in equal measure to the invectives directed at it by the Communards. For many, it was 'where once the record of our military glory was inscribed in bronze.'[22] Although few on the Commune objected to the leveling of the Column, and Félix Pyat was actually the member of the Commune who proposed its demolition, responsibility for the Column's fall settled on Courbet. Though he advocated the Column's demolition, Courbet was hardly the most strident advocate of this, and his reasoning had more to do with public art than with anti-militarism. Regardless, though, in the days prior to 16 May, Courbet received letters threatening him with stabbing, being tossed into the Seine, and poisoning.[23]

In the aftermath of the Commune, Courbet would pay dearly for his close association with the Column's destruction. Originally, sentenced to six-months imprisonment and a large fine, Courbet's work was, henceforward, rejected for inclusion in the Salon. The government issued a seizure order on all of Courbet's property and works. The worst was yet to come. When, on 30 May 1873 Marshal MacMahon, now president of the Third Republic, proposed the reconstruction of the Vendôme Column, Courbet was assessed the cost – 323,091.68 francs – to be paid in annuities through the sale of all his artwork. Exiled in Switzerland, Courbet died on 31 December 1877, the day before his first 10,000 francs payment was due.

In ordering the toppling of the Vendôme Column, the Commune had consciously endeavored to alter national memory. Obliterating a memorial to tyranny would not only constitute an expiatory act, but also an attempt at reshaping how the nation remembers and commemorates its past. Bringing down the Column was no easy feat, but most accounts focused on its symbolic import. In particular, the decapitation of Napoléon's bronze head was infused with the same metaphorical value as Louis XVI's guillotining had been in 1793. In other words, the severance of the head from the corporal vessel symbolized an irremediable severance of the body politic from its figurative head as well as a bifurcation of the nation's referential past from its reconstitutable future. In short, it represented the death of the past, and the prospects for a regenerated future. The past was a subjective topic, as testified by the 12 May discussion at the Commune regarding Thiers's art collection. Demanding that specialists be employed 'to watch over the transport of the precious objects and to safeguard the interests of art,' Communard Antoine Demay remarked: 'Don't forget that these small bronze works

of art are the history of humanity, and we want to conserve the intelligence of the past for the edification of the future. We are not barbar-
ians.'[24] In the case of the Vendôme Column, it neither represented the
intelligence of the past nor the edification of the future.

The Vendôme Column was more than the metals that composed it or
the values that it represented; its obliteration was a passion play resonant
with themes of destruction, resurrection, forgetting, and remembering.
In a thought-provoking series of essays on the relationship the past bears
to our understanding of the present, Matt Matsuda eloquently and ele-
gantly established the stakes behind the Column's toppling:

> The destruction of the Vendôme Column was much more than an anti-
> militarist statement or attempt to mock one Napoleonic dictator by
> bringing down another. To break the column would break and collapse
> many different histories – those of the Napoleonic regimes of course,
> but also classical, cosmological, cultural, and national narratives. To
> efface one without disturbing the others was impossible. As the Emperor
> fell, so also did the patriotic genius of the French revolutionary armies.
> Tyranny conquered meant a cultural heritage endangered. Virtuous
> republics tumbled down alongside ambitious dictators.[25]

Perhaps sensing the enormity of the Column's destruction, and the
emotions it evoked, Courbet disingenuously defended his opposition to
the monument along artistic lines, characterizing the monument's
phallic verticality as an aesthetic blight on the otherwise horizontal
urban landscape.

For MacMahon and countless other opponents of the Commune, the
Column was also rich in visceral symbolism. In May 1871, as he prepared
to lead his troops into Paris, MacMahon incited their hatred for the
Communards by referring to the Column's destruction as follows:

Soldiers,
The Vendôme Column has fallen.
The foreigner respected it. The Commune has toppled it. Some so-
called Frenchmen had the nerve, under the eyes of the Prussians, to
destroy this witness to the victories of your fathers over the European
coalition.
Do these worthless authors of an assault on our national glory hope to
efface the memory of military virtues of which this monument was the
glorious symbol?

Soldiers! If the memories that the column recalled are no longer engraved in bronze, they remain alive in our hearts. Inspired by them, we will give France a new pledge of bravery, devotion, and patriotism.[26]

The Communards certainly held no monopoly over the effacement of historical memory. When he became president of the Third Republic, nearly two years to the day that he led his troops into Paris, MacMahon committed himself to a project whose origins predated the Commune. As he fled Paris at the commencement of the Prussian besiegement, Alexandre Legentil, a prosperous bourgeois, vowed to lead efforts to construct a sanctuary dedicated to the Sacred Heart if God delivered Paris from the Prussians. He enlisted the help of Hubert Rohault de Fleury, another staunch conservative and notable denizen of the capital.

The Commune added a sense of urgency to their project. Whereas Legentil originally wanted to build his cathedral at the site of the uncompleted Paris Opera House, which he considered to be 'a scandalous monument of extravagance, indecency and bad taste,' the new archibishop of Paris was more interested in the bluffs of Montmartre, from whose heights the Church could manifest its supremacy over Paris. Because the coveted land at Montmartre, 6 Rue des Rosiers, was private property, governmental action was necessary to secure rights of eminent domain.

A committee of the National Assembly, a quarter of whose membership had taken a vow to see the project through to fruition, reported that a cathedral at Montmartre was of public utility 'to efface by this work of expiation, the crimes which have crowned our sorrows.' Presumably the crimes to which the Committee made reference did not include the brutal murder of Eugène Varlin on the very spot where, ironically, would be dedicated the Chapel to Jésus-Ouvrier (Jesus the Worker). No, the political value was made clear on 16 June 1875, the day that the foundation stone for the Basilica of Sacré-Cœur was laid. Rohault de Fleury was ebullient that 'it is here where Sacré-Cœur will be raised up that the Commune began, here where generals Clément Thomas and Lecomte were assassinated.' While it was a foregone conclusion that the Third Republic would never construct monuments commemorative of the Commune, the selection of Montmartre by a monarchist assembly temporarily in control of the Republic, stood as an affront to both the Commune and the tradition of republican anticlericalism.[27]

Visualizing the Commune

In what is now the seminal work on the relationship between art, artists, and the Commune (published in 2004), Bertrand Tillier writes of the relative paucity of sculpture and painting of the Commune. According to Tillier, to the extent that sculptural and painterly production requires a longer, slower gestation period for 'the maturation of the idea . . . the transformation of material and the realization in a more concrete form of the abstraction', the rapidity by which events unfolded during the Commune was more conducive to the production of prints (especially caricatures) and photographs.[28] But artistic representation of the Commune was also hindered by other factors. On one level, several artists took part in the administration of Paris or were otherwise politically involved during the Commune. On another level, their incomprehension of the meaning and enormity of the event and its unsettled nature prevented some artists from representing it. But, above all, the official prohibition against the diffusion of images, photographs, caricatures that could be construed as favorable to the Commune, promulgated on 28 December 1871 and effectively in force for several decades thereafter, severely restricted the production of artistic works.[29]

In contrast to the traditional fine arts, photographs of the Commune proliferated, making it the first French revolution to be photographed. Although newspapers exclusively illustrated their accounts with realistic engravings or caricatures, photographs appeared to offer evidence shorn of artistic manipulation. Art historian Jeannene Przyblyski's look at the photographic evidence of the Commune explores how, at the time of the Commune, the occurrence or play of events increasingly required the authentication provided by the camera's lens. Przyblyski's principal point is that the widely disseminated photographs by Eugène Appert, doctored visual reconstructions of the Commune's most notorious crimes, were not received by their audience as faithful renderings of events; rather, contemporaries understood them for what they were: 'clever simulacrum,' part of a culture of constructed spectatorship in which photography was historically sandwiched between dioramas and cinematic recreations as mediums that 'mixed reality and artifice' in the service of 'illusionistic entertainment.'[30]

As Przyblyski acknowledges, images such as those produced by Appert 'were deeply implicated in the public relations game by which the national government sought to construct its own version of the events of spring 1871, and Appert was well rewarded with official titles and support for his diligent services to the government.'[31] Whether nineteenth-century audiences received Appert's photographs as entertainment or as a faithful visual record of the past is historically intangible; on the other hand, unlike the plethora of caricatures produced by both sides during the Commune, photographs had an intrinsic objectivity. While audiences might have been able to discern that, given the limitations of photography at the time, the events depicted were staged, it is questionable whether they would have identified them as being just as ideologically charged as caricatures. How else, for example, can we explain the inclusion of Appert's photographs in both pro- and anti-Communard accounts?[32]

Several monographs that have appeared within the past decade have examined the influence of the Franco-Prussian War and Commune on painterly output.[33] Though Manet and Renoir produced lithographs of the Bloody Week, few of the artists who initiated the Impressionist Exhibition of 1874 committed the actual events of the Commune to canvas. While artists like Edgar Degas, Edouard Manet, and Pierre Renoir were republicans and abhorred the repression meted out by the Versaillais, their views on the Commune are less readily identifiable. Manet, for example, had been elected to the Federation, but remained outside of Paris until either the Bloody Week or shortly thereafter. In fact, most of the artists who, in the aftermath of the Commune, dominated the world of Impressionist art, remained outside of Paris during the Commune, some having left during the Franco-Prussian War.

Hailing from solid bourgeois backgrounds, the artists appeared more inclined towards conciliation between Paris and Versailles.[34] Although the personal stories of several of the Communards sketched in Chapter 4 verify that social class did not automatically determine one's predisposition towards the Commune, stability was crucial to artistic production; the Franco-Prussian War had caused more than its share of disruptions. Beyond this, social class did matter to artists. Though many of the artists had connections to the world of revolutionary republicanism, their political convictions were more premised on utopian ideals than class conflict. In his classic study of the hostility of the literary community to the Commune, Paul Lidsky emphasized that one must separate out artistic contempt towards bourgeois monotony and structure from the bourgeois patronage that ensured an artist's livelihood.[35] Furthermore, to the artists, bourgeois Philistinism paled in comparison to the working-class's lack of cultural refinement that, to many artists, approached the point of barbarism, savagery, and ignorance.[36]

When such French literary giants of the nineteenth century as George Sand, Victor Hugo, Gustave Flaubert, Edmond de Goncourt, Alphonse Daudet, Émile Zola addressed the Commune, either in their personal correspondences or published works, they fixated on the reports (since none were in Paris during the Bloody Week) of death and destruction. The subtext of each of these author's perspectives on the Commune was class, and, in particular, their fears of working-class autonomy.

While Sand, Hugo, and Zola expressed sympathy either for some of the Communards' objectives or for the plight of their working-class constituency, all blamed the Commune, at least in part, for the violent divisions that tore at the nation's fabric. In their letters and works, Sand and Hugo expressed support for some of what the Commune stood for; but as republicans, both decried how the internecine violence and destruction carried out by both sides laid waste to their undying faith in human and societal progress, national renewal, and unity through evolutionary and conciliatory means. Though Zola was sympathetic to the circumstances of individual workers, he maintained a deep suspicion of workers as a collective body and the influence of Parisian intellectual currents on them, sharing the same prejudices against educated and politicized workers as Daudet, Goncourt, and Flaubert, all violent opponents of the Commune.

On the precipice of the amnesty for the exiled Communards, several works took a more positive literary approach to the Commune. The publication in 1879 of the last volume of Jules Vallès's semi-autobiographical *Jacques Vingtras* trilogy – *L'Insurgé* – and Léon Cladel's *INRI* countered the conventional depiction of the Communard as a destructive, sociopath. Set against the backdrop of historical events and individuals, Vallès and Cladel's protagonists adhered to the Commune out of a sense of idealism and historical destiny to complete the French Revolution.[37]

Many artists who returned to the capital after the Commune's repression found that, in the wake of the ravages of war and revolution, Paris was hardly recognizable. Destruction, death, and disorder hung over the once ordered and prosperous Parisian landscape. The artists felt both culturally and economically dislocated by the events of 1870–1 but, according to Boime, over the ensuing years, metaphorically and realistically sought to convey through their art the 'convalescence, purification, restoration, and regeneration' of the mutilated capital.[38]

Boime sees in many visual works a conscious effort by the Impressionists to portray an urban space in which 'bridges are repaired, trees replanted and flourishing, the rubble of ruins removed, and the pace of life returned to normal.'[39] Consequently, Claude Monet, Edgar Degas, and Renoir depicted the Parc Monceau, Montmartre, Pont Neuf, and the bridges that spanned the Seine at Argenteuil and Pontoise as no longer threatening, disturbing, or endangering.[40]

Reconstituting the bourgeoisie as masters of Paris and reestablishing the pre-Commune social-class hierarchy lent a sense of predictability and order that rendered the city less ominous and chaotic. For example, in *Floor-scrapers* (1875), Gustave Caillebotte positioned three workers, consumed by their labors in refinishing the flooring in an up-scale dwelling, beneath the gaze of those observing them; no longer in political control of the capital, the workers have once again been returned to a subordinate position, both in terms of their labors and their spatial relationship to those viewing them.[41] Caillebotte's most famous work, *Paris Street, Rainy Weather* (1877), a work of enormous proportions, conveys a sense of social order as well-dressed (and presumably bourgeois) Parisians promenade on a rainy day in the capital, once again restored to its Haussmannesque splendor. As a metaphorical cleansing agent, the rain purifies and sanitizes the streets of the residue of worker control and the blood that, like a good old-fashioned bloodletting, flowed in order to reconstitute the social body.[42]

Eviscerating the Commune from the urban topography simply opened up a new front: the Commune's effacement from the collective memory.[43] Whether or not the Impressionist artists consciously encoded their works with conservative values, their representations of the public space belied any suggestion of the Commune's occurrence. In 1885, a former Communard recently returned from New Caledonia, Maxime Lisbonne, opened a Montmartre cabaret (2 Boulevard de Clichy), the Taverne du Bagne (Jailhouse Tavern). Whereas patrons at the other two Montmartre cabarets were offered the opportunity to step into either the world of the bohemian or the demimonde, the Taverne du Bagne invited the public to experience the punishments meted out to Communards.[44] Lisbonne's stated reason for opening the cabaret was to resurrect memories of the Commune, its repression, and its martyrdom.[45] But in his preservation of the Commune's memory had Lisbonne also vulgarized it as a participatory spectacle? In the final analysis, we need to inquire whether reducing the Commune to the level of entertaining distraction produced a more pernicious result than its elimination from the collective memory.

Caricatures and the Commune

Although very little fine art was produced during the Commune, the ten weeks were notable for the proliferation of caricatures, a veritable 'war of images' to employ the title of an article on the subject.[46] As a popular art form, and the predecessor to political cartooning, the art of caricature entailed a number of elements. First, it typically required exaggeration, either of a subject's physical attributes, moral turpitude or virtue, leadership qualities, or actions in a particular circumstance. As such, caricature typically reduced discourse to its lowest common denominator, a pictorial soundbite that closed off serious discussion. Second, and related to the first point, caricature relies upon negative imagery.[47] With the exception of quasi-spiritual images of resurrection or regeneration or adulatory cartoons of identifiable or abstract heroes, the focus of Commune-era caricatures was squarely on the side the artist opposed. Third, caricatures rely on tropes familiar to, and recognizable by, their audience; often as not the allegory titillated with ribald humor and sexual references. Because of their incendiary nature and easy discernability, caricatures were more susceptible to repression than textual polemics.

The Second Empire's relaxation of press laws in 1868 did not apply to caricatures. Nonetheless, the perception of a relaxed political atmosphere unleashed a torrent of anger pent up over the preceding 17 years.[48] A good portion of the hostility towards the Empire was expressed through caricatures that satirized everything from the Empire's decadence to its corrupt and destructive governance.

Caricaturists soon found another target; the inability of the Government of National Defense (and especially the three Jules – Favre, Trochu, and Simon) to measure up to its titular mandate and its capitulation in January 1871 encouraged an even greater proliferation of images focused on its cowardice, duplicity, and treason. During the Commune, pro-Commune caricaturists shifted the target of their attacks from Favre to Adolphe Thiers. Many artists highlighted Thiers's questionable commitment to republicanism, drawing attention to his past service to Louis-Philippe and his disembowelment of the Second Republic. In other cases, Thiers's physiognomy and diminutive stature were exaggerated and employed as indices of his lack of leadership qualities or as an explanation for his brutal propensities.

Ridicule, however, was not the exclusive province of the pro-Commune caricaturists. Artists opposed to the Commune lampooned it as a class war waged by the dangerous, brutal, and undeserving against the industrious, enterprising, and civilized in which the very essence of civil society – property and order – was at stake. More so than textual polemics, visual images left no doubt as to the identity of the perpetrators of violence and the threats they posed to societal stability.

Perhaps the most ubiquitous figure in caricatures was the female image. On one level, she was personified in the form of Marianne, the symbol of French republicanism whose ethereality and corporeality represented the conflation of ideal and real attributes. In opposition to the inextricable connection between the image of a particular monarch and monarchial sovereignty, the selection of an individual who lacked a personal identity to represent the republic expressed the ideal of a republic comprised of anonymous sovereigns. The image is much more than just a composite: Marianne is a woman, and thus was outside the community

10 Anti-Commune caricature: 'La terreur sous la Commune'. Interpretation of 'the terror under the Commune, 1871.' Note the presence of women and children among the combattants; the execution of clerics; and the collapse of the Vendôme Column amid scenes of unimaginable chaos
Source: © Photothèque des musées de la ville de Paris, France.

11   Anti-Commune caricature: 'Les folies de la Commune' (The insanity of the
     Commune). A Communard, torch in hand, pays homage to his historical
     inspiration
     Source: © Photothèque des musées de la ville de Paris, France.

of sovereigns possessing a civic identity. As Marina Warner has observed:
'If women had had a vote or a voice, Marianne would have been harder
to accept as a universal figure of the ideal.'[49] As the republic incarnate,
images of Marianne alternated between fortitude, virtue, stoicism, and
vulnerability depending upon the circumstances faced by the republic.[50]
However, she remained no more than an abstraction, an ideal that did

not correspond with a living and breathing woman, and she was never meant to be a statement on women's inclusion in the public space.

Inasmuch as the central purpose of caricature is to strike either a humorous or opprobrious visceral chord by highlighting the opposition's foibles, pro-Commune caricaturists, understandably, did not address positive images of female adhesion to the Commune. On the other hand, anti-Commune artists employed both metaphorical and real female imagery to underscore the social disorder unleashed by the Commune. Predictably, the *pétroleuse* became both the signifier of the Commune's excesses and a living, albeit constructed, representation of the inherent threat posed by women when they enter the public space. Lurking beneath this construction was a very real fear in which '[t]he virginal mother [Mary] who nurtured men could turn into the unfaithful Eve who would deceive and steal from them.'[51]

An example of this dualistic paradigm of womanhood is found in Plate 12, a pro-republican, but anti-Commune, print. Though its material gratification (a cradle stocked with toys) appears guaranteed, 'la France'

12 Anti-Commune caricature: 'On demande une bonne nourrice' (A wetnurse is needed)
Source: McCormick Library of Special Collections, Northwestern University Library.

is not satisfied, and demands maternal attention. Thiers, Napoléon III, and the duc d'Aumale, the Orléanist pretender to the throne, dressed as nursemaids lack the maternal nurturing craved by France. The gaunt and haggard woman in the background, armed with a guillotine, is the most troubling image, though. Similar to the cross-dressing males, the 'Commune' typifies a transgressed gender boundary; unlike the males who are simply attempting a ruse, she has become somewhat desexualized to the point of having lost all trace of female virtue. In contrast, a robust and maternal woman, a model of domesticity, clad in an apron emblazoned with 'république' on the fringe is, alone, capable of providing the requisite moral sustenance.

In the *pétroleuse*, anti-Communard artists reworked the Marianne allegory into a cautionary tale of the fine line separating abstract portrayals of a woman's private virtue from the danger posed by her very real public persona. Gullickson reminds us that, '[t]he pétroleuse was a compelling figure not because she had acted like a man but precisely because she was a woman.'[52] As became apparent from the paucity of criminal convictions, the pétroleuse was a fiction. Even Appert understood the credibility perils of including the pétroleuse amongst his reconstructed images in 'Crimes de la Commune.'[53]

The allegorical image of the pétroleuse, then, was meant to be less a faithful rendering of what occurred during the final week of the Commune than a signifier of the true nature of the Commune's disorder in that unmistakable and quintessential harbinger of disorder: the public woman. The caricatural syntax that identified the Commune in the form of a debased and subverted Marianne left no room for ambiguity. For the Commune's opponents, the Communarde, by virtue of appearing on the Commune's public stage, was no longer simply an abstract allegory; rather, she was a real woman, atavistically indulging her baser instincts and, in the process, reversing the allegorical coin.

In Plate 13, an image that confounds the Commune with the Communarde and appropriates and distorts the Marianne allegory, a brutish, muscular, almost maniacal-looking virago is surrounded by the infamous symbols of disorder and irrational violence of past revolutions. Lacking any trace of conventional femininity and devoid of maternal instincts, she is the woman tranfigured as an abomination, an identifiable beast who devalues all that is worthy in women. As Marianne's alter ego, the figure directly confronts us with the dangerous aspect of woman's essence. However, she also symbolizes the excesses to which revolutions degenerate, and from which her gender is indistinct. Literally enrobed

13 Anti-Commune caricature: 'Republique dont les honnêt gens ne veulent pas'
(The republic that decent people don't want')
Source: McCormick Library of Special Collections, Northwestern University
Library.

in a shroud bearing the names of victims of June 1848, decapitated
heads and discarded legion of honor medals strewn at her feet, a guillotine bearing a standard emblazoned '1793' and a level of equality supported by two skulls to her left, while the *vile multitude* enthusiastically
follows her from the right, she incarnates destruction. The torch held
aloft in her right hand directly references the pétroleuses, while the

expression 'guerre civile' (civil war) billowing out of the smoke from its flame, connects her to the torment France had endured. As the *pétroleuse*, Marianne was corporealized from the abstract ideal of womanhood to a personification of conventional ideas on female irrationality and the scandalized representation of the republic promised by the Commune.

Postscript: Neglect and Resonance

Beginning with Victor Hugo and François Raspail's 1876 introduction of amnesty bills in the Senate and Chamber of Deputies, respectively, until the final amnesty bill was voted on 10 July 1880, the Commune continued to cast a shadow over French parliamentary politics, in general, and to reverberate discordant notes within the republican movement, in particular.[1] With the amnesty issue settled, the moderate-to-conservative republicans (known as 'the Opportunists') who held power in the legislature struggled mightily to relegate the Commune to historical oblivion; any glorification of the Commune threatened to mutate into a recrudescence of the revolutionary tradition the Republic sought to minimize.

Even as they defended political liberty as the bedrock of republicanism, the Opportunists simultaneously limited, orchestrated, and controlled ceremonies, rituals, and meaning within the public space.[2] Cemeteries, in particular, became contested public spaces. The Père-Lachaise cemetery in eastern Paris, the site of one of the Commune's last stands and the final resting spot for many Communards, achieved symbolic importance. Beginning in 1884, a conflict developed between the Parisian municipal council, led by a majority coalition of radicals and socialists, and the Opportunist-led national Government over the latter's refusal to permit the addition of the epitaph, 'Member of the Commune,' to the gravestones of several Communards buried at Père-Lachaise (most notably, Delescluze and Pottier).[3] Under contention was both the commemoration of the Commune and, ironically, its most benign issue – Parisian municipal autonomy. The conflict over epitaphs initiated a series of battles between the Paris Municipal Council and the national Government over every conceivable public function that smacked of the Commune, including Communard funerals, a monu-

183

ment at Père-Lachaise dedicated to the anonymous Communards massacred and thrown into a common grave, and renaming of streets after
Communards.

Within the Third Republic's cosmos, republican cohesion entailed
negotiating between what the imagined nation shared in common and
the divisions it must forget. Education, long held to be a panacea by
republicans of all stripes, assumed a new urgency, with history serving as
the vehicle for molding the republican citizenry and structuring its collective memory. But public education could not be allowed to devolve
into ideological Petri dishes, cultivating different republican traditions.
Reforms instituted by Jules Ferry between 1881–2 situated republican
principles within the ambit of the principles of 1789 – liberalism, critical
inquiry, and moderation. The conditions that rendered revolution an
option in the past no longer existed under a stable republic. The Third
Republic's redefiniton and enlargement of political activity successfully
disoriented the revolutionary left, many of whom abandoned the revolutionary path.[4] Schoolteachers, even those with leftist political orientations, cited national reconciliation, rather than class struggle or violent
revolution as being at the heart of their socialist convictions; rarely, if
ever, did they cite the Commune, or writings favorable to it, as formative
of their political affinities.[5] School textbooks marginalized the
Commune as a historical aberration, the result of a disastrous war, and
an anomalous election in February 1871; the revolutionary issues at the
core of the Commune – class conflict, cultural and ideological divides,
and competing historical memories – were buried under depictions of
disorder, crime, and degeneracy. It is little wonder that today, more
than 130 years later, the Commune is either excised from, or minimized
in, the history curriculum in French schools.

In other countries and through a variety of media, the Commune
found greater resonance. However, for the most part, the Commune's
significance was tied to perceptions of its relationship to communist revolutions in the twentieth century. Despite Lenin's criticisms of the
Commune's practices, the Soviet Union included the Commune in its
revolutionary pantheon, thus creating, in many Western eyes, an inextricable, though erroneous, association between the self-styled communist
state and the Commune. The Soviet Union did its part to cultivate a historic affinity between it and the Commune. At Lenin's death in 1924,
surviving members of the Commune provided a flag that would be dis-
played for many years behind Lenin's tomb in Red Square before being
transferred to the Lenin Museum. Another flag from the Commune

reportedly accompanied the first manned Soviet spaceflight, Voskhod I, in 1964. In 1971, the Soviet Union, as well as the People's Republic of China, and other self-styled communist states, paid official recognition to the Commune at its centenary through the issuance of postage stamps, a commemoration denied it by all Western states, including France.

In the last decades of the nineteenth century, the Commune was more likely to serve as a cautionary tale. In spite of their distance from France and the absence of significant numbers of exiled Communards on their soil, Americans viewed the Commune with a mixture of macabre interest and fright; rare was the American commentator who saw anything positive in the Commune.[6] In large measure, American fears were accentuated by the interchangability with which they employed the terms 'communard' and 'communist,' and the connotations that the latter carried in American discourse.[7] The Commune reached a greater level of immediacy for Americans when a general strike in 1877 by railway workers, dockers, and freight handlers spread from the east to the west coast, causing paroxysms of fear that the Commune had, at long last, reached America.[8]

The Commune has also featured prominently, if only sporadically, in popular culture on both sides of the Atlantic. Three noted international playwrights produced plays about the Commune. Befitting their Marxist sympathies Nordahl Grieg's *Defeat*, Bertolt Brecht's *The Days of the Commune*, and Arthur Adamov's *The Spring of 1871* are polemical and didactic, but not without their artistic merits (particularly so with Adamov's piece which, in its employment of pantomine technique and guignol-like tropes, conveyed the 'theatre of the absurd' style he helped pioneer). All the works are grounded in historical events (though each contains its share of historical inaccuracies), but each play is distinct for the interpretative spin given the Commune by its respective author.[9]

Beginning with Armand Guerra's 13-minute short film in 1914, the Commune has been the subject, or an aspect, of 17 filmic treatments and 18 documentaries,[10] most notably, in the stirring 1929 Soviet agit-prop epic, *The New Babylon*, featuring Dmitri Shoshtakovich's first film score. In 2000, British filmmaker Peter Watkins produced the most ambitious treatment of the Commune. Clocking in at just under six hours, *La Commune de Paris*, a modern-day docudrama that explores the Commune through the lens of modern-day news reportage, features a cast of actors chosen more out of a need for ideological balance than due to acting experience. Watkins intended *La Commune de Paris* to establish a new standard for cinéma vérité; actors were cast as either Versaillais or Communards according to their political convictions and, in the spirit of the times, to engage each other in constant discussion about the event and their perspectives on it.

The film is both a commentary on the state of the news media and on the Commune's continuing relevance to contemporary issues. According to Watkins, 'we are now moving through a very bleak period in human history,' characterized by an education system that neglects humanistic and critical thinking, a society driven by greed, the destruction of the environment through globalization, the exploitation of the poor, and an emphasis on stultifying conformity and standardization.

In such a world as this, what happened in Paris in the spring of 1871 represented (and still represents) the idea of commitment to a struggle for a better world, and of the need for some form of collective social Utopia – which WE now need as desperately as dying people need plasma.

The French arts channel, Arte, originally screened the film between 10:00 p.m. and 4:00 a.m., a decision, Watkins claims, that further marginalized the Commune within French culture.[11]

Though the French school curriculum largely neglects the Commune, French interest in it has recently been revived by the publication of the first three volumes of internationally renowned cartoonist Jacques Tardi's four-volume series of graphic novels based on Jean Vautrin's 1999 book *Le Cri du Peuple*. Echoing Watkins, Vautrin, in the forward to Tardi's first volume, conceives of the Commune as a neglected episode of French history whose utopian vision of fraternity and social harmony remains an inspiration.[12]

The Paris Commune's brevity all but insured that its idealism – expressed in its rhetoric, debates, and discourse – would not be fulfilled. But as the limitations of its actual accomplishments faded in comparison to its real or imagined objectives, the Commune assumed a transcendency beyond the temporality of nineteenth-century class, urbanization, republicanism, and war. Instead, in its defeat it became the quintessential revolutionary experience, supple enough to be construed by its detractors as humanity's descent into the abyss or by its supporters as the expression of its highest ideals.

The Commune was revolutionary theatre resplendent in conflict, violence, heroism, and idealism. It was a polyphonic revolution whose harmoniously blended chords included neo-classicism's emphasis on civic virtue, romanticism's quest for freedom, and social realism's unexpurgated depiction of a brutal world. The resulting sound would be a utopia forged out of a new political culture premised on associations of active citizens. In this respect, the Commune anticipated 1968's Situationist movement and its assault on the stifling and alienating passivity that derives from social, cultural, political, and economic relationships in bourgeois society. In the present era of economic globalization, cultural homogenization, and commodity fetishization, the Commune still resonates via the renewed urgency of the Situationist critique.

In their respective contests of political authority, alterations of Parisian social space, subversions of cultural hierarchies, and in the challenges they posed to meaning, representation, and consciousness in the public space, the French Revolution and the Paris Commune, separated by the better part of a century, were bonded together in the French revolutionary compact. Drawing on France's previous revolutionary experiences, the Communards and their supporters imagined themselves as the heirs to France's rich revolutionary tradition with a mission to complete its unfulfilled promise. They were also revolutionary pioneers, though, existing in very different circumstances, yet still insisting on socialism (through the agency of social republicanism) as a panacea for exploitation, authoritarianism, and hierarchy. The defeat of the Paris Commune marked the final manifestation of the revolutionary republican tradition spawned by the French Revolution. But just as the French Revolution's heroic and epic struggle to regenerate society had resonance with the Communards, so too, succeeding generations constructed the Commune as a historical phenomenon whose ideals, drama, and unrealized ambitions loomed far larger than the immediate issues that engendered it, the specific challenges it confronted, the individuals who led it, and the insurmountable challenges that overwhelmed it.

Notes

Introduction: Revolutionary Antecedents

1. Without going deeply into a concept that has generated considerable debate in both history and semiotics, *mentalité*, broadly speaking, refers to the collective attitudes, practices, and actions of a given social unit. In the nineteenth century, the revolutionary *mentalité* consisted of practices, rhetoric, and symbols that referred to the French Revolution and that became an integral component of French political culture.
2. Cynthia Kudlick, *Cholera in Post-Revolutionary Paris* (Berkeley: University of California Press, 1996).
3. Alain Maillard, *La Communauté des Égaux.* (Paris: Éditions Kimé, 1999).

Chapter 1: The Second Empire

1. Pamela M. Pilbeam, *Republicanism in Nineteenth-Century France, 1814–1871* (Basingstoke: Macmillan Press – now Palgrave Macmillan, 1995), 240.
2. Sudhir Hazareesingh, *From Subject to Citizen: The Second Empire and the Emergence of Modern French Democracy* (Princeton, NJ: Princeton University Press, 1998), 30–1.
3. Robert Tombs, *France, 1814–1914* (Harlow: Addison Wesley Longman, 1996), 395–7.
4. Alain Plessis, *The Rise and Fall of the Second Empire, 1852–1871*, Jonathan Mandelbaum, trans. (Cambridge: Cambridge University Press, 1985), 116.

5. Plessis, 98–102.
6. David Jordan, *Transforming Paris: The Life and Times of Baron Haussmann* (Chicago: University of Chicago Press, 1995), 13–14.
7. Jordan, ch. 12.
8. David H. Pinkney, *Napoleon III and the Rebuilding of Paris* (Princeton, NJ: Princeton University Press, 1958), ch. 4.
9. Jordan, 289.
10. Jordan, 290.
11. Proudhon defies interpretation. At various times, he has been characterized as a communist, a revolutionary, a reactionary nationalist, and a harbinger of fascism. Alan Ritter, *The Political Thought of Pierre-Joseph Proudhon* (Princeton, NJ: Princeton University Press, 1969), 3–10. We are less concerned, in this study, with an accurate understanding of Proudhon's philosophy than with the ideas that attracted his followers in the 1850s and 1860s.
12. Robert L. Hoffman, *Revolutionary Justice: The Social and Political Theory of P.-J. Proudhon* (Urbana, IL: University of Illinois Press, 1972), 284.
13. Hoffman, 291.
14. Hoffman, 242–3.
15. Hoffman, 145–67.
16. Hoffman, 277.
17. William Serman, *La Commune de Paris* (Paris: Fayard, 1986), 49–51.
18. Plessis, 161.
19. Bernard Moss, *The Origins of the French Labor Movement, 1830–1914* (Berkeley: University of California Press, 1980), 52.
20. Quoted in Plessis, 161.
21. Serman, 60.
22. Hazareesingh, 260–5.
23. Samuel Bernstein, *Auguste Blanqui and the Art of Insurrection* (London: Lawrence & Wishart, 1971), 258.
24. Bernstein, 262.
25. Auguste Blanqui, 'Le communisme, avenir de la société (1869–1870),' *Blanqui. Textes Choisis* (Paris: Éditions sociales, 1971), 145–73.
26. Maillard, 166.
27. Dominique Aubry, *Quatre-vingt-treize et les Jacobins. Regards Litteraires du 19e Siècle* (Lyon: Presses Universitaires de Lyon, 1988), 98.
28. Patrick Hutton, *The Cult of the Revolutionary Tradition: The Blanquists in French Politics, 1864–1893* (Berkeley, Los Angeles, and London: University of California Press, 1981), 49–51.

29. Bernstein, 252–3.
30. For a survey of nineteenth-century Jacobinism, see: Aubry, 107–10.
31. Serman, 82–90; Charles Rihs, *La Commune de Paris. Sa Structure et ses Doctrines (1871)* (Geneva: Librairie E. Droz, 1955), 143–55.
32. An example of this occurred at a meeting in the working-class district of Belleville on 17 January 1869 when neo-Hébertists violently clashed with neo-Jacobins. Alain Dalotel and Jean-Claude Freiermuth, 'Socialism and Revolution,' in Adrian Rifkin and Roger Thomas, eds, *Voices of the People: The Politics of 'La Sociale' at the End of the Second Empire* (London: Routledge & Kegan Paul, 1988), 248.
33. Blanqui, 'Coopération et Réaction,' *Blanqui. Textes Choisis*, 193–4.
34. Bernstein, 287–96.
35. Alain Faure, 'The Public Meeting Movement in Paris from 1868 to 1870,' in *Voices of the People*, 188–90.
36. Dalotel and Freiermuth, 239.
37. Dalotel and Freiermuth, 316–17.
38. Dalotel and Freiermuth, 241, 294–5.
39. Dalotel and Freiermuth, 283, 303–15.
40. Pilbeam, 256.
41. Dalotel and Freiermuth, 235–7.
42. Faure, 197.
43. Hazareesingh, 248–9.

Chapter 2: Prelude to the Commune

1. Gustave Lefrançais, *Souvenirs d'un révolutionnaire* (Bordeaux: Éditions de la Tête de Feuilles, 1972), 313.
2. Victor Desplats, *Lettres d'un homme à la femme qu'il aime pendant le siège de Paris et la Commune* (Paris: Éditions Jean-Claude Lattès, 1980), 9.
3. Victorine Brocher, *Souvenirs d'une morte vivante* (Paris: François Maspero, 1977), 99.
4. Sudhir Hazareesingh, *From Subject to Citizen: The Second Empire and the Emergence of Modern French Democracy* (Princeton, NJ: Princeton University Press, 1998), ch. 4.
5. Stewart Edwards, *The Paris Commune 1871* (London: Eyre & Spottiswoode Publishers, 1971), 65.
6. Brocher, 104.
7. Desplats, 37.
8. An aggressive foreign policy, predicated on a somewhat self-right-

eous nationalism, had been one of the ideological leitmotifs of French republicanism.

9. William Serman, *La Commune de Paris* (Paris: Fayard, 1986), 121–2.

10. Bertrand Taithe, *Defeated Flesh: Medicine, Welfare, and Warfare in the Making of Modern France* (Lanham, MD: Rowman & Littlefield Publishers, 1999), 99–106.

11. Martin Phillip Johnson, *The Paradise of Association: Political Culture and Popular Organizations in the Paris Commune of 1871* (Ann Arbor: University of Michigan Press, 1996), 22.

12. Two of the appointed mayors became more popular after having become confrontational with the Government. The candidates elected in the nineteenth and twentieth *arrondissements* were, respectively, Charles Delescluze and Gabriel Ranvier, revolutionary republicans, later elected to the Commune. Taithe, 104.

13. In fact, Marseille has been called the 'capital of the "no" vote'. Jeanne Gaillard, *Communes de Province, Commune de Paris, 1870–1871* (Paris: Flammarion, 1971), 29.

14. Serman, 119.

15. Gaillard, 151.

16. Maurice Moissonnier, '1869-1871, Lyon des insurrections entre tradition et novation' in *La Commune de 1871: Utopie et Modernité?*, ed. Gilbert Larguier and Jérôme Quaretti (Perpignan: Presses Universitaires de Perpignan, 2000), 115.

17. Serman, 127.

18. Moissonnier, 116–117.

19. Maurice Moissonnier, *La Première Internationale et la Commune à Lyon* (Paris: Éditions Sociales, 1972), 287.

20. Moissonnier, *La Première Internationale*, 297.

21. Moissonnier, '1869–1871,' 112–13.

22. Moissonnier, '1869–1871,' 118.

23. Alistair Horne, *The Fall of Paris: The Siege and the Commune, 1870–1871* (New York: St. Martin's Press, 1965), 85.

24. Horne, 144–6; Geneviève D. Sée, *Aujourd'hui Paris, ou les 133 jours du siège 1870–71 par ceux qui les ont vécus* (Versailles: Éditions les Sept Vents, 1988), 194–6.

25. Horne, 84–5, 121–31.

26. The *francs-tireurs* was a guerilla army comprised of individuals who wanted to show their devotion to *la patrie*, but not serve in the regular army. Battalions were characterized by their very individualistic fashion sense and ideological unity. Michael Howard, *The Franco-Prussian War* (London: Methuen, 1979), 249–56.

27. Desplats, 85.
28. Edmond Goncourt, *Paris Under Siege, 1870–1871* (edited and translated by George Becker) (Ithaca, NY, and London: Cornell University Press, 1969), 90.
29. Taithe, 128–9.
30. Howard, 340.
31. Rebecca Spang, '"And they ate the zoo": Relating Gastronomic Exoticism in the Siege of Paris.' *Modern Language Notes*, 107 (1992), 758–60.
32. Desplats, 57.
33. Goncourt, 128.
34. Horne, 128–9.
35. Spang, 758.
36. Towards the end of the siege, when foodstocks were at their lowest, bread comprised of wheat, rice, and straw appeared under the name *pain Ferry*, a reference to Jules Ferry, the appointed mayor of Paris responsible for provisioning the capital. Horne, 180.
37. Melvin Kranzberg, *The Siege of Paris, 1870–1871: A Political and Social History* (Ithaca, NY: Cornell University Press, 1950), 120.
38. Raoul DuBois, *À l'assaut du ciel. La Commune racontée* (Paris: Les Éditions ouvrières, 1991), 54.
39. Kranzberg, 120–1.
40. Edwards. 100. According to Goncourt, 'The salt meat delivered by the government cannot be desalted or eaten.' Goncourt, 158. On 18 December, Desplats wrote that the three-day supply of cooked beef he received was only enough for one meal. Desplats, 128.
41. Henry Labouchere, *Diary of the Besieged Resident in Paris* (New York: Macmillan, 1872), 228–9. Labouchere's account of the siege is full of anecdotal information regarding food, including the prices for various animal meats. Labouchere, 224.
42. Taithe, 115.
43. Kranzberg, 108–9.
44. An excellent description of the various foods available and the efforts by the government and Academies of Science and Medicine to sustain the Parisian population during the siege can be found in Taithe, 106–29.
45. Labouchere also demonstrated gustatory skills in assessing the delectability of different animals. For example, after confessing his shame at eating dog, Labouchere wrote that, '[e]picures in dog-flesh tell me that poodle is by far the best, and recommend me to avoid bull-

dog, which is coarse and tasteless.' He also described *salami de rat* as tasting almost like a cross between rabbit and frog. Labouchere, 242.

46. The bodies of Castor and Pollux, the two 6-year old elephants who were the principal attraction at the Jardin d'acclimatation, sold for 27,000 francs! The trunk and filet sold for 40 francs per pound, while the feet fetched 20 francs.

47. Rupert Christiansen, *Paris Babylon* (London: Penguin Books, 1995), 245. Spang also asserts that eating the zoo animals was strictly a function of 'fantastical cookery': the combination of Paris' gastronomic culture and efforts to relieve the tedium of the siege by indulging in the exotic. Spang's entertaining article is, however, undercut by its focus on the elite, thereby encouraging her somewhat glib approach to the conditions endured by the besieged Parisians.

48. Spang, 772.

49. Taithe, 113.

50. Goncourt, 177–8.

51. Brocher, 117, 122.

52. Kranzberg, 123.

53. Goncourt, 177.

54. Kranzberg, 97–103.

55. Gustave de Molinari, *Les Clubs Rouges Pendant le Siége de Paris* (Paris: Garnier Frères, 1871), 8–9.

56. Desplats, 141.

57. Edwards, 105.

58. Edwards, 112–13; Serman, 164

59. Rougerie, Jacques, *Paris Libre, 1871.* (Paris: Éditions du Seuil, 1971), 82.

60. Brocher, 147.

61. Edwards, 117. Candidates were permitted to stand in multiple electoral districts and, if elected, determine which constituency to represent.

62. Charles Rihs, *La Commune de Paris. Sa Structure et ses doctrines (1871)* (Geneva: Librairie E. Droz, 1973), 19.

63. Rougerie, 91.

64. Rougerie, 96–100. Six 'bourgeois' *arrondissements* (I, II, VII, VIII, IX and XVI) sent no delegates to the Central Committee, while four others sent incomplete delegations.

65. The march of 30,000 German soldiers through the Étoile and down the Champs-Élysées took place on 1 March. For the most part, there were no protests during the march. The Germans remained either

in central or western Paris, not daring to venture into the more hostile popular districts such as Montmartre or Belleville. The only violence appears to have been meted out to individuals who fraternized with the Germans or businesses that served them. Most Parisians appear to have greeted the Germans with silent contempt. In the evening, according to Goncourt, German soldiers felt anxious as they walked in groups of four in the 'dead city.' Two days later, the Germans began their departure from Paris. Goncourt, 222–4; Horne, 261–4.
66. Dubois, 74.
67. Desplats, 191–2.
68. On the other hand, according to Robert Tombs, the efforts to confiscate the cannons were 'less evidence of a desire to provoke civil conflict than of a desparate attempt to avert it.' Robert Tombs, *The War Against Paris, 1871* (Cambridge: Cambridge University Press, 1981), 51.
69. Edwards, 138.
70. Rougerie, 102.
71. Goncourt, 229.

Chapter 3: The Commune

1. Victorine Brocher, *Victorine B . . . Souvenirs d'une morte vivante* (Paris: François Maspero, 1977), 161.
2. Jacques Rougerie, *Paris Libre 1871* (Paris: Éditions du Seuil, 1971) 109.
3. Gustave Lefrançais, *Souvenirs d'un révoluionnaire* (Paris: Futur Antérieur, 1972), 366.
4. To some, Lullier singularly gave Versailles its most significant victory. Lefrançais, 383. However, Lullier's apparent service to Versailles did not spare him the wrath of the Versaillais. Arrested during the repression, his original death sentence was commuted to life imprisonment. Exiled on New Caledonia, he informed on an escape attempt by some of his fellow inmates.
5. Stewwart Edwards, *The Paris Commune, 1871* (Newton Abbot: Readers Union, 1971), 154.
6. Edith Thomas, *Louise Michel* (Montreal: Black Rose Books, 1980), 79.
7. Moreau was a gifted writer and lawyer. When war with Prussia broke

out he was living in London; returning to Paris, he joined the National Guard and distinguished himself at Buzenval.

8. Rougerie, 113.

9. Lefrançais, 367.

10. Edwards, 166.

11. A.M. Blanchecotte, *Tablettes d'une femme pendant la Commune* (Charente: Idéographies, 1996), 26.

12. Edwards, 167.

13. For example, in a letter dated 24 March, Desplats wrote that 'it is necessary that the 40,000 men at Versailles resolutely march on Paris .... France is expiring under the thumb of these shameless bandits who, unbelievably, have just named Garibaldi as commander of their army. This is ignoble and a thousand times more humiliating than the Prussian occupation.' Victor Desplats, *Lettres d'un homme à la femme qu'il aime pendant le siège de Paris et al Commune*, correspondence présentée par Pierre Lary (Paris: Éditions Jeane-Claude Lattès, 1980), 199 (translations mine).

14. Georges Soria, *Grande Histoire de la Commune* (vol. II), (Paris: Club Livre Diderot, 1971), 142.

15. Reprinted in *Journal Officiel de la Commune*, 27 March 1871.

16. After a couple of postponements, a second round of elections was held on 16 April to fill the seats of those who had been victorious in more than one *arrondissement*, those who refused their mandate for ideological reasons, and those who, previously elected to the National Assembly, chose to sit in that body.

17. Blanqui, however, was captured at Figeac (Lot) on 17 March and imprisoned for the duration of the Commune. Nonetheless, he was elected in the eighteenth and twentieth *arrondissements*.

18. See also Rihs, the most notable of the studies to have explored the ideological divide on the Commune. Rihs concluded that, after the supplemental elections in April, 12 Communards were Blanquists, 40 were Jacobins, and over 30 were Socialists (though only one, Léo Frankel, was a Marxist). In 1973 Rihs produced a new edition of his classic work which, while accounting for publications produced in the interim 18 years, did not alter his original thesis. Charles Rihs, *La Commune de Paris. Sa Structure et ses doctrines (1871)* (Geneva: Libraire E. Droz, 1973).

19. Edwards, 185–6.

20. Edwards, 188.

21. Lefrançais, 373–4.

22. *Le Cri du Peuple*, 29 March 1871.
23. Edmond Goncourt, *Paris Under Seige, 1870–1871* (edited and translated by George Becker) (Ithaca, NY, and London: Cornell University Press, 1969), 236.
24. William Serman, *La Commune de Paris* (Paris: Fayard, 1986), 265.
25. *Journal Officiel de la Commune*, 30 March 1871.
26. Louis M. Greenberg, *Sisters of Liberty: Marseille, Lyon, Paris and the Reaction to a Centralized State, 1868–1871* (Cambridge: Harvard University Press, 1971), 4.
27. Jeanne Gaillard, *Communes de Province, Commune de Paris 1870–1871* (Paris: Flammarion, 1971), 69.
28. Ronald Aminzade, *Ballots and Barricades: Class Formation and Republican Politics in France, 1830–1871* (Princeton, NJ: Princeton University Press, 1993), 215–16.
29. Raymond Huard, 'Un Échec du Mouvement Communaliste Provincial: Le Cas de Nîmes,' in *La Commune de 1871: Utopie et Modernité?*, ed. Gilbert Larguier and Jérôme Quaretti (Perpignan: Presses Universitaires de Perpignan, 2000), 122.
30. For Lyon, see: Maurice Moissonnier, *La Première Internationale et la Commune à Lyon* (Paris: Editions Sociales, 1972); Marseille: Roger Vignaud, *Gaston Crémieux. La Commune de Marseille un rêve inachevé . . .* (Aix-en-Provence: Edisud, 2003); Antoine Olivesi, *La Commune de 1871 à Marseille et ses origines* (Paris: Marcel Rivière, 1950); Saint-Etienne and Toulouse: Aminzade; Narbonne: Marc César, *La Commune de Narbonne (mars 1871)* (Perpignan: Presses Universitaires de Perpignan, 1996); Limoges: John M. Merriman, *The Red City: Limoges and the French Nineteenth Century* (Oxford and New York: Oxford University Press, 1985). In addition, see the collection of articles on the provincial communes in *La Commune de 1871: Utopie et Modernité?*, eds Larguier and Quaretti.
31. Aminzade, 228–9; Gaillard, 150.
32. Gaillard, 154.
33. Serman, 432.
34. Gaillard, 146.
35. Desplats, 203.
36. Prosper Lissagaray, *History of the Paris Commune* (reprinted by New Park Publications, London, 1976), 133–4.
37. Goncourt, 239–40.
38. Lefrançais, 382.
39. Bernard Noël, *Dictionnaire de la Commune* (Paris: Champs

Flammarion, 1978), 288–90; Edwards, 199.

40. Edwards, 342.

41. Vignaud, 176. In fact, after having taken control of Marseille, Espivent led his troops through a triumphal march shouting, '"Vive Jesus! Vive the Sacred Heart!"'

42. Robert Tombs, *The War Against Paris, 1871* (Cambridge: Cambridge University Press, 1981), 111.

43. Brocher, 188.

44. Tombs, 90.

45. Émile Maury, *Mes souvenirs sur les événements des années 1870–1871* (Paris: La Boutique de l'Histoire éditions, 1999), 56.

46. Lissagaray, 243.

47. Serman, 480.

48. Edwards, 201.

49. For example, Serman notes that two-thirds of the 200,000 rifles and 50,000 revolvers distributed to the National Guard were never fired. Serman, 475.

50. Serman, 470–1.

51. Quoted in Serman, 441.

52. Philip Nord, 'The Party of Conciliation and the Paris Commune,' *French Historical Studies*, vol. 15, no. 1 (Spring, 1987), 1–35.

53. Serman, 446.

54. Serman, 451–6.

55. Nord, 28.

56. Maury, 62.

57. Lefrançais, 405.

58. Edwards, 243–4.

59. Georges Bourgin and Gabriel Henriot, eds, *Procès – Verbeaux de la Commune de 1871*, 2 vols (Paris: Imprimerie A. Lahure, 1945), vol. I, 507–8.

60. Bourgin and Henriot, vol. II, 359–60.

61. Jean Dubois, *Le vocabulaire politique et social en France de 1869 à 1872. À travers les oeuvres des écrivains, les revues et les journeaux* (Paris: Larousse, 1962), 295.

62. Bourgin and Henriot (eds), vol. II, 470–523.

63. Victor Debuchy, *La Vie à Paris sous la Commune* (Paris: Éditions Christian, 2001), 189.

64. *Paris Under Siege. A journal of the events of 1870–1871 kept by contemporaries and translated and presented by Joanna Richardson* (London: The Folio Society, 1982), 179–80.

65. Goncourt, 294.
66. Desplats, 215.
67. Dubois, 143.
68. Stewart Edwards, ed., *The Communards of Paris, 1871.* (London: Thames and Hudson, 1973), 162–3.
69. Serman, 463.
70. An army of provincials, battling Paris, also conjured up images of the Revolution when provincial rebels, known as Chouans, became the principal source of counter-revolution. Robert Tombs, 'Paris and the Rural Hordes: An Exploration of Myth and Reality in the French Civil War of 1871,' *The Historical Journal,* vol. 29, no. 4 (Dec., 1986), 795–808.
71. Tombs, 805–8.
72. Dubois, 143–4.
73. Serman, 498.
74. Edwards, 313–14.
75. Serman, 494.
76. Lissagaray, 270.
77. Edwards, 337.
78. Tombs, 78–9.
79. Lissagaray, 152.
80. Professional hostilities surfaced over Chaudey's arrest. Acting in the capacity of special commissioner of the Commune, caricaturist Georges Pilotell ordered Chaudey's arrest. Artist Gustave Courbet, who resented Pilotell's opportunistic pursuit of authority, condemned Pilotell's actions and demanded his dismissal. Bertrand Tillier, *La Commune de Paris. Révolution sans Images?* (Seyssel: Champ Vallon, 2004), 126.
81. Edwards, 330.
82. Serman, 516–17.
83. Quoted in Edwards, 343.
84. Tombs, 178–9.
85. Tombs, 165.
86. Tombs, 173–5; 183–5. According to Tombs, although he had a reputation for both honesty and stupidity, 'MacMahon must have been broadly aware of the events. He received reports and visited areas where mass executions were regularly carried out. The sound of shooting could be heard over long distances.'
87. Tombs, 172–3.
88. Edwards, 344.

89. Bertrand Taithe, *Citizenship and Wars* (London and New York: Routledge, 2001), 124–43.

90. George L. Mosse, *Fallen Soldiers: Reshaping the Memory of the World Wars* (New York and Oxford: Oxford University Press, 1990), 159.

91. Taithe, 138–9; Tombs, 109–23.

92. Robert Tombs, 'Reflexions sur la semaine sanglante,' in *La Commune de 1871. L'événement, les hommes et la mémoire* (Saint-Etienee: Publications de l'Université de Saint-Etienne, 2004), 237–45. Though the Versaillais soldiers might have been stirred by emotions, Tombs largely exculpates them from responsibility for the carnage, characterizing them as having become 'amoral and more or less passive instruments of a structure of authority that appears to them wise, powerful, and legitimate.'

93. Serman, 463.

94. For Algeria, see Jacques Frémeaux, *La France et l'Algérie en guerre: 1830–1870, 1954–1962* (Paris: Économica, 2002), ch. 7. For Mexico, see Jean-François Lecaillon, *Napoléon III et le Méxique. Les illusions d'un grand dessein* (Paris: Éditions l'Harmattan, 1994), 171–5. Durieu, a Commandant of the Volunteers of the Seine, a unit that carried out some of the most vicious atrocities against Communards, had been a veteran of the anti-guerilla forces in Mexico, noted for their use of torture. Tombs, 'Reflexions', 167.

95. Patricia M. E. Lorcin, *Imperial Identities: Stereotyping, Prejudice and Race in Colonial Algeria* (London and New York: I. B. Tauris Publishers, 1995), 96.

96. In fact, Tombs cites an example whereby, after the body of an apparently executed Versaillais soldier was found, the Communards were characterized as 'worthy imitators of the savages of Lake Chad.' Tombs, 'Reflexions' 120.

97. Serman, 518–20.

98. Lissagaray, 308–9.

99. Rougerie, 257.

100. *Paris Under Siege*, 189.

101. W. Pembroke Fetridge, *The Rise and Fall of the Paris Commune in 1871* (New York: Harper and Brothers Publishers, 1871), 341, 379.

102. Lissagaray, 314–22. Gay Gullickson, *The Unruly Women of Paris* (Ithaca, NY, and London: Cornell University Press, 1996), 192–5.

103. Vignaud, 239. Espivent is described as 'one of the most fervent antisemites of the marseillais bourgeois reaction. He personally insisted that Gaston Crémieux benefit from no particular favors.'

104. Robert Aldrich, *Greater France: A History of French Overseas Expansion* (Basingstoke and New York: Palgrave – now Palgrave Macmillan, 1996), 71.

105. Alice Bullard, *Exile to Paradise: Savagery and Civilization in Paris and the South Pacific, 1790–1800* (Stanford, CA: Stanford University Press, 2000).

106. Bullard, 200–9.

107. On general questions regarding the communards in exile, see Marc Vuilleumier, 'L'exil des communeux,' in *La Commune de 1871. L'événement . . .* , 265–88.

108. Renaud Morieux, 'Le prison de l'exil. Les réfugiés de la Commune entre les polices françaises et anglaises (1871–1880),' in *Police et migrants. France 1667–1939* (Rennes: Presses Universitaires Rennes, 2001), 133–50.

109. Serman, 535–7.

110. Bourgin, 422–3.

111. Jérôme Grévy, *La République des opportunistes, 1870–1885* (Paris: Perrin, 1998), 27.

112. Maxime du Camp, *Les Convulsions du Paris*, 4 vols (Paris: Librairie Hachette et Cie, 1878–1880).

113. Patrick Hutton, *The Cult of the Revolutionary Tradition: The Blanquists in French Politics, 1864–1893* (Berkeley, Los Angeles, CA, and London: University of California Press, 1981), 23, 114.

Chapter 4: A Socialist Revolution?

1. Jacques Rougerie, 'La Commune: utopie, modernité?,' in *La Commune de 1871: Utopie ou Modernité?* (Perpignan: Presses Universitaires de Perpignan, 2000), 23–4.

2. Karl Marx, 'The Civil War in France,' in *Karl Marx and Friedrich Engels on the Paris Commune* (Moscow: Progress Publishers, 1971), 75.

3. 'The great social measure of the Commune was its own working existence. Its special measures could but betoken the tendency of a government of the people by the people.' Marx, 80.

4. '[T]his was merely the rising of a city under exceptional circumstances, the majority of the Commune was in no wise socialist, nor could it be.' Marx, 293.

5. Benoît Malon, *La Troisième Défaite du Prolétariat Français* (Neuchâtel: G. Guillaume Fils, 1871).

6. Prosper Lissagaray, *History of the Paris Commune*, Eleanor Marx, trans. (London: New Park Publications, 1976).

7. E.g., Frank Jellinek, *The Paris Commune of 1871* (London: Victor Gollancz, 1937), 418–19. While Jellinek saw the Commune as riven by conflicting revolutionary theories, he felt that it was 'compelled, by force of circumstances, even more than by inclination, to adopt many of the forms of the proletarian dictatorship.'

8. Maxime du Camp, *Les Convulsions de Paris*, 4 vols, (Paris: Hachette, 1877–1880).

9. Edward S. Mason, *The Paris Commune: An Episode in the History of the Socialist Movement*, reprint (New York: Howard Fertig, 1967), 370.

10. Louis M. Greenberg, *Sisters of Liberty: Marseille, Lyon, Paris and the Reaction to the Centralized State, 1868–1871* (Cambridge, MA: Harvard University Press, 1971), 6, 341.

11. William Serman, *La Commune de Paris* (Paris: Fayard, 1986), 571.

12. Jacques Rougerie, *Paris libre, 1871* (Paris: Éditions du Seuil, 1971), 234.

13. Robert Tombs, 'Prudent Rebels: the 2nd *arrondissement* during the Paris Commune of 1871,' *French History*, vol. 5, no. 4 (1991), 393–413, 411.

14. Philip Nord, 'The Party of Conciliation and the Paris Commune,' *French Historical Studies*, vol. 15, no. 1 (Spring, 1987), 33.

15. Jacques Rougerie, 'Autour de quelques livre étrangers. Réflexions sur la citoyenneté populaire en 1871,' in *La Commune de 1871. L'événement, les hommes et la mémoire* (Saint-Étienne: Publications de l'Université de Saint-Étienne, 2004), 231. Rougerie directed his critique at the works of Martin Phillip Johnson and Roger Gould, both of which will be discussed below.

16. Rougerie, *Paris libre, 1871*, 215–48.

17. Jacques Rougerie, *Procès des Communards* (Paris: Gallimard Julliard, 1971), 238.

18. David Harvey, 'Paris, 1850-1870,' in *Consciousness and the Urban Experience* (Baltimore, MD: Johns Hopkins University Press, 1985), 165–8.

19. Harvey, 'Paris,' 183–7.

20. Harvey, 'Paris,' 206–20.

21. Roger V. Gould, *Insurgent Identities: Class, Community, and Protest in Paris from 1848 to the Commune* (Chicago: University of Chicago Press, 1995), 105, 119.

22. Gould, 165–71.

23. Gould, 175.
24. David Harvey, *Paris, Capital of Modernity* (New York and London: Routledge, 2003).
25. Harvey, *Paris, Capital of Modernity*, 242.
26. Rougerie, 'Autour de quelques livres . . . ', 226–36.
27. Jerrold Seigel, *Bohemian Paris: Culture, Politics, and the Boundaries of Bourgeois Life, 1830-1930* (New York: Viking, 1986).
28. Seigel, 212.
29. Kristin Ross, *The Emergence of Social Space: Rimbaud and the Paris Commune* (Minneapolis: University of Minnesota Press, 1988), 41.
30. Ross, 61 (emphasis original).
31. Edith Thomas, *Louise Michel*, Penelope Williams, trans. (Montreal: Black Rose Books, 1980), 63.
32. Mason, 18.
33. Charles Delescluze, 'Le Droit d'Association devant la Justice,' *Le Réveil*, 9 July 1868, no. 2.
34. Charles Delescluze, 'Libéraux et Radicaux,' *Le Réveil*, 6 August 1868, no. 6.
35. Ernest Hamel, 'La Question Sociale,' *Le Réveil*, 13 August 1868, no. 7; A. Morel, 'Transaction,' *Le Réveil*, 1 February 1870, 2nd series, no. 250.
36. Bertrand Taithe, *Citizenship and Wars: France in Turmoil, 1870-1* (London: Routledge, 2001), 165.
37. Robert Wolfe, *The Origins of the Paris Commune: The Popular Organizations of 1868-1871* (Ph.D. diss., Harvard University, 1968); Alain Dalotel, Alain Faure and Jean-Claude Freiermuth, *Aux Origines de la Commune: Le mouvement des réunions publiques à Paris, 1868–1870* (Paris: François Maspero, 1980).
38. It has also been suggested that Parisian cafés not only served a social function, but also contributed to the politicization of its habitués and also contributed to working class political culture. W. Scott Haine, *The World of the Paris Café: Sociability Among the French Working Class, 1789-1914* (Baltimore, MD, and London: Johns Hopkins University Press, 1998).
39. Martin Phillip Johnson, *The Paradise of Association: Political Culture and Popular Organizations in the Paris Commune of 1871* (Ann Arbor: The University of Michigan Press, 1996), 133.
40. Johnson, 4–5.
41. Johnson, 141–2.
42. Serman, 280.

43. Serman, 276–7.
44. Stewart Edwards, (ed.), *The Communards of Paris, 1871* (London: Thames & Hudson, 1973) 212.
45. Quoted in V. Daline, *Hommes et Idées* (Moscow: Éditions du Progès, 1983), 152.
46. Prosper Lissagaray, *History of the Paris Commune*, Eleanor Marx, trans. (London: New Park Publications, 1976), 165–7. Lissagaray wrote that after the early sorties against Versailles resulted in defeats, Pyat, hoping to save his life, vacillated between violent rhetoric at the Commune and expressions of conciliation in his newspaper.
47. Edwards, 214.
48. André Decouflé, *La Commune de Paris (1871). Révolution Populaire et Pouvoir Révolutionnaire* (Paris: Éditions Cujas, 1969).
49. Sudhir Hazareesingh, *From Subject to Citizen: The Second Empire and the Emergence of Modern French Democracy* (Princeton, NJ: Princeton University Press, 1998), 69.
50. 'Déclaration au Peuple Français,' *Journal Officiel de la Commune*, 20 April 1871.
51. Rougerie, *Paris Libre*, 150.
52. Alain Dalotel and Jean-Claude Freiermuth, 'Socialism and Revolution,' in *Voices of the People: The Politics of 'La Sociale' at the End of the Second Empire* (London: Routledge & Kegan Paul, 1988), 263–5.
53. Patrick Hutton, *The Cult of the Revolutionary Tradition: The Blanquists in French Politics, 1864-1893* (Berkeley: University of California Press, 1981), 48–52.
54. Hutton, 81–4.
55. Serman, 393–4.
56. Johnson, 159–60.
57. Victor Debuchy, *La Vie à Paris sous la Commune* (Paris: Éditions Christian, 2001), 125–34; Edwards, 283–7.
58. Jacqueline Lalloutte, *La libre pensée en France, 1848–1940* (Paris: Albin Michel, 1997), 30–40.
59. Bernard Noël, *Dictionnaire de la Commune* (Paris: Champs Flammarion, 1978), vol. I, 243.
60. Mona Ozouf, *L'École, l'Église et la République, 1871–1914* (Paris: Éditions Cana, 1982), 30.
61. *Journal Officiel de la Commune*, 12 May 1871.
62. Lissagaray, 373–6.
63. Serman, 354–5.
64. René Bidouze, *72 Jours Qui Changèrent la Cité. La Commune de Paris*

dans l'histoire des services publics (Paris: Le Temps des Cerises, 2001), 122.

65. Bidouze, 122–4.
66. Taithe, 130–46.
67. Geneviève Bréton, *'In the Solitude of My Soul.' The Diary of Geneviève Bréton, 1867–1871*, James Palmes, trans. (Carbondale: Southern Illinois University Press, 1994), 191–2.
68. Victor Desplats, *Lettres d'un homme à la femme qu'il aime pendant le siège de Paris et la Commune* (Paris: Éditions Jean-Claude Lattés, 1980), 211.
69. Quoted in Alain Dalotel, 'Maintiens de l'ordre public à Paris et polices en 1870–1871,' in *Maintiens de l'ordre et Polices en France et en Europe au XIXe siècle* (Paris: Créaphis, 1987).
70. Serman, 398. In fact, Serman notes that, during the two months, the police jailed more than 3500 lawbreakers.
71. Edwards, 250–1.
72. There has been some speculation that the Versaillais actively facilitated Beslay's escape to Switzerland. On the other hand, the Third Council of War condemned Jourde to deportation to New Caledonia.
73. Serman, 349–50.
74. Lefrançais, 392.
75. Lefrançais, 448.
76. *Journal Officiel de la Commune*, 30 March 1871.
77. Rougerie, *Paris Libre*, 168.
78. Arthur Arnould, *Histoire Populaire et Parlementaire de la Commune de Paris*, reprint (Lyon: Jacques-Marie Laffont, 1981), 161.
79. *Journal Officiel de la Commune*, 1 May 1871.
80. Bidouze, 134–5.
81. Georges Bourgin and Gabriel Henriot, *Procès-Verbaux de la Commune de 1871* (Paris: Éditions Ernest Leroux, 1924), vol. I, 81–82, 94. The Communards also considered a proposal by Fränkel to remunerate elected Communards at the daily rate of 10 francs and 5 francs extra for their attendance at sessions.
82. Edwards, 207. Industrial wages fluctuated wildly according to region and industry. For example, in 1870, a male textile worker in Mulhouse earned an average daily wage of 22 francs while his foreman received 52.50 francs per day.
83. Arnould, 168. In fact, according to official sources, functionaries' salaries under the Second Empire ranged from 20,000 to more than 50,000 francs per year. Bidouze, 139.

84. Rougerie, 166.
85. Serman, 337.
86. Bourgin and Henriot, vol. II, 34.
87. *Journal Officiel de la Commune*, 4 May 1871.
88. *Journal Officiel de la Commune*, 4 May 1871.
89. Bourgin and Henriot, vol. II, 34.
90. Serman, 343–4.
91. Serman, 278–9.

Chapter 5: Women and the Commune

1. Claire Goldberg Moses, *French Feminism in the Nineteenth Century* (Albany: State University of New York Press, 1984), 133.
2. Moses, 144–5.
3. Robert L. Hoffman, *Revolutionary Justice: The Social and Political Theory of P.-J. Proudhon* (Urbana: University of Illinois Press, 1972), 250–2.
4. Moses, 155–6.
5. David A. Shafer, '*Plus que des ambulancières*: women in articulation and defence of their ideals during the Commune (1871),' *French History*, vol. 7, no. 1 (1993), 88.
6. Alain Dalotel, *Paule Minck, communarde et féministe, 1839–1901* (Paris: Éditions Syros, 1981), 14.
7. Varlin's perspective did represent a minority viewpoint. When prostitutes offered their services as *ambulancières*, the Commune rejected them, claiming that 'the wounded must be tended by pure hands.' Louise Michel defended the women as victims of capitalist rapaciousness during the Empire and signed them on to the Eighteenth *Arrondissement* Vigilance Committee. Edith Thomas, *Louise Michel*, Penelope Williams, trans. (Montreal: Black Rose Books, 1980), 89.
8. Paule Lejeune, *Eugène Varlin. Pratique militante et écrits d'un ouvrier communard* (Paris: François Maspero, 1977), 25.
9. Edith Thomas, *The Women Incendiaries*, James and Starr Atkinson, trans. (New York: George Braziller, 1966), 40.
10. Louise Michel, *Mémoires de Louise Michel écrits par elle-même*, reprint (Paris: François Maspero, 1977), 121–2.
11. Eugene Schulkind, 'Socialist Women during the 1871 Paris Commune,' *Past and Present*, 106 (1985), 135.
12. Thomas, *Louise Michel*, 96.
13. Thomas, *Louise Michel*, 33.

14. Thomas, *Louise Michel*, 54–7.
15. Thomas, *Louise Michel*, 83–4.
16. According to George Clemenceau's recollection of her at Issy, 'In order not to be killed herself, she killed others . . . I have never seen her to be more calm. How she escaped being killed a hundred times over before my very eyes, I'll never know. And I only watched her for an hour . . . .' Thomas, *Louise Michel*, 87.
17. Thomas, *Louise Michel*, 91.
18. Alice Bullard, *Exile to Paradise.* (Stanford, CA: Stanford University Press, 2000), 274–6.
19. Thomas, *The Women Incendiaries*, 79.
20. Woodford McClellan, *Revolutionary Exiles: The Russians in the First International and the Paris Commune* (London: Frank Cass, 1979), 156–7.
21. McClellan, 242. Upon her return to Russia, Dmitrieff remarried, but her husband was soon convicted of heading a gang of gambling swindlers. Dmitrieff joined him in exile in Siberia before returning to her ancestral village in northwest Russia.
22. Stewart Edwards, *The Paris Commune, 1871* ((London: Eyre & Spottiswoode Publishers, 1971), 271–2.
23. A jury in each *arrondissement*, presided over by a member of the Commune from that district, would make a determination that the claimant was not a prostitute, but a woman who 'truly and honestly lived with the man she had chosen.' Arthur Arnould, *Histoire Populaire et Parlementaire de la Commune de Paris* (Lyon: Éditions Jacques-Marie Laffont et Associés, 1981), 165.
24. Thomas, *The Women Incendiaries*, 80.
25. Thomas, *The Women Incendiaries*, 83.
26. William Serman, *La Commune de Paris* (Paris: Fayard, 1986), 370.
27. Thomas, *The Women Incendiaries*, 114–115.
28. Bernard Noël, 'Crèche,' in *Dictionnaire de la Commune*, 2 vols (Paris: Champs Flammarion, 1978), vol. I, 179–80.
29. Alain Corbin, *Women for Hire: Prostitution and Sexuality in France after 1850*, Alan Sheridan, trans. (Cambridge, MA, and London: Harvard University Press, 1990), 21.
30. The mayors of the eleventh and fourteenth *arrondissements*, on 10 and 18 May, respectively, authorized the police in their districts to arrest any women 'exercising their shameful profession on the public thoroughfares.' On 18 May, the mayor of the second *arrondissement* ordered the closure of all bordellos in his district.

Noël, 'Prostitution,' in *Dictionnaire* , vol. II, 179.

31. Bertrand Taithe, *Defeated Flesh: Medicine, Welfare, and Warfare in the Making of Modern France* (Lanham, MD: Rowman & Littlefield Publishers, 1999) 227–9.

32. Moses, 193; Martin Phillip Johnson, *The Paradise of Association: Political Culture and Popular Organizations in the Paris Commune of 1871* (Ann Arbor: University of Michigan Press, 1996), 270.

33. Johnson, ch. 7; Darline Gay Levy and Harriet B. Applewhite, 'Women and Militant Citizenship in Revolutionary Paris,' in *Rebel Daughters: Women and the French Revolution* (New York and Oxford: Oxford University Press, 1992).

34. Johnson, 244–5.

35. Johnson, 250.

36. Johnson, 253.

37. Johnson, 240–1.

38. Gay L. Gullickson, *The Unruly Women of Paris* (Ithaca, NY, and London: Cornell University Press, 1996), 4.

39. Gullickson, 77–9.

40. Shafer, 85; Moses, 117–31.

41. Gullickson described the first violent incident on 18 March when a Captain Saint-James ordered his troops to charge a crowd at Place Pigalle. His troops refused, but Saint-James went ahead, whereupon the National Guard shot him and his horse. His dead horse was subsequently butchered and the meat taken by some of the assembled. Whereas more dispassionate accounts of the event attributed it to men and women still suffering the privations of the siege, conservative writers ascribed it exclusively to women, characterizing it as 'the return to a "primitive brutality"' and a harbinger of things to come under the Commune. Gullickson, 45–8.

42. Thomas, 155.

43. Noël, 'Incéndies,' in *Dictionnaire*, vol. II, 16–17.

44. Thomas, 166–7.

45. Thomas, 170.

46. While it never officially sanctioned 'free union marriages,' the Commune approved of pensions to the domestic partners of National Guardsmen killed in combat.

47. Charles Bernheimer, *Figures of Ill Repute: Representing Prostitution in Nineteenth Century France* (Cambridge, MA: Harvard University Press, 1989), 209. Though the Commune did not deregulate prostitution, this did not prevent its opponents from attributing to it the encour-

agement of a spirit of libertinism and sexual license. According to Alain Corbin, the Commune's 'antiregulationism was accompanied in principle by an attempted prohibition on the part of municipal authorities and an increase in libertarianism in reality.' Corbin, 21.

48. Quoted in Thomas, *The Women Incendiaries*, 178.
49. Gullickson, 208–9.
50. Gullickson, 85.
51. Bernheimer, 210–11.

Chapter 6: Revolution, Culture, and the Commune

1. Warren Roberts, *Jacques Louis David, Revolutionary Artist* (Chapel Hill: University of North Carolina Press, 1989), 18.
2. Quoted in Thomas Crow, *Painters and the Public Life in Eighteenth-Century Paris* (New Haven, CT: Yale University Press, 1985), 227–228.
3. Philippe Bordes, 'L'Art et le Politique,' in *Aux Armes et Aux Arts!* (Paris: Éditions Adam Brio, 1988), 103–35.
4. Emmet Kennedy, *A Cultural History of the French Revolution* (New Haven, CT: Yale University Press, 1989), 237.
5. Gonzalo J. Sánchez, *Organizing Independence: The Artists Federation of the Paris Commune and Its Legacy, 1871–1889* (Lincoln: University of Nebraska Press, 1997), 21.
6. T. J. Clark, *Image of the People: Gustave Courbet and the 1848 Revolution* (London: Thames & Hudson, 1982). Clark points to confusion over whether those depicted in the work are peasants or bourgeois.
7. Sánchez, 42–4.
8. This included the commercialized and industrialized decorative arts. At the time of the Commune, the sharp distinctions between creative and commercial artistic works had yet to become an indelible line of demarcation. Sánchez, 64–6.
9. Sánchez, 48–50.
10. Sánchez, 55–8.
11. Matt Matsuda, *The Memory of the Modern* (New York and Oxford: Oxford University Press, 1996), 33–4.
12. Sánchez, 133–48.
13. Georges Bourgin and Gabriel Henriot, eds., *Procès-Verbaux de la Commune de 1871*, 2 vols (Paris: Éditions Ernest Leroux, 1924), vol. II, 413.
14. Bourgin and Henriot, vol. II, 425–30.

15. *Journal Officiel de la Commune*, 10 April 1871; William Serman, *La Commune de Paris* (Paris: Fayard, 1986), 308–9.

16. André Decouflé, *La Commune de Paris (1871). Révolution Populaire et Pouvoir Révolutionnaire* (Paris: Éditions Cujas, 1969), 58–9.

17. Stewart Edwards, *The Paris Commune, 1871* (Newton Abbot: Readers Union, 1971), 300–1.

18. Matt K. Matsuda, *Memory of the Modern* (New York and Oxford: Oxford University Press, 1996), 21.

19. Edwards, 301.

20. Bourgin and Henriot, vol. I, 190.

21. Bourgin and Henriot, vol. I, 522–3.

22. Goncourt, 289.

23. Maxime Vuillaume, *Mes Cahiers Rouges au Temps de la Commune* (Paris: Babel, 1998), 297.

24. Bourgin and Henriot, vol. II, 360.

25. Matsuda, 30.

26. Georges Bourgin, *La Guerre de 1870–1871 et la Commune* (Paris: Les Éditions Nationales, 1939), 288.

27. David Harvey, 'Monument and Myth: The Building of the Basilica of the Sacred Heart,' in *Consciousness and the Urban Experience: Studies in the History and Theory of Capitalist Urbanization*, David Harvey ed. (Baltimore, MD: The Johns Hopkins University Press, 1985), 221–49. Harvey extends his discussion of the selection of Montmartre to the tension between clerical and political justifications for the basilica, and the historical evolution of the project.

28. Bertrand Tillier, *La Commune de Paris. Révolution sans Image? Politique et Représentations dans la France Républicaine (1871–1914)* (Seyssel: Champ Vallon, 2004).

29. While the 1871 law was modified over the years, efforts at repressing the anarchist movement included the interdiction of anything associated with its encouragement; this included images of the Commune. Tillier also noted that, after the repression, Courbet, an elected member of the Commune and Manet, sometimes critical of, sometimes sympathetic to the Commune, concealed their political affinities in works largely confined to their studios. Tillier, 247–65; 278–90.

30. Jeannene M. Przyblyski, 'Moving Pictures: Photography, Narrative, and the Paris Commune of 1871,' in *Cinema and the Invention of Modern Life*, ed. Leo Charney and Vanessa R. Schwartz (Berkeley and Los Angeles: University of California Press, 1995), 253–78.

31. Przyblyski, 273.
32. Przyblyski, 270.
33. On the Franco-Prussian War, the most incisive analysis is found in Hollis Clayson, *Paris in Despair: Art and Everyday Life under Siege (1870–71)* (Chicago: University of Chicago Press, 2002). John Milner, *Art, War and Revolution in France 1870–1871: Myth, Reportage and Reality* (New Haven, CT, and London: Yale University Press, 2000) is less interpretative and more descriptive of art as a narrative medium of events. On the Commune, Albert Boime, *Art and the French Commune: Imagining Paris after War and Revolution* (Princeton, NJ: Princeton University Press, 1995) is a provocative study of the psychodynamic impact of the Commune on the work of Impressionist artists. Philip Nord, *Impressionists and Politics: Art and Democracy in the Nineteenth Century* (London and New York: Routledge, 2000) examines the republican convictions of Impressionist artists and how they weathered major crises of the Third Republic from the Franco-Prussian War and Commune to the Dreyfus Affair.
34. Philip Nord, *Impressionists and Politics: Art and Democracy in the Nineteenth Century* (London and New York: Routledge, 2000) 43.
35. Paul Lidsky, *Les écrivains contre la Commune* (Paris: Éditions La Découverte & Syros, 1999), 160. As with the painters, Lidsky noted exceptions to the rule. Victor Hugo was generally more sympathetic to the Commune than were most of his contemporaries. Seventeen-year-old Arthur Rimbaud actively supported the Commune; at the time of the Commune, he was experiencing 'inner turmoil or revolution ... that corresponded to the political revolution of the Commune.' Wallace Fowlie, 'Rimbaud and the Commune,' in *Revolution and Reaction: The Paris Commune of 1871*, John Hicks and Robert Tucker, eds (Amherst: The University of Massachusetts Press, 1973).
36. Lidsky, 19–28. Even Émile Zola, whose social realism was the literary complement to Courbet's art, was contemptuous of working-class political independence. Whereas nearly every work in his Rougon-Macquart series contains a 'bad worker,' Lidsky asserts that the focus on that character-type qualifies it as representative of the whole working class. Lidsky, 138.
37. Géraldi Leroy, *Batailles d'Écrivains. Littérature et politique, 1870–1914* (Paris: Armand Colin, 2003), 43–78; Luce Czyba, 'La représentation de la Commune dans INRI de Léon Cladel: épopée et martyrs,' in

Écrire la Commune. Témoignages, récits et romans (1871–1931), Roger Bellet and Philippe Régnier, eds (Tusson: 'Idéographies' Du Lérot, 1994), 175–86.

38. Boime, 51.
39. Boime, 96.
40. Boime, 96–106; 114–39.
41. Boime, 79–81.
42. Boime, 93.
43. That said, the Commune, and its deconstruction of social space had a formative influence on Arthur Rimbaud's view of order in both its accepted literary and societal senses. Kristin Ross, *The Emergence of Social Space: Rimbaud and the Paris Commune* (Minneapolis: University of Minnesota Press, 1988).
44. Michael L. J. Wilson, 'Portrait of an Artist as a Louis XIII Chair,' in *Montmartre and the Making of Mass Culture*, Gabriel P. Weisberg, ed. (New Brunswick, NJ, and London: Rutgers University Press, 2001), 198–200.
45. Tillier, 409–16.
46. James Leith, 'The War of Images Surrounding the Commune,' in *Images of the Commune/Images de la Commune*, James A. Leith, ed. (Montreal and London: McGill-Queen's University Press, 1978), 101–50.
47. Leith, 143.
48. Robert Justin Goldstein, *Censorship of Political Caricature in Nineteenth-Century France* (Kent, OH, and London: Kent State University Press, 1989), 184–5.
49. Marina Warner, *Monuments and Maidens* (New York: Atheneum, 1985), 292.
50. David A. Shafer, 'Viragos, Virgins, and Matrons: The Confluence of Gender and Political Constructs in French Republican Imagery,' in *Histoire, Images, Imaginaire*, Pascal Dupuy, ed. (Pisa: Edizioni Plus – Università di Pisa, 2002), 85–6.
51. Gay L. Gullickson, *The Unruly Women of Paris* (Ithaca, NY, and London: Cornell University Press, 1996) 224.
52. Gullickson, 225.
53. Jeannene Przyblyski, 'Between Seeing and Believing: Representing Women in Appert's *Crimes de la Commune*,' in *Making the News: Modernity and the Mass Press in Nineteenth-Century France*, Dean de la Motte and Jeannene M. Przyblyski, eds (Amherst: University of Massachusetts Press, 1999).

Postscipt: Neglect and Resonance

1. The most complete discussion of the debates on the amnesty remains Jean T. Joughlin, *The Paris Commune in French Politics, 1871–1880: The History of the Amnesty* (Baltimore, MD: The Johns Hopkins Press, 1955).

2. James Lehning, *To Be a Citizen: The Political Culture of the Early Third Republic* (Ithaca, NY, and London: Cornell University Press, 2001).

3. Danielle Tartakowsky, *Nous irons chanter sur vos tombes. Le Père-Lachaise, XIXe–XXe siècle* (Paris: Aubier, 1999), 44–6. Amazingly, the employment of 'Commune' on a gravestone was not authorized until 1906. Tartakowsky, 72.

4. Lehning, 102.

5. Jacques and Mona Ozouf, *La République des instituteurs* (Paris: Gallimard, 1992), 144–5, 160, 194, 202.

6. Philip M. Katz, *From Appomattox to Montmartre: Americans and the Paris Commune* (Cambridge, MA, and London: Harvard University Press, 1998). Katz believes that American fears of the Commune were likely *heightened* by the distance as they lacked 'the rich raw material of immediate experience to construct an explanation.' Katz, 84. The most notable example of an American who took a positive view of the Commune is Walt Whitman. Katz, 75–8.

7. Katz provides numerous examples where American commentators employed the term 'communist' in place of 'communard'. It is nearly impossible to say whether this was due to ideological or phonetic considerations.

8. David A. Shafer, 'Les répercussions de la Commune aux États-Unis. Le cas de la presse, la Commune de Paris et la grève générale de 1877,' *Cahiers d'histoire*, 44 (1981), 7–23. Katz, 161–83.

9. Gerhard Fischer, *The Paris Commune on the Stage: Vallès, Grieg, Brecht, Adamov* (Frankfurt am Main and Bern: Peter Lang, 1981).

10. perso.club-internet.fr/lacomune/pages/savoir.html

11. www.peterwatkins.lt/a_trecia.htm

12. Jacques Tardi, *Le Cri du Peuple. Les Canons du 18 Mars* (Paris: Casterman, 1999), vol. 1, 5.

Select Bibliography

The following list represents only a selection of the numerous works devoted to the Commune. With few exceptions, the list is limited to works in English. A far more extensive list of French-language works can be found in the notes to the various chapters.

Reference Works

Dubois, Jean. *Le vocabulaire politique et social en France de 1869 à 1872. À travers les œuvres des écrivains, les revues et les journaux.* Paris: Larousse, 1962.

Le Quillec, Robert. *La Commune de Paris. Bibliographie Critique 1871–1997.* Paris: La Boutique de l'Histoire, 1997.

Noël, Bernard. *Dictionnaire de la Commune* (2 vols.). Paris: Champs Flammarion, 1978.

Second Empire

Aubry, Dominique. *Quatre-vingt-treize et les Jacobins. Regards du 19e siècle.* Lyon: Presses Universitaires de Lyon, 1988.

Dalotel, Alain, Alain Faure and Jean-Claude Freiermuth. *Aux origines de la Commune. Le mouvement des réunions publiques à Paris, 1868–1870.* Paris: François Maspero, 1980.

Hazareesingh, Sudhir. *From Subject to Citizen: The Second Empire and the Emergence of Modern French Democracy.* Princeton, NJ: Princeton University Press, 1998.

Jordan, David. *Transforming Paris: The Life and Times of Baron Haussmann.* Chicago: University of Chicago Press, 1995.

Moss, Bernard. *The Origins of the French Labor Movement, 1830–1914.* Berkeley: University of California Press, 1980.

Pilbeam, Pamela M. *Republicanism in Nineteenth-Century France, 1814–1871.* Basingstoke: Macmillan Press – now Palgrave Macmillan, 1995.

Pinkney, David H. *Napoleon III and the Rebuilding of Paris.* Princeton, NJ: Princeton University Press, 1958.

Plessis, Alain. *The Rise and Fall of the Second Empire, 1852–1871.* Translated by Jonathan Mandelbaum. Cambridge: Cambridge University Press, 1985.

Rifkin, Adrian, and Roger Thomas, eds. *Voices of the People: The Politics of 'La Sociale' at the End of the Second Empire.* Translated by John Moore. London: Routledge, Kegan Paul, 1988.

Tombs, Robert. *France, 1814–1914.* Harlow: Addison Wesley Longman, 1996.

Franco-Prussian War and the Commune

Castells, Manuel. *The City and the Grassroots.* Berkeley, Los Angeles and London: University of California Press, 1983.

Derfler, Leslie. *Paul Lafargue and the Founding of French Marxism, 1842–1882.* Cambridge, MA: Harvard University Press, 1991.

Edwards, Stewart. *The Paris Commune 1871.* Newton Abbot: Readers Union, 1971.

Gould, Roger V. *Insurgent Identities: Class, Community, and Protest in Paris from 1848 to the Commune.* Chicago and London: University of Chicago Press, 1995.

Harvey, David. *Paris, Capital of Modernity.* New York and London: Routledge, 2003.

Horne, Alistair. *The Fall of Paris: The Siege and the Commune, 1870–71.* New York: St. Martin's Press, 1965.

Howard, Michael. *The Franco-Prussian War.* London and New York: Methuen, 1961.

Jellinek, Frank. *The Paris Commune of 1871.* London: Victor Gollancz, 1937.

Johnson, Martin Phillip. *The Paradise of Association: Political Culture and*

Popular Organizations in the Paris Commune of 1871. Ann Arbor: University of Michigan Press, 1996.

Kranzberg, Melvin. *The Siege of Paris, 1870–1871: A Political and Social History.* Ithaca, NY: Cornell University Press, 1950.

Marx, Karl, and Friedrich Engels. *On the Paris Commune.* Moscow: Progres Publishers, 1980.

Mason, Edward S. *The Paris Commune: An Episode in the History of the Socialist Movement.* New York: Howard Fertig, 1967.

Nord, Philip. 'The Party of Conciliation and the Paris Commune.' *French Historical Studies.* 15:1 (1987), 1–35.

Rougerie, Jacques. *Paris libre 1871.* Paris: Éditions du Seuil, 1971.

Rougerie, Jacques. *Procès des Communards.* Paris: Julliard, 1978.

Rougerie, Jacques. *Paris insurgé. La Commune de 1871.* Paris: Decouvertes Gallimard, 1995.

Serman, William. *La Commune de Paris.* Paris: Fayard, 1986.

Taithe, Bertrand. *Defeated Flesh: Medicine, Welfare, and Warfare in the Making of Modern France.* Lanham, MD: Rowman & Littlefield Publishers, 1999.

Taithe, Bertrand. *Citizenship and Wars: France in Turmoil, 1870–1871.* London: Routledge, 2001.

Tombs, Robert. *The War Against Paris, 1871.* Cambridge: Cambridge University Press, 1981.

Tombs, Robert. *The Paris Commune, 1871.* London: Longman, 1999.

Tombs, Robert, 'Paris and the Rural Hordes: An Exploration of Myth and Reality in the French Civil War of 1871.' *The Historical Journal.* 29:4 (1986), 795–808.

Tombs, Robert. 'Prudent Rebels; the 2nd arrondissement during the Paris Commune of 1871.' *French History.* 5:4 (1991), 393–413.

Wolfe, Robert. 'The Parisian "Club de la Révolution" of the 18th arrondissement, 1870–71', *Past and Present.* 39 (1968), 81–119

Culture and the Commune

Bellet, Roger, and Philippe Régnier, eds. *Écrire la Commune. Témoignages, récits et romans (1871–1931).* Tusson: Éditions du Lérot, 1994.

Boime, Albert. *Art and the French Commune: Imagining Paris after War and Revolution.* Princeton, NJ: Princeton University Press, 1995.

Clayson, S. Hollis. *Paris in Despair: Art and Everyday Life Under Siege (1870–1871).* Chicago: University of Chicago Press, 2002.

Ferguson, Priscilla Parkhurst. *Paris as Revolution: Writing the 19th-Century City.* Berkeley, Los Angeles and London: University of California Press, 1994.

Fischer, Gerhard. *The Paris Commune on the Stage: Vallès, Grieg, Brecht, Adamov.* Frankfurt am Main: Peter Lang, 1981.

Leith, James A. *Images of the Commune, Images de la Commune.* Montreal and London: McGill-Queen's University Press, 1978.

Leroy, Géraldi. *Batailles d'Écrivains. Littérature et politique, 1870–1914.* Paris: Armand Colin, 2003.

Lidsky, Paul. *Les écrivains contre la Commune.* Paris: Éditions la Découverte, 1999.

Milner, John. *Art, War & Revolution in France, 1870–1871: Myth, Reportage and Reality.* New Haven, CT: Yale University Press, 2000.

Nord, Philip. *Impressionists and Politics: Art and Democracy in the Nineteenth Century.* London: Routledge, 2000.

Prendergast, Christopher. *Paris and the Nineteenth Century.* Cambridge, MA, and Oxford: Blackwell, 1992.

Ross, Kristin. *The Emergence of the Social Space: Rimbaud and the Paris Commune.* Minneapolis: University of Minnesota Press, 1988.

Sánchez, Gonzalo J. *Organizing Independence. The Artists Federation of the Paris Commune and its Legacy, 1871–1889.* Lincoln and London: University of Nebraska Press, 1997.

Seigel, Jerrold. *Bohemian Paris: Culture, Politics, and the Boundaries of Bourgeois Life, 1830–1930.* Baltimore, MD, and London: The Johns Hopkins University Press, 1986.

Tillier, Bertrand. *La Commune de Paris. Révolution sans Images? Politique et Représentations dans la France Républicaine (1871–1914).* Paris: Champ Vallon, 2004.

Women and the Commune

Barry, David. *Women and Political Insurgency: France in the Mid-Nineteenth Century.* Basingstoke: Macmillan Press – now Palgrave Macmillan, 1996.

Jones, Kathleen, and Françoise Vergès. '"Aux cityoennes!": Women, politics and the Paris Commune of 1871.' *History of European Ideas.* 13 (1991), 711–32.

Gullickson, Gay L. *Unruly Women of Paris: Images of the Commune.* Ithaca, NY, and London: Cornell University Press, 1996.

Schulkind, Eugene. 'Socialist Women during the 1871 Paris Commune', *Past and Present*. 106 (1985), 124–63.

Shafer, David. 'Plus que des ambulancières; Women in Articulation and Defence of their Ideals during the Paris Commune', *French History*. 7:1 (1993), 85–101.

Thomas, Edith. *The Women Incendiaries*. Translated by James and Starr Atkinson. New York: George Braziller, 1966.

Thomas, Edith. *Louise Michel*. Translated by Penelope Williams. Montreal: Black Rose Books, 1980.

Post-Commune

Bullard, Alice. *Exile to Paradise: Savagery and Civilization in Paris and the South Pacific, 1790–1900*. Stanford, CA: Stanford University Press, 2000.

Hutton, Patrick. *The Cult of the Revolutionary Tradition: The Blanquists in French Politics, 1864–1893*. Berkeley, Los Angeles, and London: University of California Press, 1981.

Joughin, Jean T. *The Paris Commune in French Politics, 1871–1880: The History of the Amnesty of 1880*. Baltimore, MD: The Johns Hopkins University Press, 1955.

Lehning, James R. *To Be a Citizen: The Political Culture of the Early Third Republic*. Ithaca, NY and London: Cornell University Press, 2001.

Nord, Philip. *The Republican Moment: Struggles for Democracy in Nineteenth-Century France*. Cambridge, MA, and London: Harvard University Press, 1995.

The Commune's Echo in the Provinces and Abroad

Aminzade, Ronald. *Ballots and Barricades: Class Formation and Republican Politics in France, 1830–1871*. Princeton, NJ: Princeton University Press, 1993.

Gaillard, Jeanne. *Communes de province, commune de Paris, 1870–1871*. Paris: Flammarion, 1971.

Greenberg, Louis M. *Sisters of Liberty: Marseille, Lyon, Paris and the Reaction to the Centralized State, 1868–1871*. Cambridge, MA: Harvard University Press, 1971.

Katz, Philip Mark. *From Appomattox to Montmartre: Americans and the Paris Commune*. Cambridge, MA: Harvard University Press, 1998.

McClellan, Woodford. *Revolutionary Exiles: The Russians in the First International and the Paris Commune.* London: Frank Cass, 1979.

Primary Sources

Allen, James Smith. *'In the Solitude of My Soul.' The Diary of Geneviève Bréton, 1867–1871.* Translated by James Palmes. Carbondale and Edwardsville: Southern Illinois University Press, 1994.
Becker, George J., ed. *Paris Under Siege, 1870–1871:. From the Goncourt Journal.* Translated by George J. Becker. Ithaca, NY, and London: Cornell University Press, 1969.
Bourgin, Georges, and Gabriel Henriot, eds. *Procès-Verbaux de la Commune de 1871. Édition Critique* (2 vols). Paris: Éditions Ernest Leroux, 1924.
Edwards, Stewart, ed. *The Communards of Paris, 1871.* London: Thames & Hudson, 1973.
Harrison, Royden, ed. *The English Defence of the Commune (1871).* London: Merlin Press, 1971.
Labouchere, Henry. *Diary of the Besieged Resident in Paris. Reprinted from 'The Daily News,' with Several New Letters.* London: Macmillan, 1872.
Lissagaray, Prosper. *History of the Paris Commune of 1871.* Translated by Eleanor Marx. London: New Park Publications, 1976.
Réimpression (in extenso) du Journal Officiel de la Commune. Paris: Victor Bunel, 1872.
Schulkind, Eugene, ed. *The Paris Commune of 1871: The View from the Left.* London: Jonathan Cape, 1972.
Vizetelly, Ernest A. *My Adventures in the Commune.* New York: Duffield, 1914.

Photographs, Caricatures, Images

Bourgin, Georges. *La Guerre de 1870–1871 et la Commune.* Paris: Les Éditions Nationales, 1939.
Bruhat, Jean, Jean Dautry and Émile Tersen. *La Commune de 1871.* Paris: Éditions Sociales, 1970.
Soria, Georges. *Grande Histoire de la Commune* (5 vols). Paris: Éditions Robert Laffont, 1970.

Index

219